D1244102

STOPPING A STALKER

A Cop's Guide to Making the System Work for You

Previous Plenum Trade books by

Captain **Robert L. Snow**

Family Abuse: Tough Solutions to Stop the Violence

SWAT Teams: Explosive Face-Offs with America's Deadliest Criminals

Protecting Your Life, Home, and Property: A Cop Shows You How

STOPPING A STALKER

A Cop's Guide to Making the System Work for You

Captain **Robert L. Snow**

PERSEUS PUBLISHING

Cambridge, Massachusetts

Library of Congress Cataloging-in-Publication Data

Snow, Robert L.
    Stopping a stalker : a cop's guide to making the system work for
you / Robert L. Snow.
        p.   cm.
    Includes bibliographical references and index.
    ISBN 0-306-45785-7
    1. Stalking--United States--Prevention.   2. Stalking victims-
-United States--Psychology.   I. Title.
HV6594.2.S56   1998
362.88--dc21   98-9571
                                                            CIP

Perseus Publishing books are available at special discounts for bulk purchases
in the U.S. by corporations, institutions, and other organizations.
For more information, please contact
the Special Markets Department at the Perseus Books Group,
11 Cambridge Center, Cambridge, MA 02142, or call (617) 252-5298.
or (800) 255-1514 or e-mail j.mccrary@peseusbooks.com

ISBN 0-7382-0627-x

© 1998 Robert L. Snow

Published by Perseus Publishing
A Member of the Perseus
Books Group

Printed in the United States of America

To Melissa, who will always be Daddy's Little Girl

➤   ➤   ➤   ➤   ➤

ACKNOWLEDGMENTS

Writing a book about a subject as complex as stalking could never be done without help from many people. I particularly want to thank my editor at Plenum, who saw the need for this book and acquired it. I also want to thank my agent, who is always able to find work for me.

I naturally received both advice and information from many people who work with stalkers and stalking victims, and I want to thank everyone who assisted me. But most of all I want to thank the stalking victims who helped me. Although I have seen many cases of stalking during my 30 years as a police officer, I have never experienced the long-term fear and terror that accompany it. Therefore, I want to express my deepest gratitude to the stalking victims who opened up their souls to me and let me see exactly what stalking does to a person. Only through their very candid descriptions and recollections was I able to visualize what it must feel like to be a stalking victim. I hope they feel I have given a true and accurate picture of their victimization.

CONTENTS

STALKING IN AMERICA

A friendship turned to terror. What began as a friendly 4th of July 1992 outing to the Orange County (California) Fair ended on 9 May 1993 with two people murdered and seven others shot. In between lay a nightmarish 10 months of stalking.

Kim Springer, a 29-year-old postal employee at the Dana Point post office in Orange County, during testimony before a grand jury, told of how 38-year-old fellow postal employee Mark Hilbun, almost immediately following their outing to the Orange County Fair, had begun making overtures that he wanted to have an intimate relationship with her. Kim tried, as gently as possible, to make Mark understand that she didn't want anything more than just friendship. Mark, though, wouldn't be put off by her refusals. Soon, he began calling her repeatedly on the telephone and sending her gifts. Then came love letters. Dozens of them. Mark reportedly even told a relative that he intended to marry Kim, though the extent of their relationship had been just the one trip to the fair.

For the next several months, Kim kept refusing to have anything to do with Mark. She told him many times, plainly, and finally bluntly, how she felt, yet he continued his pursuit. He refused to accept that she didn't want to know him intimately. His phone calls to her persisted and he would show up wherever she went, even following her on her mail route.

"He'd follow me everywhere I'd go," Kim said. "I mean, at one point it was like three or four times a day he'd show up. I told him to go back and deliver his mail."[1]

Eventually, because of Kim's continued refusal of his advances, Mark's declarations of undying love began changing to something much darker. Instead of love letters she now started receiving bizarre and threatening messages, including one that said because she wouldn't have him as a lover she should bring popcorn to the beach and watch him commit suicide. Because of Mark's constant threats and obscene messages left on her answering machine, Kim changed her telephone number twice, but that didn't help. He always was able to get her new number. Whereas Mark's behavior at first had been just a constant annoyance, as the threats and obscene messages escalated, it became scary and frightening. Kim was now living a nightmare.

When at last Mark's obsessive behavior became so frightening that Kim began to fear for her safety, she complained to the postal authorities about him. Mark's supervisors at the post office met with him and warned him to stop harassing Kim. Although promising he would, he didn't, and continued to follow and harass her. Eventually, this led to Mark's dismissal from the post office.

Although not seeing as much of Kim any longer because of his firing, Mark continued stalking her. And in May 1993 his threatening behavior reached its apex. Mark left a message for Kim that said: "I love you. I'm going to kill us both and take us to hell."[2] This so frightened her that she applied for a restraining order against him. However, Kim discovered, as have many other stalking victims, that to obtain a restraining order, individuals are often required to pay a substantial filing fee ($182 in California at that time). To her dismay, Kim couldn't afford the $182 filing fee and would have to wait until payday. That turned out to be one day too late.

On 6 May 1993, wearing a tie-dyed T-shirt with "Psycho" written on it, Mark stormed into the Dana Point post office waving a handgun and screaming, "Kim! Kim!" Kim was at the post office getting ready to go to work on her delivery route when she heard Mark's screams and quickly hid.

"I saw him with a bandanna around his face, waving a gun back and forth coming down the middle of the bay," Kim said. "I went under my mail case. He was calling my name."[3]

Mark searched fruitlessly for Kim. Frustrated at not finding her, he shot and killed Charles Barbagallo, his best friend and fellow postal worker, when Charles tried to persuade him to leave. Then losing all control, Mark shot and wounded Peter Gates, another friend and postal worker, who struggled with him over the gun, and finally fired a shot through the door of the postmaster's office, fortunately not hitting anyone inside. Kim continued to successfully evade him, and Mark eventually fled the post office in his Toyota pickup, shooting a 65-year-old man working in a garage a few blocks away. Later, Mark shot and critically wounded a female motorist who followed him after she saw him steal some magnetic placards from her car in an apparent attempt to disguise his truck.

After the police responded to the shooting at the Dana Point post office, officers went to Mark's mother's house in nearby Corona del Mar, hoping to obtain some information about where he might have gone. Instead they discovered Mark's 63-year-old mother, Frances Hilbun, murdered, stabbed repeatedly by Mark. They also found her cocker spaniel with its throat cut.

Mark eluded the police for several days, during which time he shot several other people in apparent robbery attempts. On 9 May 1993, police found him sitting in a Huntington Beach (California) sports bar, his long hair now cut short and his moustache shaved off in an attempt to disguise himself. He told the police after his arrest that he wanted Kim because they had been chosen as "husband and wife of the human race."[4]

At his trial, Mark pled innocent by reason of insanity. The jury, however, found him guilty of two counts of murder and seven counts of attempted murder.

Undoubtedly, one of the greatest benefits of living in America is the freedom our citizens enjoy. Freedom to move about without restriction, to congregate where and with whomever we choose, to preach whatever we believe in, and to say whatever is on our minds. Unfortunately, it is these very freedoms that allow stalkers like Mark Hilbun to harass, intimidate, and terrorize others, and for years prohibited the police from doing much about such behavior until it was too late. It is the freedoms enjoyed by people like Mark Hilbun that force others to become terrified prisoners in their own homes. Afraid to venture out, they are trapped, knowing that the stalkers are out there somewhere, watching and waiting for them. Until very recently, stalking fell into the gray area of perhaps being morally wrong, but not against the law, as much of stalking involved what appeared to be constitutionally protected behavior. Fortunately, this has now changed with the recent passage of antistalking laws.

But what does the new crime of stalking encompass? Each state defines it a little differently. In Pennsylvania, stalking is defined as: "engaging in a course of conduct or repeatedly committing acts toward another person, including following the person without proper authority, under circumstances which demonstrate either of the following: an intent to place the person in reasonable fear of bodily injury, or an intent to cause substantial emotional distress to the person."

In Florida, stalking is defined as: "any person who willingly, maliciously, and repeatedly follows or harasses another person; or who harasses another person and makes a credible threat with the intent to place that person in reasonable fear of death or bodily injury."

In Indiana, stalking is defined as: "a knowing or intentional course of conduct involving repeated or continuing harassment of another person. This conduct must be such that it would cause a reasonable person, and did in fact cause the victim, to feel terrorized, frightened, intimidated, or threatened."

In light of the untimely death of Princess Diana, who, on 31 August 1997, died in a car crash while being chased by several members of the paparazzi, many readers may wonder why the police cannot arrest the paparazzi, who often act more like stalkers than reporters or photographers, before such an incident can occur. While I'm not intimately acquainted with the laws of France, where the unfortunate incident involving Princess Diana took place, in the United States the paparazzi usually hide behind one of two defenses. Their first defense is that their actions do not meet the requirements of the various state laws against stalking. In truth, their conduct, while certainly reprehensible, usually doesn't *legally* constitute stalking because, although they certainly harass their victims, they don't terrorize or put them in fear of bodily harm (even though this was the end result in the case involving Princess Diana). The second defense, used by those members of the paparazzi who do appear to skirt close to the statutes against stalking, is that their actions are protected under the First Amendment. In cases involving the paparazzi, often the only avenue of relief available for victims is a restraining order, which the late Jackie Onassis was forced to obtain in order to stop a particularly aggressive photographer.

Putting the legal jargon and the issue of the paparazzi aside, to truly understand the crime of stalking as ordinary individuals are likely to experience it, put yourself in the following scenario: A person you may or may not know watches your home day and night. Whenever you leave home the person follows you wherever you go, sitting for hours on end outside wherever you have gone, including your workplace, friends' homes, and shopping malls. This person calls you on the telephone, both at work and at home, dozens of times every day. During the calls the person makes sure you're aware that he or she knows where you've been, who you've talked to, and what you're wearing. You change your telephone number to an unlisted number, but somehow the person discovers the new number and the calls continue. Letters and messages from this person pour into your home and workplace by the dozens. You find that this person has been asking family members, friends, and business acquaintances about you, apparently compiling reams of information from any source he or she can gain access to, legally or not.

At first, the person claims during the calls and letters that his or her actions are out of love for you. But after a while, as you continue to refuse the person's demands for an intimate relationship, things turn dark and sinister. The telephone calls and letters become obscene, threatening, or bizarre, and you hear such things as "Soon we'll be in heaven together." You find your property vandalized, a family pet is killed. Other family members are threatened and their property is vandalized. One day you find that the person has been inside your home. Now you feel terrorized. The threats become more than just words. Every time the telephone rings you jump, every time you hear a noise at night your heart stops. You're certain it is the person coming for you. Soon your appetite disappears, as does your ability to sleep. Then you have trouble concentrating, and begin having problems at your job.

You now realize you are a prisoner. You no longer control your own life, the stalker does. You can no longer go wherever you want or do whatever you want. You must now make any plans or life decisions based on the stalker's actions. Your life is no longer yours. The stalking may go on for months, even years. You may eventually be assaulted, or even the victim of a murder/suicide.

This is what stalking is. Stalking is not a crime of love or desire, but an attempt at domination. "It's about power and control," said Karen Phillips, director of Project Assist/Legal Aid of Western Missouri. "Stalkers keep someone in line by frightening them."[5] According to an article in *Essence* magazine: "Similar to the way a jackal tracks and kills its prey, human stalkers wage a campaign of terror against their victims, and often the hunt ends only when the stalker moves on to another [victim], or kills [them]."[6]

Stalking will likely become the crime of the twenty-first century. Those of us who study crime trends see that it is already well along the path followed by similar crimes that have risen from obscurity to become nationwide plagues. Although probably in existence for as long as humankind, stalking has only recently become recognized by law enforcement officials as a serious problem.

"It's a brand new area," said Sergeant Bob Drago of the Broward County (Florida) Police Department. "Many, many people just don't understand the severity of it."[7]

Lieutenant John Lane, head of the Los Angeles Police Department's Threat Management Unit, which investigates stalking complaints, adds, "We just put a label on it in recent years. It's like domestic violence or child abuse were ten years ago. Both have been around a long time, but law enforcement saw them as family matters."[8]

Many people in law enforcement believe stalking will become the next "in-vogue" crime in America because we are a nation of copycat criminals. Whenever a spectacular crime occurs that generates large amounts of media attention, similar crimes quickly follow. Examples are plentiful for anyone who doubts this assertion. Following the 1971 hijacking of Northwest Orient Flight 305, aircraft hijackings became *the* crime to commit. Because this initial crime received unbelievable levels of news coverage, raising the perpetrator to near legend status, hundreds of copycat aircraft hijackings occurred over the next decade. However, once the authorities learned how to deal successfully with these, hijackings declined dramatically. In the 1980s hostage taking became the in-vogue crime, again because the initial crimes received such intense media coverage. After this, mass killings at fast-food restaurants and other public places moved to center stage.

Like the crimes above, stalking has recently begun to receive extensive press coverage. This publicity can propel a perpetrator from a nobody to an instant media celebrity, as it did with hijackers, hostage takers, and mass murderers. For example, John Hinckley, who stalked movie star Jodie Foster and attempted to assassinate President Ronald Reagan in an effort to impress her, reportedly asked Secret Service agents who questioned him, "Is it on TV? Am I somebody?" In a letter sent by Hinckley to *New York Times* reporter Stuart Taylor, Hinckley said, "At one time, Miss Foster was a star and I was an insignificant fan. Now everything is changed."[9]

After the 1984 mass murder of 21 people at the McDonald's restaurant in San Ysidro, California, other demented individuals across the country imitated this crime, committing mass murders in their desire for instant media stardom. After a massive shooting spree at the McDonald's in Kenosa, Wisconsin, the killer left behind a videotape praising former mass murderers. In Los Angeles, the police had to use tear gas to flush out a man who had barricaded himself inside his home with over a dozen weapons and had told family members he wanted to emulate James

Huberty, the killer at the San Ysidro McDonald's. Stalking, unfortunately, is following the same path as these other crimes and before long will likely become the next major crime wave.

"Unfortunately, the media's increasingly sensationalized reporting of stalking incidents feeds the imaginations of those who have always wanted to indulge in such behaviors but never had the courage to," says Linden Gross in his book *To Have or to Harm*.[10]

Actually, stalking has now become so common in some locations that it is almost an accepted fact of life, like robberies and murders. "In Hollywood, having an erotomaniac [a person with delusions of love] stalk you has become a form of status," said Dr. Park Dietz, a psychiatrist who has studied stalkers for a number of years.[11] Indeed, while reading the local newspaper the other day I saw that the comic strip *Non-Sequitur* had a strip titled: "The New Hollywood Status Indicator." The comic strip showed a restaurant with a sign that said: "This section reserved for patrons with stalkers."

But stalking is not a joke. "It's terrorism," said John Stein, deputy director of the National Organization for Victim Assistance in Washington, D.C. "To feel that you can't get away from this person and that you're at risk no matter where you go is tantamount to living in Beirut."[12]

Stalking is now illegal in all 50 states. It is defined in most jurisdictions as a *repeated* pattern of harassment that presents a threat to the victim. Although the laws vary from state to state, the majority require more than just one act, that the victim feel threatened by these acts, and that there be an intent on the part of the stalker to instill fear. Of course, how this fear is instilled is up to interpretation. It can be something obvious such as threatening notes or messages, or something symbolic such as dead flowers or animal carcasses left on the doorstep. Sometimes fear can be instilled by looks and gestures.

Yet, while stalking is now illegal in all 50 states, the laws against it did not appear before 1990. The first state to pass an antistalking law, California, passed it in 1990 after a stalker murdered actress Rebecca Schaeffer and other stalkers had harassed, threatened, and finally murdered four more women in southern California within a short time after the Schaeffer murder. Because antistalking laws have only been around for a few years, most law enforcement agencies, prosecutors, and judges don't have much experience in enforcing them, so much of the protection that victims need is simply not yet available. Thus, many of the measures necessary for protection against stalking must be taken by the victims themselves.

Interestingly, although celebrity stalkings often receive considerable media coverage, the most common victims are not stars like Jodie Foster, Olivia Newton-John, Sharon Gless, Vanna White, Michael J. Fox, David Letterman, and others. The largest number of stalking victims are ordinary people who have for some reason had another person fixate on them. These stalkers can be complete strangers or, as in the incident in Dana Point related earlier, someone who is only a casual acquaintance, but more often than not the stalker is an ex-spouse or ex-intimate partner who feels he or she has been wronged in the breakup of the relationship. A case I handled demonstrates just how far these stalkers will go to intimidate and harass their victims.

➤   ➤   ➤   ➤

One day, while working as a district police officer on the south side of Indianapolis, another officer and I received a run from the dispatcher reported as "an ex-husband threatening his ex-wife." The dispatcher then added the chilling warning: "The victim says that her ex-husband is walking around the outside of her house right now threatening her with a scythe."

When we arrived at the address, we found an angry and determined-looking young man standing in the front yard of a house shouting for his ex-wife to come out, all the while waving a scythe (we later learned that he worked as a weed cutter for a construction company). Because just a few weeks earlier a police officer in Indianapolis was killed while responding to a domestic disturbance, most of us went to these runs with a gallon of adrenaline racing through our systems. The other officer and I quickly unsnapped our holsters and kept our hands on our guns as we approached the man and ordered him to put the scythe down, which he did immediately. We then placed him in the rear seat of my police car, and, while the other officer stayed with him, I went inside the house to speak with his ex-wife.

They had been divorced, I learned, for almost 5 years. The woman told me that since then her ex-husband had shown up at her house and threatened her weekly. She also said that, because of her ex-husband's harassment, she had moved four times in the 5 years, and had had her telephone number changed at least a half-dozen times. Somehow though, she said, he always got her new telephone number and the phone calls and threats would begin again. He also always found out where she had moved to, and would begin showing up at her home at least weekly. Although disturbed and frightened by his stalking of her, she really didn't want her ex-husband arrested or prosecuted. She only wanted him to leave her alone. The woman told me that he frightened her because during their marriage he had been physically abusive to her many times. Nevertheless, she felt sorry for him, and although she didn't want him to go to jail, she feared that some day he was going to do more than just threaten her. She feared that some day he would snap and either seriously injure or kill her.

Because at that time we had no law against stalking in Indiana, and the victim didn't want any legal action to be taken, my options for a solution were limited. I went to my police car to talk with the man, who I discovered was crying and pleading with the other officer not to arrest him. When he realized that he wasn't going to jail, the man immediately regained his composure and told us that he still loved his ex-wife intensely, and that he would never give up until she took him back. On talking further with the man, I discovered that he lived almost 10 miles away, had no money, and had walked over to his ex-wife's house. The best solution to the problem, I felt (though temporary at best), was to drive him back home. At least that would put some miles between him and his ex-wife, who said she planned to spend the night with some friends.

On the ride to the man's home we talked about what he had done that day and about his relationship with his ex-wife. I tried to discuss rationally with him the idea that he ought to give up his quest for his ex-wife, as she obviously didn't want him back. I also discussed his tactic of trying to threaten her into reconciling with him, hoping to be able to make him see the obvious problems with this approach. However, I found that this man, as with almost all stalkers I have encountered in my almost 30 years as a police officer, appeared completely oblivious to any logical arguments about his behavior. He seemed totally fixated on his ex-wife, and was completely obsessed with the idea of getting her back. It was as if he couldn't think of anything else or see any other goal in life. She had married him, he told me, and so that meant she was his forever. He said that he would never, as long as he lived, give his ex-wife a moment's peace until she took him back as her husband.

By the time I dropped him off at his residence, I had had a truly chilling and frightening glimpse into the mind of an obsessed and likely very dangerous man. His quest to regain his ex-wife appeared to totally dominate his thoughts, squeezing out any rational considerations. It was as if he felt he wouldn't have a life or be a real man again until he got her back. But most frightening, he truly felt that by continuing his obsessive and threatening behavior he would eventually obtain his goal. I wondered with a shudder what would happen when he finally realized he wouldn't.

Since I began writing this book I have often thought about what it must feel like to be a stalking victim, to experience the uncertainty and terror of it. I have tried many times to imagine living with this intense fear for months or even years, and then to only have it get worse and worse. For those of us who have never experienced stalking, it is difficult to imagine or comprehend how people can function under this level of stress, how they can get through their daily lives knowing there is an obsessed and likely dangerous person watching and following them at any moment.

Most stalkers, the police find, are just as obsessed as the ex-husband in the incident above either with obtaining the love and attention of their victims or with winning them back. A woman in St. Paul, Minnesota, found out the depth of this obsession when she left her husband and moved into a new home. Unbeknownst to her, her estranged husband secretly crept into the crawlspace under her home and lived there for a week, apparently in an attempt to keep an eye on what she was doing. In another case, a California woman continued to be stalked by a man even after he had been incarcerated in a maximum security prison. The stalker had his name legally changed to that of the father of the woman's daughter, and consequently gained access to the child's school records and to the victim's tax returns.

Dr. Park Dietz, a psychiatrist specializing in the type of people who become stalkers, estimates that there are presently 5 million psychopaths loose in America, and that 5 percent of our work force is "clinically depressed."[13] Dr. Dietz also assisted in a study conducted by the U.S. Justice Department that estimated there are at least 150,000 stalkers on the streets of America, and that 1 in every 20 women in the United States has been or will be the victim of a stalker.[14] Other experts in the field believe the chances are closer to 1 in 10. This means there are or will be nearly as many victims of stalking as there are victims of all other types of major crime every year.

However, because stalking is such a new crime, it was until recently not reported as a specific offense on the national crime statistics kept by the FBI. Therefore, although the U.S. Justice Department has estimated the size of the stalking problem, no one is certain just how prevalent it is in our country, but most of us who deal regularly with crime believe it is likely much more prevalent than most members of the public suspect. The 1994 Crime Bill passed by the U.S. Congress mandates tracking and compilation of stalking statistics. Also, the National Institute of Justice, in collaboration with the Centers for Disease Control and Prevention, plans to conduct a national survey of crime victims, which will include a section on stalking. However, it will still be several years before we have exact numbers and a clearer picture of this crime's actual prevalence.

A quick measure of just how prevalent stalking may be in America, however, comes from the New York telephone company NYNEX, which says it receives 6000 reports of threatening phone calls and 9000 reports of obscene phone calls (both integral parts of stalking) every month. "The emotional toll is unbelievable," said Dena Raymer of NYNEX. "The [victims] who call us are uniformly scared, often hysterical."[15] That's 15,000 calls a month from just one of the many telephone companies in the United States. And no one knows how many victims do not report threatening or obscene calls.

Another measure of the extent of stalking in America can be seen in the plots of many recent Hollywood movies that involve stalking. Examples of these popular movies are *Fatal Attraction*, *Cape Fear*, *The Cable Guy*, *Sleeping With The Enemy*, and *The Fan*. A little deeper research into the movies made during the past 10 years could undoubtedly find many, many more that used stalking as their plot.

Occasionally, however, stalking is not as intense as depicted in the movies mentioned above. Some stalking doesn't even involve threats, but just a constant annoyance, such as repeated telephone calls or approaching over and over for dates, even though the victim has refused the request many times. Although this type of stalking may not be as dangerous as other types, the constant harassment can still wear on the victim, causing stress-related ailments, and leading to problems domestically or socially. The following case demonstrates just how disturbing this kind of stalking can be to the victim.

When I was in charge of the Indianapolis Police Department's Personnel Branch, a male employee who worked as a security guard at some property occupied by the police department came to me to complain about being stalked by another employee. For some reason, the man said, he had attracted the attention of a co-worker, a female security guard. The man was married, the female stalker wasn't. What started out as requests from the woman for dates soon became a constant presence near him, and when he continued to refuse her request for dates she began sending him obscene cards and notes. There was no violence or even threats, just a constant presence and annoyance. The man told me what he really feared was that his wife would find out about the stalking. His wife, being a very insecure woman, might not understand.

I called the female security guard into my office and talked with her. I told her about the complaint made concerning her behavior and asked her whether she and the male employee had ever had any type of relationship. She said no, it was just that her mental telepathy had revealed both that he was unhappy in his marriage and that they would make a much better couple than he and his wife. As we talked I could find no rational explanation for her behavior, only the obsession that she and the man were meant for each other. Finally, I told her that since the man apparently didn't agree, and her advances were obviously not wanted, she needed to leave the man alone or else she would be fired.

Although while sitting in my office the woman assured me she would leave the man alone, she didn't. The stalking began again almost immediately, in fact later that afternoon. I eventually had to fire the woman. I left my position in the Personnel Office soon afterward and don't know if the firing had any effect on the stalking or not.

Stalking, as shown by the incidents related up to this point, is a crime on a continuum that can run from constant annoyance to harassment to threatening behavior to assault and homicide. National statistics show that 90 percent of the women killed every year by current or former spouses were stalked by these men before being murdered.[16] However, those stalkers who ended up becoming murderers often didn't start out planning to kill, but usually began at the low end of the continuum and worked their way up in seriousness. Unfortunately, no one knows which stalkers will stay at the low end and which ones will move up the violence continuum. Because of this, any stalking, even on a minor level, should be taken seriously. If ignored, stalking can quickly grow to dangerous levels.

Unfortunately, far too many victims of stalking, the police find, view the initial actions of stalkers as harmless infatuation, or even as flattering, though unwanted, attention, and so they ignore it, believing the person's interest in them will wane and eventually disappear because of their lack of response. However, stalking victims very often find to their dismay that, rather than waning and disappearing, the interest and actions of the stalkers instead become even more bold and intense. Victims can occasionally even act to increase this intensity by unknowingly sanctioning the stalkers' behavior.

Because of their desire to let unwanted suitors down easily, often future stalking victims, rather than directly saying they do not and never will want a relationship with the stalkers, inadvertently sanction the stalkers' behavior by saying something much softer and noncommittal, such as they are just not ready for a relationship right then. Few people can bring themselves to flatly state the firm, no-nonsense answers that are needed. However, anything beyond a firm "no" to most stalkers is a sanction of their behavior. It means "yes, keep trying." Consequently, the stalkers persist, believing that, in order to win the victims, they have only to convince them that they are ready for a relationship. Later, the victims discover that they can no longer pick up their telephone when it rings, answer their door, open their mail, or go anywhere. A firm and blunt "no" to the stalkers' initial approach is the best course.

Interestingly, scientists who have recently begun studying stalkers find that their behavior is actually just a deviant variance of acceptable behavior. Stalking is an outgrowth, they find, of the way male/female relationships are viewed in our society. People, for example, often say no to others with whom they actually want to have a relationship, not because they don't like the individuals, but because they don't want to appear to be too easy to win. I and most people have had the experience of learning that a person we believed didn't even know we were alive, or seem to show the least bit of interest in us, actually was very interested in us. In his book *To Have or to Harm*, author Linden Gross relates the case of a man brought to trial after months of pestering a woman for a date. The man handled his own defense and asked the women on the jury and those present in the courtroom how many of them had initially said no to a man they actually wanted to date. The large show of hands eventually won him an acquittal.[17]

In any group of nonstalkers, a large number would likely admit to actions typical of stalkers, although on a smaller scale of intensity. A large number of us would admit to checking on the marital status of some person, or to finding the person's address and telephone number in some manner other than by asking the person. Some would admit to calling someone just to see who would answer the phone, or to driving by someone's home to see if he or she was there. And how many of us know of an individual who relentlessly pursued another person and eventually won that person? This is the plot of hundreds of books and movies. The movie *Money Can't Buy You Love* tells of an infatuated, but unpopular, young man who finally pays a popular girl to date him, and in the end wins her. The movie *The Graduate* portrays Dustin Hoffman as a relentless stalker who, through perseverance, eventually wins the stalking victim's love. The standard script for many movies and books is: boy meets girl; boy fails to capture her heart; boy perseveres against all odds; boy eventually wins girl. Through movies and books, our society sanctions and encourages extreme perseverance. Is it any wonder many stalkers believe that if they just continue their stalking and harassment they will eventually win?

Another possible explanation of stalking behavior relates to the fact that men and women view social situations very differently. A study reported in the *Journal of Vocational Behavior* may explain why some stalkers believe a person is interested in them. Men and women in this study viewed films of neutral and professional interaction between a man and a woman, and then were asked to describe what they believed happened during the observed interaction. Men more often than women saw sexual clues or connotations in the interactions, and more often reported that they thought the woman's behavior was a sexual come-on.[18]

Regardless of how we view situations, if we look at our own experiences, most of us can understand a little of how stalkers feel, even though we abhor their actions. Anyone who has ever been in love with another person knows how important being close to that person can be, how being around that special person is intoxicating and exhilarating, and how receiving love in return can be euphoric. But those who do not receive the same feelings in return know how heartbreaking the experience can be. Still, we recover and move on.

Stalkers, however, don't recover and don't move on. They stay fixated on the person to the exclusion of everything else. Stalkers make it their life's work to follow and harass a person who doesn't want them, unrealistically believing that such behavior will eventually win the person's love. Finally, when they discover that they can't be the object of the person's love, they settle for being the object of that person's attention, even though this attention is born of fear. Very often, when the stalkers do realize that they are not going to obtain the person's love, the quest turns ugly, brutal, and occasionally deadly.

"All people have a small amount of obsessiveness in their personalities," said Maurice Rappaport, former president of the Northern California Psychiatric Society. "It becomes a mental disorder when the pursuit of the obsession becomes the life's focus, the one issue that dominates thoughts."[19]

It is a fuzzy line the stalker steps over when he or she first moves from acceptable to unacceptable behavior. Few people will agree where this line is drawn. Stalking cases seldom start out as drastic and dramatic as they eventually become. Few stalkers introduce themselves as such. Many simply appear to be lovesick individuals with an infatuation for someone. Although at first this infatuation may even be flattering, stalking cases often escalate from words of love to threats of death.

Being a stalking victim, therefore, no matter at what level, can change a person's life forever. Stalking victims must restrict their movement because they know with certainty that the stalker is waiting outside and will follow them, and most victims can never be sure what the stalker will do. The unpredictability of stalking causes enormous stress for the victims. "The reality is you can't know for certain what a stalker may do," said Assistant Attorney General for Virginia Mark Bowles.[20] Because of this uncertainty, stalking victims come to dread whenever the phone rings or someone knocks on the door. And, the victims discover, the longer the stalking goes on, the more likely it will turn violent. Victims become very aware of just how extraordinarily vulnerable they are.

The crime of stalking can be more damaging than even a random act of violence. A violent crime, once committed, is over with and victims can usually recover and go on with their lives. Stalking, however, is a crime that goes on day after day, and occasionally year after year. Fortunately, there are methods to stop stalking from beginning as well as methods for stopping it once it has begun. In Chapter 16, I will give readers advice and tips on how to spot potential stalkers before becoming involved with them, how to discourage stalking from beginning, and how to stop stalking if it has begun. Victims are not totally defenseless.

WHO AND WHAT ARE STALKERS?

Melvin Phillips simply refused to accept that the relationship with his girlfriend, Brenda, was over. For a year and a half, Melvin, Brenda, and her children had lived together in Illinois. But because they fought constantly and Melvin had tried to control her life, and especially because Brenda now feared for her and her children's lives since Melvin had recently begun threatening her with a gun, Brenda decided to end their relationship. Against Melvin's protests, Brenda and her children moved out and into a home whose location was unknown to Melvin. Within a year's time, however, she and her children would be forced to move four times throughout Illinois, each time Melvin somehow tracking them down and harassing them. Finally, Brenda confided in a counselor, who suggested that she and her children move to the Salvation Army shelter in Indianapolis, which they did.

However, within a month of moving to Indianapolis, Melvin showed up at the shelter, stopping people as they entered and exited and questioning them as to the whereabouts of Brenda and her children. This type of confrontation naturally disturbed the shelter's residents, and an assistant director went outside to speak with Melvin.

Melvin at first claimed he was there looking for his wife and children, but once inside the assistant director's office he revealed who he really was, and said he was certain that if he could just talk with Brenda he could persuade her to move back to Illinois with him. The assistant director would not confirm or deny that Melvin's girlfriend and her children were residents there, but did say that if Melvin would leave his name and number she would put up a notice. She also advised Melvin of the shelter's

17

policy of not allowing anyone to come onto the shelter property and question people about the residents. Melvin assured the assistant director that he would respect the shelter's rules, and then left.

Melvin not only began calling the shelter repeatedly, he also returned there asking once again about Brenda and her children's whereabouts. He also showed up at the school the children attended and attempted to find out where the family was living. Now fearing that it would only be a matter of time before Melvin found them, and unsure what he might do, Brenda and her children became virtual prisoners inside the shelter.

Because of Melvin's persistence and the very real danger he presented, the shelter staff decided to move Brenda and her children to another location. The staff's reasoning for this, according to later court records, was: "She was very upset and the children were terrified and they felt very unsafe. They were like imprisoned in the shelter. Children couldn't go to school or anything."

Finally, however, exhausted from running and hiding, and feeling that she couldn't go on like this much longer, Brenda went to the local prosecutor's office to file charges against Melvin for stalking. Soon after she arrived at the prosecutor's office, Melvin, who had apparently been following her, also showed up there. After a loud confrontation with Brenda, Melvin left but was stopped by sheriff's deputies alerted to the problem in the prosecutor's office. Although at first claiming to be someone else, Melvin finally admitted who he was. The deputies arrested him for stalking, and a court eventually convicted him. He received a sentence of 6 months in jail.

Stalkers like Melvin Phillips are obviously not normal people. Although many stalkers are worse than him and have mental problems that demand immediate institutionalization, and others have problems that demand, at minimum, long-term psychiatric help, almost all stalkers have some type of mental or emotional problem. Stalkers will go across town, country, or even to different continents in order to continue their stalking. Stable people simply do not continue, often in the face of years of rejection, to pursue someone.

"None of the people who engage in stalking behavior are normal individuals," said Dr. Park Dietz. "There's something wrong with each of them."[21]

Stalkers, no matter what or how bad their mental disorder, can usually be sorted into one of three major groupings:

Simple Obsession Stalkers

These stalkers have previously been involved in an intimate relationship with their victims. Often, the stalking victims have attempted to call off the relationship, but the stalkers, like Melvin Phillips in the anecdote above, simply refuse to accept this. Although this category of stalker may not have serious mental disorders that demand immediate institutionalization, they do suffer from personality disorders, including being emotionally immature, extremely jealous, and insecure; suffer from low self-esteem; and quite often feel powerless without the relationship.

According to *The Terror of Batterer Stalking* by Michael Lindsey: "The injury can be real or perceived leaving the individual feeling devastated, annihilated, betrayed, or abandoned. Stalkers often express the belief that everything for which they have worked has been stripped from them, creating a vast emptiness that is unbearable....While reconciliation is the goal, stalkers believe they must have a specific person back or they will not survive."[22]

The stalkers of former spouses and intimate partners, as the title of Lindsey's work suggests, and as researchers have found, are often domineering over and abusive to their partners during the relationship, and use this domination as a way to bolster their own low self-esteem. The control the abusers exert over their partners gives them a feeling of power they can't find elsewhere. Because of this, they try to control every aspect of their partners' lives. The abusers' worst fear becomes losing the people over whom they have control.

When they realize this fear as the relationship finally does end, the stalkers suddenly believe that their lives are destroyed. Their total identity and feelings of self-worth are tied up in the power experienced through their domineering and abusive relationship. Without this control, they feel that they will have no self-worth and no identity. They will become nobodies, and, in desperation, they begin stalking, trying to regain their partners and the basis of their power.

It is this total dependence on their partners for identity and feelings of self-worth that makes these stalkers so very dangerous. They will often go to any length and stop at nothing to get their partners back. If they can't have the people over whom they can exert dominance and total control, their lives are truly not worth living. Unfortunately, along with becoming suicidal, they also often want to kill the intimate partners who have left them.

"Stalking doesn't always begin with violence or trying to terrorize, it usually starts with, 'Can I just talk to you?'" said FBI agent James Wright, supervising agent for the National Center for the Analysis of Violent Crime, in Quantico, Virginia. "He wants her back, and she won't come back. Everything escalates from there...and sometimes he snaps and assaults or kills her. In his mind, he makes the decision, 'If I can't have you, no one else will.'"[23]

Dr. Park Dietz adds, "Typically, the woman beater tries to hide his dependence on women with macho displays. When he says, 'If I can't have her, nobody can,' he is attempting to cover his fear that she'll meet another man and leave him."[24] Far too often, the police find that these stalkers follow through on their threats, killing the victims and then many times committing suicide. For them death is better than having to face the humiliation of the stalking victims leaving them for someone else, and the humiliation of having to face their own powerlessness.

Love Obsession Stalkers

These are individuals who become obsessed with or fixated on a person with whom they have had no intimate or close relationship. The victim may be a friend, a business acquaintance, a person met only once, or even a complete stranger. One stalker, for example, met his victim when she gave him a ride in her car after learning that he was headed in the same direction she was. He didn't see her again for 31 years. The woman became a stalking victim when the man found her through an obituary notice for her mother. Once he had located her, the man began a relentless pursuit of the victim. When arrested by the police, the man had in his possession 62 presents purchased over the years since he had last seen the woman, one for every Christmas and birthday during the 31 years. He also had a set of wedding rings, a bottle of champagne, and a pair of toasting glasses.

Love obsession stalkers believe that a special, often mystical, relationship exists between them and their victims. Any contact with the victims becomes a positive reinforcement of this relationship, and any (even the slightest) wavering of the victims from an absolute "no!" is seen as an invitation to continue the pursuit. These stalkers often imagine that they and their victims, whom they may never have met, are married, have had an affair, or have had a child together. Love obsession stalkers will often read sexual meanings into neutral responses from the victims. Yet, as the victims will usually have nothing to do with them, these stalkers many times resort to collecting in-depth personal information about the victims so as to give them a feeling of intimacy with the victims. These stalkers are often loners with an emotional void in their lives. Any contact with the object of their infatuation, even negative, helps fill this void.

"Chronic failures in social or sexual relationships through young adulthood may be a necessary predisposing experience for obsessional followers," said Reid Meloy, an associate clinical professor of psychiatry at the University of California at San Diego. "In fact, failed relationships are the rule among these individuals."[25]

According to the National Victim Center: "The vast majority of love obsessional stalkers suffer from a mental disorder—often schizophrenia or paranoia. Regardless of the specific disorder, nearly all display some delusional thought patterns and behaviors. Since most are unable to develop normal personal relationships through more conventional and socially acceptable means, they retreat to a life of fantasy relationships with persons they hardly know, if at all."[26]

Dr. Maurice Rappaport adds, "We're not really dealing with true love for another person. It's more childlike emotion. If a child is unable to get the gratification he wants, he acts childlike. He kicks the cat. In an adult person it takes the form of mayhem."[27]

Many love obsession stalkers suffer from a condition known as erotomania or de Clerambault's syndrome. Stalkers suffering from this disorder have the delusion that they are loved intensely by another person, usually a person of higher socioeconomic status than them or an unattainable public figure. This delusional love relationship is often seen by the stalkers as an idealized love or a perfect pairing. Love obsession stalkers are totally convinced that the stalking victims love them dearly and truly, and would return their affection, except for some external influence.

Included in this group are those stalkers who pursue movie stars or other famous people, believing that they are married or have some secret relationship with the star. A woman named Margaret Ray has stalked late night television host David Letterman for 8 years. She has the delusion that she and Letterman are married. As a part of the stalking, she has broken into Letterman's house, stolen his car, and shown up at his home with a child in tow, who she claims is hers and Letterman's.

Gavin DeBecker, who serves as a security consultant for many Hollywood stars and celebrities, finds that most of the stalkers he deals with are loners, without any strong emotional relationships. Most seem to have a need to be recognized as someone of importance and value, and consequently attach themselves to the star or celebrity in the desperate hope that this will give them that status.[28]

During questioning, the police find that most love obsession stalkers have fantasized a complete relationship with the person they are stalking. However, when they attempt to act out this fantasy in real life, they expect the object of their obsession to return the affection. When no affection is returned, the stalker, frustrated, often reacts with threats and intimidation. These stalkers, when the threats and intimidation don't accomplish what they hoped, can often become violent, and even deadly.

"Their ultimate possession is murder," said Dr. Bruce Danto, a forensic psychiatrist and former police officer. "They really look at homicide and suicide as a change of address—their death is not extinction, but the killer plans on a reunion with the victim so they will live happily ever after in ga-ga land."[29]

Other Stalkers

Some stalkers harass their victims not out of love but out of hate. Occasionally, stalking becomes a method of revenge for some misdeed against the stalker, real or imagined. Stalking can also be used as a means of protest. This is the smallest group, but this type of stalking, for revenge and protest, can be especially dangerous. For example, there have been several killings in recent years by stalkers at abortion clinics, and a number of mass murders around the country by employees who have been fired and then returned to stalk and eventually kill those who have fired them.

In an attempt to determine the numbers in each of the three groups of stalkers, the Los Angeles Police Department's Threat Management Unit, in 1992, analyzed 74 cases of stalking in Los Angeles and reported the following breakdown for stalking victims: 38 percent were ordinary citizens stalked by ex-spouses or intimate partners, or stalked by a neighbor or complete stranger; 49 percent were celebrities and entertainers (it must be remembered that this analysis was done in Los Angeles, and so this group of victims is very likely overrepresented); and 13 percent were corporate executives stalked by former or current employees, supervisors stalked by disgruntled subordinates, or psychotherapists stalked by patients.[30]

Although most stalkers will fit into one of the three groupings, there are certain traits that all stalkers will usually possess, regardless of grouping. It is important to know these traits, because they can alert you to the possibility that a potential suitor or even a friend or acquaintance could become a stalker.

1. Stalkers will not take no for an answer. They refuse to believe that a victim is not interested in them or will not rekindle their relationship, and often believe that the victim really does love them, but just doesn't know it and needs to be pushed into realizing it. Most stalkers have little sense of self or identity. So, if the object of their desire rejects them, they have nothing, no life or self, to fall back on. Consequently, as long as they continue pursuing their victims, the stalkers can convince themselves they haven't been completely rejected yet.

2. Stalkers display an obsessive personality. They are not just interested in, but totally obsessed with the person they are pursuing. Their every waking thought centers on the victim, and every plan the stalker has for the future involves the victim.

"Friends and co-workers who wonder whether a person's interest has become an obsession should evaluate their answer to a certain question," said James Torkildson, executive director of Associates for Psychological Services. "Is the energy involved disproportionate to the positive return?"[31] In other words, is the person totally involved in and completely overwhelmed with pursuing someone who has no, and never will have any, interest in him or her?

Along with obsessive thinking, stalkers also display other psychological or personality problems and disorders. They may suffer from erotomania, paranoia, schizophrenia, and delusional thinking.

"They tend to have rigid personalities and a maladaptive style," said Professor Reid Meloy. "These personality disorders in themselves are very stable and not treatable."[32] And although there are drugs to treat certain specific mental disorders, stalkers, when given the choice, seldom continue with their medication or treatment.

3. Stalkers are above average in intelligence, and are usually smarter than the run-of-the-mill person with mental problems. They will often go to great and even ingenious lengths to obtain information about their victims or to find victims who have secretly moved. Stalkers have been known to hack into computers, tap telephone lines, take jobs at public utilities that allow them access to the victims or information about the victims, and even to travel thousands of miles and spend thousands of

dollars to gain information about or find their victims. They are also often smart enough to gain access to people who have established stringent security measures. In addition, stalkers many times use their intelligence to throw others off their trail. A stalker at Florida State University, for example, allegedly tapped into his victim's telephone line and then called himself in an effort to make it look as though the victim was harassing him, rather than the other way around.

Although many victims may feel that they have been selected at random by the stalkers and immediately approached, this isn't always so. Stalkers, being above average in intelligence, often make elaborate plans even before the stalking begins. Many times, stalkers trail their victims for weeks or months and spend a considerable amount of time and money researching their victims' habits and vulnerabilities before actually approaching them. Stalkers want someone they know they can control and manipulate with fear and intimidation.

"It is easier to go after someone who seems safe to pursue than someone you think would reject you," said Dr. Park Dietz.[33]

4. Most stalkers don't have any relationship outside the one they are trying to reestablish or the one they have imagined exists between them and their victim. Because they are usually loners, stalkers become desperate to obtain this relationship.

"Many [stalkers] were deprived of their parents for some time when they were children," said Professor Reid Meloy. "Early on, some of these individuals had a disturbance in parenting. They were separated at earlier than five years of age. It helps explain the difficulty in forming attachments."[34]

Irving Guller, a forensic psychologist at John Jay College of Criminal Justice, adds, "Most people who get involved in stalking are losers. The rejection, or perceived rejection, by the person they are stalking is another major blow to an ego that is weak to start with. They are almost never a 'focused, reality-oriented' person."[35]

5. Stalkers don't display the discomfort or anxiety that people should naturally feel in certain situations. Normal individuals would be extraordinarily embarrassed to be caught following other people, going through their trash looking for information about them, leaving obscene notes, and other inappropriate behavior displayed by stalkers. Stalkers, however, don't see this as inappropriate behavior, but only as a means to gain the person's love.

6. Stalkers often suffer from low self-esteem, and feel they must have a relationship with the victim in order to have any self-worth. Some stalkers believe that if they can attach themselves to famous or important people, some of this fame and importance will transfer to them.

"Usually, you have an individual with very little self esteem and who has to prop up that self-esteem by relating to someone they've put on a pedestal," said Dr. Ronald Markman, a psychiatrist and attorney. "If that relationship breaks up, which further damages their own self-esteem, they have to re-institute that relationship."[36]

Carrie Dixon, a nurse and psychologist who works with obsessive individuals, agrees. "Preoccupations with other people almost always involve someone with weak social skills and low self-esteem."[37]

7. Few stalkers can see how their actions are hurting others. Also, they display other sociopathic thinking in that they cannot learn from experience, and they don't believe society's rules apply to them. Most stalkers don't think they're really threatening, intimidating, or even stalking someone else. They think they're simply trying to show the victims that they're the right one for them.

However, to the victims stalking is like a prolonged rape. Stalkers, like rapists, want absolute control over their victims. Of course, stalkers don't regard what they're doing as a crime, or even wrong. To them it is true love, with the exception that the victims don't recognize it yet. With enough persistence, stalkers believe they will eventually convince the victims of their love.

8. Stalkers many times have a mean streak and will become violent when frustrated. How violent? Often deadly. Charlotte Garner reportedly cried tears of joy when informed by the police that her husband, Joseph Garner, had been arrested. For the 7 years since their divorce, Charlotte had been living in constant terror of him. He had stalked her, beaten her, and threatened to sneak into her house, kill her and their three children, and then commit suicide. Charlotte had seen Joseph sneaking around her house and going through her trash a number of times. In December 1995, Indianapolis police arrested Joseph after he allegedly stabbed his 76-year-old father over 200 times, butchered the body, and ate part of his brain. At his trial in 1997, a jury found Joseph guilty but mentally ill and sentenced him to 62 years, which in Indiana means he will receive psychiatric treatment, but in prison.

A rare, unique case? Unfortunately not. In Florida, police arrested a man they accused of stalking a woman with the intention of raping, killing, and then cannibalizing her. Luckily, they intercepted the stalker before he could follow through on the plans he had carefully written out in detail. In Virginia, the police arrested a man previously charged with stalking a woman after he broke into her home and raped her. As his defense the stalker claimed he didn't rape the woman; one of the other 30 personalities that inhabited his body did it. In Pennsylvania, a man accused of stalking his ex-girlfriend left a paper bag on top of her car. The bag contained a pipe bomb, which police managed to dispose of safely. In Minnesota, a man stalked his ex-wife, placing over 200 calls to her in one day, and then tried to force his way into her house. In applying for an order of protection, the woman wrote that her ex-husband had told her, "Let's sign a pact so it doesn't look like murder. I'll kill you and then kill myself." When police went to the man's house to arrest him, he set the house on fire and hung himself.[38]

These anecdotes should remind us that although much of stalking involves harassment and annoyance, stalkers can also be extraordinarily dangerous. Believing that their victims love and care for them, stalkers can become violent when frustrated in their quest for this love. This is particularly true for stalkers with serious mental disorders. And as we continue in America to dismantle and tear down the traditional state facilities for the mentally disturbed in favor of community-based mental health treatment facilities, which in most communities have not yet been built, we are letting thousands of dangerous, and possibly violent, mentally disturbed people loose to roam through our society. The National Institute of Mental Health and the American Psychiatric Association claim that during any year more than 25 percent of all Americans suffer from some type of diagnosable mental disorder, yet only a fifth of these people receive any kind of treatment.[39] And with the continuing decline of available state-run mental health facilities, this will only get worse. An increasing number of mentally disturbed stalkers will be roaming unrestrained in our communities.

"All stalkers are potentially violent," said Dr. Bruce Danto. "Some of them are blatantly psychotic. Most of them are paranoid and possessive; very insecure and very dangerous."[40]

Although the few statistics we have managed to gather in the last few years on stalking show that the majority of cases do not end in murder or grave bodily injury, enough do every year that victims should never brush aside this possibility. Victims of stalking should *never* take the crime lightly, no matter who the stalkers are or how close they've been emotionally. Look carefully at the traits listed below and be wary if someone seems to fit these.

1   Won't take no for an answer
2   Has an obsessive personality
3   Above average intelligence
4   No or few personal relationships
5   Lack of embarrassment or discomfort at actions
6   Low self-esteem
7   Sociopathic thinking
8   Has a mean streak

Many readers will likely believe that the traits listed above apply only to people occupying the bottom edge of society's social strata, the uneducated and unsophisticated. However, this is not so. Stalkers can come from any class and from any background.

"This [stalking] crosses all segments of society," said Mark Smith of the Dade County State Attorney's Office. "We've had airline pilots in here, attorneys."[41]

According to an article in *Essence* magazine: "[Stalkers] can be rich, poor, professional people, or laborers. But whatever their qualities...the one characteristic stalkers share is persistence."[42]

Even as a police officer who has seen the worse side of humanity and consequently seldom shocked, I am still surprised by the large number of people with a considerable stake in society who become stalkers. I am amazed by the number of people with a tremendous amount to lose who throw away everything and become stalkers, as the following incident demonstrates.

"You're gonna get a letter from me, and you'd better listen to every word of it and do what it tells you to do or you're gonna be in serious trouble and you're not gonna see your daughter again, you hear me?" The garbled voice on the telephone came from a stalker who had been terrorizing New York socialite and GOP fund-raiser Joy Silverman. "I'm a sick and desperate man," the voice continued. "I need the money, and you'll be hearing from me."[43]

Was this the voice of a small-time hoodlum trying to make one big score? The voice of a demented psychopath who had simply picked Ms. Silverman by chance? No, the voice, distorted by an electronic device attached to the telephone, turned out to be that of Sol Wachtler, chief justice of the New York State Court of Appeals, New York's highest court.

The story began several years earlier. Wachtler and Silverman became involved in a long extramarital affair after Wachtler had been named as executor for the estate of Silverman's stepfather. After several years, Silverman decided to end the relationship, but Wachtler, apparently upset by her decision, couldn't accept this, and began secretly stalking her soon afterward.

Often spoken of as a possible U.S. Supreme Court nominee and a likely candidate for governor of New York, Wachtler publicly kept up his staid appearance as the powerful and revered head of New York's court system. Privately, though, he had a much darker side. Soon after his and Silverman's breakup, he began making anonymous obscene and threatening telephone calls to her, and also began sending lewd and threatening letters and cards to her and her 14-year-old daughter, including one to the daughter that contained a condom. Eventually, Wachtler began making extortion demands. He told Silverman that unless she paid him $20,000 he would release embarrassing and compromising photos of her and her current lover. Those familiar with the case believe Wachtler must have thought that his actions would force Silverman to reestablish their relationship because of her fear of the unknown stalker.

Silverman, however, turned to her friend William S. Sessions, director of the FBI. After listening to her describe the anonymous threats and extortion attempts, Sessions got the FBI involved in the case, and eventually had 80 agents assigned to find the stalker. Placing a trace on Silverman's telephone, the FBI agents discovered the harassing calls came from Wachtler's mobile telephone, from a casino in Reno, Nevada, where Wachtler attended a conference, from an exclusive private club in New York, where Wachtler attended a meeting, from Louisville while Wachtler was visiting there, and from a pay phone in Roslyn, New York, from which the FBI lifted a fingerprint belonging to Wachtler.

After Silverman received instructions from the caller about where to deliver the extortion money, FBI agents set up surveillance around the money drop site: the Shanley Laundry in midtown Manhattan. Stunned agents watched as Wachtler, in his state-issued black Caprice, cruised around the area several times, then sped away. When the agents stopped him, they found on the front seat of his car an electronic device for distorting voices over the telephone. On questioning by the authorities, Wachtler admitted everything.

Judge Wachtler resigned his $120,000 a year job and eventually pled guilty to sending anonymous threats through the mail. He received a 15-month prison sentence in the federal correctional facility at Butner, North Carolina. In August 1994, following his release from prison, Wachtler entered a halfway house in Brooklyn.

➤   ➤   ➤   ➤

Although the above incident stunned everyone who knew Judge Wachtler, his case certainly doesn't stand alone as the only person of high social standing who became a stalker. My research uncovered a huge number of high-profile people who became stalkers.

New York Judge S. Barrett Hickman accused fellow Judge Lorraine Miller of stalking him after he ended their 5-year relationship. Hickman, in his complaint, said he received constant telephone hang-ups and hate mail from Judge Miller.

In San Francisco, a court found a 46-year-old attorney guilty of stalking a local judge and his 23-year-old daughter. The attorney reportedly became infatuated with the judge's daughter when they met through a mutual friend. Although the young woman thought little of their meeting and left soon afterward for Europe, the attorney began sending her love letters. When the woman returned to America and began attending a college out of state, where the attorney could not locate her, the attorney began sending dozens of poems and letters to the young girl's father, a municipal court judge. Some of the poems and letters spoke of plans to marry the judge's daughter, but others contained threats. At the trial, the court played a tape from the judge's answering machine on which the attorney said, "I will kill your mother dead and your hired gun, too."[44]

The legal profession isn't the only occupation to reveal unlikely stalkers. Quite the contrary.

John Heard, the actor who played Macaulay Culkin's father in the movie *Home Alone*, recently faced charges that he had stalked actress Melissa Leo and their 9-year-old son. He also faced charges of assaulting Miss Leo's present boyfriend. In her complaint to police, Leo said, "I fear for the safety of my son and my safety. He is stalking my son and must be stopped before something else happens." Miss Leo's boyfriend, in his complaint to police, said that Heard assaulted him at the Baltimore school the 9-year-old attends, and repeatedly threatened him over the telephone. In 1994, a judge denied Heard custody of his and Miss Leo's son because the judge said Heard lacked "temperament in parenting skills" and had a history of physical abuse with Leo.[45]

Actor James Farentino stalked television producer Tina Sinatra, Frank Sinatra's daughter, after the breakup of their 5-year romance. According to Los Angeles Deputy City Attorney Liz Gertz, "Death threats had sort of been going on for months." Gertz said Farentino telephoned Tina Sinatra after she obtained a temporary restraining order and said, "Knock it off, kid, you're going to die and so am I."[46] The City Attorney's Office charged Farentino with one count of stalking, one count of ignoring a restraining order, and two counts of making annoying phone calls. Found guilty, Farentino received a sentence of 3 years' probation and an order to undergo psychiatric and alcohol counseling.

A gynecologist in Pennsylvania allegedly followed his wife to a gathering at their children's school and threatened her. The police charged him with harassment, stalking, and violation of a protective order. A court set bond at $100,000. The previous year this same doctor pled guilty to harassing his wife by making silent calls to her house, which the police traced to his phone.

A bank president in Mississippi received a jail sentence for violating a court order not to contact his estranged wife. According to court records, the bank president made over 25 calls to his wife at her home and place of business. He also made numerous visits to the home where he and his wife had lived and his wife still resided.

Also in Mississippi, police arrested a state representative after his ex-girlfriend complained that he had been stalking and harassing her. The ex-girlfriend, who had been engaged to the state representative, said he called her after she broke off the engagement and threatened to kill her, then showed up at her apartment. The ex-girlfriend taped the telephone calls and gave them to police, who confirmed that the tapes supported her charges.

A former school superintendent and city councilman in Ohio surrendered to police after being accused of stalking a high school secretary. The woman claimed he stalked her at her apartment.

In Philadelphia, a school board member resigned after being arrested a second time for stalking a former girlfriend. The ex-girlfriend, who had broken off a 7-year relationship with the school board member, said she believed he was responsible for slashing her tires, spray-painting obscenities on her car, and sending her dozens of anonymous letters. Police arrested the former school board member after witnessing him use a 6-inch awl to scratch the side of her car.

A professor of architecture and urban design at Kansas University pled guilty to stalking a woman who had been his therapist. According to the victim, who said she and the professor were never romantically involved, the man parked by her house and kept a log of all the cars that drove down her street, claiming that all of the male drivers were her lovers. The victim said.the stalking also involved nasty telephone messages and hundreds of hang-up calls.

Even America's greatest heroes are not immune to charges of stalking. In February 1994, an aerospace engineer, Bernadette Cardenas, sued astronaut Sam Gemar, claiming that the astronaut had stalked her after she gave birth to their child 2 years before. Cardenas said that Gemar made harassing and intimidating calls to her both at home and at work. She also said that Gemar's wife attempted to get her fired after learning of the affair.

Police in Melbourne, Florida, arrested a fellow officer after he allegedly harassed his former girlfriend with telephone calls, and also attempted to break into her house. In Mount Olivet, Kentucky, the police chief, 64-year-old William Staggs, received a jail sentence for stalking a 24-year-old woman. The chief reportedly called and threatened the woman the day after he was released from probation on a previous charge of harassing her. In Saint Paul, Minnesota, police arrested a deputy sheriff after he allegedly stalked a former girlfriend despite her having a restraining order against him. In Fort Worth, Texas, police arrested former Pelican Bay, Texas, Police Chief Tom Jenkins for allegedly stalking his ex-wife, threatening her with a sawed-off shotgun, and trailing her to a busy intersection in downtown Fort Worth with a homemade bomb in the trunk of his car. In Orlando, Florida, police arrested and charged an officer with stalking another officer. The two officers, one male and one female, had apparently become friends when they met at the Training Academy. However, when the female officer was to be married, the male officer reportedly blocked her entry into the wedding chapel and insisted that she be photographed with him first. Afterward, she said, he began stalking her.

The above anecdotes reveal that anyone can become a stalker or a stalking victim. And although the incidents related above involved male stalkers, this is by no means the rule for stalking. As will be seen in the following incidents and throughout this book, men stalk women, men stalk men, women stalk men, and women stalk women.

➤   ➤   ➤   ➤

For 8 years, according to the prosecutor handling the case, Diane Schaefer trailed world-renowned cancer specialist Dr. Murray Brennan. She would show up at medical conferences the doctor attended in such places as Boca Raton (Florida), San Francisco, and Milan (Italy). She would often try to get into taxi cabs with him, and several times she managed to get herself seated next to him on airplanes. During the 8 years, Schaefer sent Dr. Brennan hundreds of letters, and called his office so many times, using different names and trying to disguise her voice, that the receptionists were forced to question the identity of every caller.

Following one of Schaefer's arrests for stalking Dr. Brennan, the police found in her purse a book containing Dr. Brennan's travel schedule, information on his children and friends, and the telephone numbers of his neighbors. Although Dr. Brennan vehemently denies it and most people connected with the case believe she fantasized the entire relationship, Schaefer remains absolutely convinced that she and Dr. Brennan had an affair.

As with most stalking cases, when after several years Dr. Brennan didn't respond to Schaefer's entreaties, her calls and letters became dark and threatening. Dr. Brennan began taping her calls and eventually took all of the evidence to the District Attorney's Office. After several years of restraining orders, legal wrangling, and more harassment, an all-female jury finally convicted Schaefer of seven counts of aggravated harassment. She received the maximum sentence: 2 years in prison.

In Lexington, Kentucky, a court sentenced a woman to 6 months in jail for stalking a woman who had dated her husband several years before the stalker and her husband were married. According to court records, for years the wife harassed the woman with hang-up calls, drive-bys, and deliveries of dresses several sizes too large for her.

In Santa Ana, California, a woman received a 5-year prison sentence for stalking a man who had spurned her romantic advances. The woman threatened to kill him, and also falsely reported him as a child molester. In addition, she threatened to burn down his house and kidnap his young son. At the trial she apologized to the victim, saying, "I don't know what possessed me to do the things that I did. I didn't mean to be malicious." Nevertheless, after the trial, the victim said he continued to receive crank calls from the woman.[47]

A woman in Bradenton, Florida, reportedly fell in love with a paramedic who responded to an emergency call at her house. When informed of her desire, he told her that he wasn't interested because he was married. The woman, however, began following him and calling his home. The victim complained to the police that the stalker telephoned him constantly and threatened him, his wife, and his daughter.

Interestingly, the crime of stalking also knows no age limits.

In Tallahassee, Florida, police charged a 72-year-old man with conducting a year-long campaign of obscene phone calls and harassment, which included publicly posting sexually explicit photographs of his ex-girlfriend. In Macomb Township, Michigan, a court issued an arrest warrant for a 79-year-old woman accused of stalking an 80-year-old man. The man claimed that for 3 years the woman had been leaving him love notes, telephoning him, blowing him kisses, and proposing marriage whenever she passed him. In Fort Lauderdale, Florida, police arrested a 66-year-old man for stalking his 75-year-old ex-girlfriend. The woman reportedly called the police 18 times in one month about him bothering and harassing her.

This lack of age discrimination for stalkers also is seen in the other direction. In Hastings, Michigan, local authorities faced a serious dilemma about what to do with a 9-year-old boy accused of stalking a 10-year-old girl. He was too young to prosecute, yet authorities knew something had to be done about the situation. The boy reportedly called the girl's house over 200 times and left messages on the answering machine saying, "I want to be your lover."[48] A judge eventually dropped the case after the boy underwent 6 months of counseling.

In Albuquerque, New Mexico, authorities brought a 10-year-old boy into domestic violence court. In a complaint filed by the parents of an 11-year-old girl, the parents claimed that the boy, who at one time had a crush on their daughter, punched her, made threatening telephone calls to their home, broke windows in their house, and stole hubcaps from their car.

From the anecdotes in this chapter, it should be exceedingly clear that stalkers come from every background and every level of society, as do stalking victims. And even though much of the stalking appears to be committed by individuals who claim to care for and love the victims, far too many times stalking ends in violence and death. For this reason all incidents of stalking should be taken seriously for what they are: crimes committed by disturbed individuals.

> ➤ ➤ ➤ ➤ ➤ **3**

INTIMATE-PARTNER STALKING

"She really and truly believed that he would kill her before it was all over with," said a friend of Bluffton, Indiana, resident Mary Ellet.[49]

Unfortunately, Mary Ellet was right. On 12 December 1994, Mary's estranged husband, Wilbur Ellet, shot her twice with a shotgun as she left work at the Bluffton Rubber Company. She died later at a local hospital. Wilbur had reportedly been stalking Mary for months.

The chain of events that led to this tragedy began in September 1994 when Mary filed for a divorce from Wilbur, citing an irretrievable breakdown of their marriage. Friends of the couple said that Wilbur had been physically and emotionally abusive to Mary during their marriage, often slapping and shoving her or calling her names.

Several times in the first month after filing for a divorce Mary called police about Wilbur, once for slashing her car tires and once for physically assaulting her. Because of her fear of Wilbur, Mary stayed for a time with some friends, who eventually had to have their telephone number changed due to Wilbur calling their home 20 to 30 times a day and making threats against both Mary and them.

Finally, Mary applied for and received a restraining order against Wilbur, which he violated regularly. In the following months, police arrested Wilbur twice on four counts of violating the restraining order, and reportedly, there were many other violations. Mary contacted police on 7 October 1994, reporting that Wilbur, in defiance of the restraining order, repeatedly drove by her house. On 8 October 1994, she again called police, this time to report that Wilbur had called her, told her he had a gun, and was going to kill himself. When officers arrived at Wilbur's apartment he shot himself in the stomach.

On 21 October 1994, after being released from the hospital, Wilbur reportedly parked his truck near Mary's house and watched her. Several days later, he parked near the house of a friend of Mary's, whom she was visiting, and again watched her. Later the same day, he called Mary at her home and demanded that she get a man out of the house. Wilbur, again parked nearby, had apparently watched Mary enter her home with a friend. Mary made a written complaint to police that day. She wrote that she and her daughter were "terrified of this man...neither of us want to be alone, because of being afraid of what this man will do next. I'm constantly looking over my shoulder, always expecting to see him."

On 30 October 1994, a burglary occurred at Mary's home. The intruder cut the gas lines, sliced electrical cords, and unhooked the washing machine water line, sending water gushing through the house.

On 2 November 1994, state police arrested Wilbur after he telephoned his wife, accusing her of adultery. "You and your son-of-a-bitch are trash," he told her, "and trash needs to be destroyed."

The police arrested Wilbur on 8 November 1994 for another violation of the restraining order. Each time police arrested Wilbur, however, a judge set a low bond, and Wilbur would be back on the street, only to once more begin harassing his estranged wife.

About this time, Mary, exhausted from the continuous stalking, began making plans if anything happened to her. Mary arranged for friends to care for her daughter and gave a friend the key to her house. In mid-November, Wilbur reportedly called Mary and told her that she wouldn't live to see the next holiday season. On 12 December 1994, he fulfilled that promise. When police arrived at the Bluffton Rubber Company they discovered Mary lying on the ground, mortally wounded from two shotgun blasts. They found Wilbur sitting nearby, waiting to be arrested. On 26 June 1995, after entering into a plea bargain, Wilbur received a 45-year prison sentence.

Along with the lethal outcome, another very disturbing aspect to this case is that legally there was little the authorities could do to stop Wilbur. Although the victims of intimate-partner stalking may be convinced that their stalkers are going to kill them, usually the stalkers can't be arrested and held for long periods until something serious happens. For this reason, stalking victims must heed the advice given in later chapters on preventative measures, which can make incidents such as this one much less likely to happen.

➤   ➤   ➤   ➤

The above incident, unfortunately, is not uncommon in stalking cases involving intimate partners, particularly when the stalker has formerly been abusive to the intimate partner. As discussed in the previous chapter, once the relationship ends, this group of stalkers, fearing they will lose their identity and self-worth, often become desperate to reestablish the dominance and control they wielded during the relationship. If they find this isn't possible they can become suicidal or homicidal, or both. According to the Bureau of Justice Statistics report *Female Victims of Violent Crime*, in 29 percent of all violence against women by a lone offender the perpetrator was an intimate; women are about seven times more likely than men to experience violence committed by an intimate; and female victims of violence by an intimate are more often injured seriously enough to require medical attention than are females victimized by a stranger.[50] But intimate-partner stalking can end in much worse than just injury. It can, as in the incident above, end in death if the stalkers cannot regain the control they so intensely and desperately need.

According to Julie Owen, a battered women's advocate in Hawaii, "The women I know who have been stalked have been in relationships with people who have power and control issues."[51]

How much control do intimate-partner stalkers want? Total control.

"One time a girlfriend was visiting me, and we were talking about some things we had done before I met my husband," explained a woman who was eventually stalked by her husband. "This infuriated him so much he threw us both out of the house. I wasn't allowed to have any past before him."

Many intimate-partner stalkers who have spent years dominating and controlling their partners simply cannot face the prospect that the people they've controlled for so long have successfully gotten away—have proven themselves stronger than the stalkers. Wayne Chaney wrote in a diary he kept about the stalking of his ex-wife, Connie: "I couldn't live with myself thinking or knowing she had won, or she got me. No! This is war." Tragically, he eventually murdered Connie.[52]

According to Linden Gross in his book *To Have or to Harm*: "We all have problems with rejection, especially if we're emotionally invested in a relationship. For the majority of us, however, rejection doesn't imply devastation. Even through the pain, however excruciating, our identities stay intact, our sense of self-worth bruised, perhaps, but still operational."[53] This isn't so, however, for intimate-partner stalkers. Because of their need for total control over someone, when the relationship breaks up their world is devastated. Their personality disorders won't allow them to accept rejection.

According to the National Victim Center: "While this kind of stalker may or may not have psychological disorders, all clearly have personality disorders."[54] A few of these personality disorders, according to the Center, include:

1   Socially maladjusted and inept
2   Emotionally immature
3   Often subject to feelings of powerlessness
4   Unable to succeed in relationships by socially acceptable means
5   Jealousy, bordering on paranoia
6   Extremely insecure about themselves
7   Often suffering from low self-esteem

According to experts, intimate-partner stalkers can be the most dangerous type of stalkers because they often have a history of violence against their victims, and consequently feel totally uninhibited about using more or heightened violence in an effort to get them back. The stalkers know that violence has worked for them in the past, and so they have no reason to believe that it won't work again. Also, intimate-partner stalkers know their victims well: their family, place of employment, recreational activities, and so forth. They know where to find their victims.

Intimate-partner stalkers, because of the dominance and control once held over their victims, often have the mind-set that the victims are their property, to do with as they wish, and to reclaim in any way they see fit. And, believing that their lives won't be worth living if they can't recapture the victims as their property, they often feel they have nothing to lose by using extreme measures. Consequently, these stalkers feel totally justified in doing just about anything in an effort to regain control over their victims. And, since the stalkers believe the victims belong to them, they show no regard for restraining orders, and may instead be infuriated by them, feeling they are being denied their God-given rights.

"When you know a person is capable of anything, and he also feels he has nothing to lose," a stalking victim told me, "you'd better be scared of him. He'll kill you."

While Mary Ellet, in the incident discussed at the beginning of this chapter, was understandably frightened of Wilbur, and consequently tried to avoid any contact with him, even to the point of hiding, murderous-minded stalkers often know just where to find their victims—a place the victims often can't change—their place of employment. Although stalkers, after committing the ultimate control crime—murder—will many times wait for police to arrive and arrest them, as Wilbur did, a stalking can end even more violently than this, as demonstrated in the following incidents.

Twenty-nine-year-old Pamela Cook and 46-year-old Crawford Outen carried on a secret affair when they both worked at the Lancaster (South Carolina) Telephone Company. Crawford was an electronics specialist and Pamela a receptionist. At the time of their affair both were married to other people. Pamela, however, apparently decided to end the affair after the phone company dismissed both her and Crawford. Crawford couldn't accept this. Soon after, in April 1994, Pamela swore out warrants against Crawford, whom she accused of harassment.

In October 1994, Pamela stood waiting in the Lancaster County Drugstore for a prescription to be filled when Crawford walked up behind her and grabbed her arm. According to the police report, he told her, "See how easy it is to find you. And you will pay."[55]

Immediately afterward, Pamela swore out a warrant against Crawford for stalking her. She told police that Crawford followed and harassed her constantly, and had threatened to kill both her and her husband. Although the police arrested Crawford, a local magistrate set a low bond, with the condition that he stay away from Pamela and her family, and so Crawford soon got out of jail.

On 5 January 1995, Crawford stormed into the City of Lancaster Finance Office, where Pamela was training for a new job. Pulling out a .25-caliber pistol, he shot Pamela three times, twice in the head and once in the upper body, sending the other employees scrambling under desks and behind doors. He then turned the gun on himself, firing one bullet into his head.

"There was nothing you could do in that situation," said an employee of the finance office. "You're just hoping he doesn't come in after you."[56]

Pamela died that day. Crawford died the following day.

In another incident, this one in New York City, Patricia Clark moved out of the apartment she shared with Stanley King, meaning to end their intimate relationship because of his possessiveness and jealousy. Stanley, however, didn't want to end the relationship. For the next year he followed

Patricia constantly and telephoned her over and over at her home and at her workplace, the Woodmere (Long Island) Nursing Center. On one occasion he went to her apartment with a gun and shouted, "I'll kill you!" Family members slammed the door and called 911.

"It was like he was her shadow," said a cousin of Patricia's. "He told her, 'I can see every move you make, but you can't see me.'"[57]

Fearing for her safety, Patricia requested and obtained a restraining order. Stanley repeatedly ignored the order and finally confronted Patricia at her job at the nursing center. Following a heated discussion, Stanley pulled out a gun, shot 26-year-old Patricia to death, and then killed himself.

Although the incidents of intimate-partner stalking given so far in this chapter involve male stalkers and female victims, this certainly isn't universal. In Pineville, Kentucky, Walter Dean Knuckles accused his estranged wife of both stalking and trying to kill him. He told police that she showed up at his house, shot him, and then waited around for an hour and a half, periodically checking his pulse to see if he was dead yet. When Walter, feeling faint and fearing he might die if he didn't get help, finally pretended to be unconscious, she left. He then crawled outside and got help.

The nightmare, however, wasn't over. Later, police arrested the wife's boyfriend when he allegedly attempted to hire a hitman to kill Walter. Believing there would be more attempts on his life, Walter had already gone into hiding. Records show that both Walter's estranged wife and her boyfriend have been charged with stalking other people in the past.

Interestingly, researchers find that intimate-partner stalking often follows a three-phase cycle. First is the tension-building phase, which can include such things as making hundreds of telephone calls and sending dozens of letters, showing up wherever the victims are, casual surveillance of the victims, and following the victims wherever they go. However, when these actions don't accomplish what the stalkers want, the tension builds, and eventually the stalkers may begin making threats, vandalizing property, and instituting more forceful attempts to make the victims give in to their demands.

The second phase is the violence phase. Once the stalkers realize that their efforts in the first phase have failed, they often resort to violence against not only the victims but also the victims' friends and family. This can include angry face-to-face confrontations, physical assaults (including rape), kidnapping, and, in extreme cases, murder.

The third phase is the hearts and flowers phase. The stalkers revert back to the less violent tactics, and will often either beg forgiveness for the violence or appear to abandon the stalking altogether. Unfortunately, any cessation is usually only temporary. This pause in the stalking can actually be an extremely dangerous period because many times the victims falsely believe that the nightmare is over, and consequently let down their guard. They then can be caught unprepared and unprotected when the stalking suddenly begins again, often violently. The following incident clearly demonstrates how this cycle of violence works in intimate-partner stalking cases.

➤　　➤　　➤　　➤

Sandy Henes, a widow with three children, lived in Ann Arbor, Michigan, when she met her future husband, John Abrahams. She found him very attractive, and he seemed taken with her, so after a few months of dating they decided to move in together. However, on the first night after moving in together John set a pattern for their future relationship: he beat her.

"I was shocked," Sandy told *Dallas Morning News* reporter Pam Maples. "No one had ever hit me. He was very apologetic, said it would never happen again."[58]

Despite this episode, Sandy married John, and in the following years he beat, kicked, and injured her regularly, always apologizing afterward and swearing that it would never happen again. More times than she can remember, though, Sandy had to go to the hospital emergency room to be treated for painful injuries.

Finally, Sandy had had enough and moved out, filing for divorce. John, however, like most physically abusive men, was emotionally dependent on Sandy, and wouldn't be gotten rid of that easily. John began stalking her. Finally, he tracked her down, broke into where she was staying, and beat her.

After the beating, John, in the hearts and flowers phase, became repentant, calling Sandy on the telephone over and over, and begging her to take him back. After a year had gone by with no new violence, their divorce not yet finalized, Sandy took John back and they bought a house together. But almost as soon as they moved back in together the beatings began again.

During this time, John's brother, a high school coach, murdered his ex-wife with an ax, and John sought to win custody of his 12-year-old nephew. John stopped beating Sandy because he didn't want to jeopardize his chances of getting the custody he was seeking. He lost the request for custody when Sandy spoke to the social worker handling the case about John's violence.

Sandy and John separated again shortly after this, and John moved to California. However, Sandy's respite was short-lived, as John soon returned to Michigan and began stalking her once more. He would call her on the telephone continuously, cycling rapidly through the phases, one time screaming what he was going to do to her, and the next time begging her to forgive him. He also began following her and keeping her under surveillance.

Finally, one Friday morning, as Sandy walked from the bus stop to work, John came up behind her, brandished a .357 magnum revolver, and forced her into a car. He kept her prisoner for 16 hours in both Ann Arbor and Detroit, sexually assaulting her twice.

Fortunately, before they left Ann Arbor for Detroit, Sandy managed to make a telephone call to a friend. The friend notified authorities, and the Detroit Police Department SWAT Team rescued Sandy several hours later. Although John attempted at the scene to persuade the SWAT officers that Sandy had come along with him willingly, her pain from the many injuries that John had inflicted on her during the ordeal convinced them otherwise, and John was taken into custody.

A court eventually convicted John and sentenced him to prison for kidnapping and rape. However, after serving only 4½ years, the state of Michigan paroled him.

"He hadn't been out two weeks and he found me," Sandy said.[59]

Because of this resumption of the stalking, Sandy moved, but John found her again. When John finished his parole, though, he moved to California, got married again, and had a child. Sandy thought her troubles with John were over, but then he began making trips back to Michigan.

"In my soul, I don't think this will be over until I have to kill him," said Sandy. "I hope I'm wrong, but I just feel the day will come and it will be him or me. And it's not going to be me. It's never going to be me again."[60]

Sandy obtained a gun permit. She now carries a handgun wherever she goes.

➤   ➤   ➤   ➤

An important point for victims or potential victims of intimate-partner stalking to remember about this cycle of stalking is that it is not uniform or predictable. In the above incident, John moved through the phases fairly rapidly, at times changing from being loving to brutal in only seconds. For other stalkers, it may take years to move from one phase to another, and some may never move out of the first phase. But most important, because a stalker may cycle from being a minor nuisance to a physical threat extremely rapidly, intimate-partner stalking victims must always be on guard. Fortunately, as we shall see, there are measures stalking victims can take that will make their lives much safer.

CASUAL ACQUAINTANCE STALKING

"**I** will get you before I die; it might be my death, but I will get you, Marc, I will get you."

The words of a spurned lover? The vindictive statement of a wife abandoned for a younger woman? No. These are the words of a client of Minneapolis attorney Marc Kurzman, a client whom he successfully defended against attempts by her family to have her committed. According to Kurzman, when the case ended she thanked him and went on her way. That was the extent of their relationship. He thought.

Soon after the case ended, however, Kurzman began receiving strange, rambling letters from the former client. When Kurzman first began getting the letters, over a decade ago, he was more amused than frightened by them. "I was getting one or two letters a day," Kurzman said. "They were filled with poetry and wild imaginings, almost as if someone were writing fiction. I used them as a reward for my staff. My 'employee of the week' would get to open them."

However, after a while the letters lost their humor because the woman began following and threatening Kurzman. In addition, she would demand Kurzman's help on nonexistent lawsuits and insist that he acknowledge a romantic relationship that she imagined they had had.

Soon, the letters also began to change in tone. Rather than poetry, they contained references to her willingness to die as long as she could take Kurzman with her. Once, the woman broke into Kurzman's house and left behind a rose, a teddy bear, and a pair of eyeglasses. The next day the woman called Kurzman's office and told the staff that she had left her glasses at his home when she visited him, hinting at their romantic involvement. She also kept Kurzman constantly under surveillance, telling him one time how the color of his car matched the color of his eyes and made it easy to follow him.

Although Kurzman had an unlisted telephone number at his home, the woman somehow obtained it and made hundreds of harassing calls. During her more than one decade of stalking the attorney, she has left messages on Kurzman's voice mail that filled 28 cassette tapes. Once, after a court released the woman following an appearance because of her harassment of Kurzman, she smashed out the headlights of Kurzman's automobile. She left a note behind that said: "Bet you thought you were rid of me for a while."

Recently, Kurzman leaped out of bed late at night, electrified with terror, when he heard his front door being smashed in. Several embarrassed police officers told him that they had received a call reporting he had shot himself. While the officers were there the woman phoned.

Ironically, Kurzman recently represented several clients arrested under Minnesota's stalking law because of their activities involving abortion rights. While he was attempting to get his clients off on the stalking charges by challenging the constitutionality of the law, he was at the same time the victim of stalking and would eventually look to the law to protect him. "It's ironic as hell," he said. After he got the charges dropped against his clients, Kurzman began pushing for stiffer penalties for stalking.

Fortunately for Kurzman, his stalker recently moved to California. Reportedly, she is still a stalker, but now has found a new target.[61]

Many people have become involved in lobbying for new or stiffer laws against stalking because of their experience as victims of this crime. Kathleen Krueger, wife of Texas Senator Bob Krueger, testified before a Senate Judiciary Committee, telling the members how being a stalking victim can turn a happy, normal life into a never-ending nightmare of paranoia. How every day becomes an endless trauma of never knowing when the stalker will call or show up, but knowing with certainty that he will. She and her husband have been victimized by a stalker for over a decade.

"Please, I urge you to pass a strong antistalking law for our sake and for the sake of thousands of victimized families," Kathleen told the Senate committee members.[62]

The nightmare for the Kruegers began in 1983 when Bob Krueger, then a Texas rancher and businessman, decided to seek a U.S. Senate seat.

Once he had entered the race, Bob began forming a campaign staff, which came to include Thomas Humphrey, a pilot who owned a single-engine airplane. Thomas's job would be to fly Bob to his various campaign appearances around Texas. Everyone on the staff liked Thomas, who appeared to be a solid, reliable employee who enjoyed his work.

In May 1984, however, Bob lost the primary election by one-tenth of a percentage point. Naturally, this deeply disappointed Bob and all of his campaign staff. Thomas, however, was more than deeply disappointed. He appeared devastated, as if his life had ended. He seemed totally destroyed by the defeat, as if he had invested his entire life and identity in the campaign.

After the campaign ended, other members of the staff moved on to other jobs, but not Thomas. He often stopped at Bob and Kathleen's house to visit. He seemed deeply troubled, and it appeared that all he could think of and talk about was the campaign loss. Bob tried, without success, to talk Thomas out of his funk, to convince him this wasn't the end of the world. Finally, when the visits continued unabated, Bob insisted that Thomas get on with his life, and that he respect his and Kathleen's privacy.

That event seemed to change Thomas from a troubled ex-employee into an obsessed stalker. He suddenly began telephoning the Kruegers at all hours, at one point calling them over a 100 times a day. He would ring their doorbell, frightening Kathleen who would peek out and watch him stand staring at the door for 20 minutes at a time, waiting for someone to open it. He began leaving bizarre, rambling, and threatening notes in their mailbox. One note read: "Look how close I can get to you. See, I could kill you right now if I·wanted to."

For a time, to the distress of the Kruegers, Thomas rented the house across the street from them. They would see him peeking out at them from behind the curtains when they entered and left their home. Although Thomas finally moved from Texas to California, his obsession with the Kruegers never waned, nor did his telephone calls to their home. For 3 years the daily harassment continued, and because Bob was by then both a congressman and ambassador-at-large to Mexico, their home number was listed in the phone book. When Kathleen became pregnant, however, she insisted that they get an unlisted number. There was little else they could do. At that time Texas had no law to stop Thomas's stalking.

"It was baffling to me that there was this gaping hole in our laws that would allow someone to do this," Kathleen said. "I just kept thinking, 'How could this be possible in the United States of America?'"[63]

Getting an unlisted home number, however, didn't stop Thomas. He now began calling Bob's office, again often over 100 times a day. During one call from California, he said, "I'm going to kill you. I'm going to kill you. I'm going to kill you. I've hired a killer to put a .22-caliber to your head while you're sleeping next to your wife. You won't be much of an ambassador with a hole in your head."[64]

Because this threat was made between states, the FBI became involved in the case, and went to Thomas's home in California to arrest him. They didn't find him there, though, and immediately feared he was en route to Texas to carry out his threat. However, when they traced a telephone number Thomas gave when he called Bob again, the FBI tracked him to a hotel in California, where they arrested him.

In May 1989, Thomas pled guilty to making death threats and received a 12-month sentence. Within a few months of being released from prison, though, Thomas began the stalking again, and a judge sent him back to prison. Released once more, he again immediately began the stalking and was once again sent back to prison.

The Kruegers are convinced that the prison sentence, though giving them a respite from the stalking, will not stop Thomas from beginning again as soon as he is released. Senator Krueger cosponsored a bill making stalking a federal offense if the stalker crosses state lines to stalk or uses the mail to make a threat.

As the two incidents related above clearly show, stalking need not involve an intimate relationship with the victims. The relationship can be as minor as a business arrangement, or, as in the following incident, even much less than that.

Janet Lee Pyles worked at Sue's Handy Mart at the intersection of Kentucky Highways 90 and 92 in Monticello, Kentucky. Michael Alley was a customer there. That was the extent of Janet and Michael's relationship. Michael, however, apparently became infatuated with Janet and began showing up constantly at the store whenever she worked, following her wherever she went, and leaving behind barely readable notes, pleading for a date.

Michael first began visiting the Handy Mart in the summer of 1995. Janet had never met him before that. On 4 August 1995, Janet swore out her first complaint against Michael for harassment. "He followed me in public places (around my apartment and workplace) and left notes for me," she said in her complaint. "Not for any legitimate reason, but only to alarm and annoy me."

On 24 August 1995, Janet filed another complaint against Michael, this time for stalking. In her complaint it became apparent that she was becoming more alarmed and frightened by Michael. "The defendant has stalked me around my house and workplace and made implicit threats which have placed me in fear of injury, death or sexual assault," she said.

The police arrested Michael, who quickly posted the $1000 bond a local judge set. The court ordered him to stay away from Janet. He didn't.

On 24 October 1995, Janet filed a third complaint against Michael. "He is still stalking me," she said in her complaint, "thereby implicitly threatening me with reasonable fear of sexual assault, all of which occurred while a criminal complaint for stalking is pending."

The police again arrested Michael and he again quickly got out of jail, this time upon posting a $5000 bond. The court once more ordered him to stay away from Janet.

"He just kept on and on," said Janet's 14-year-old son. "Coming back and back. I knowed about it well. I was there several times when he come by."[65]

At just after noon on 27 November 1995, Michael stormed into Sue's Handy Mart while Janet was working. This time he brought along a .22-caliber rifle. He allegedly shot Janet four times, three times in the body and once in the head, killing her. He then reportedly shot another employee, Dolly Hogue, in the hip, afterward fleeing from the Handy Mart to his home. Although at first firing at police when they surrounded his mobile home, Michael eventually surrendered.

"Just write in the paper," Janet's son said, "that my mom was nice." Apparently, Janet's good nature and kindliness were what sparked Michael's stalking of her.[66]

As shown by the incidents discussed in this chapter, befriending or even just being polite to potential stalkers can be exceedingly dangerous. Any acts of kindness are often interpreted by stalkers as a sign of the true love that they are convinced exists between them and their victims. Even the most casual interaction, such as a momentary conversation, a quick lunch together in a crowded restaurant, or a smile across a room, can be seen as a romantic encounter by a potential stalker. A large number of people every year become stalking victims because they felt sorry for someone and showed him or her compassion, as demonstrated in the following incident.

> ➤ ➤ ➤ ➤

It was a "pity date," Christine Sloan said of her outing to the state fair with a man she had said hi to as she sat with some friends in a nightspot popular with college students in Columbia, South Carolina. When he asked her out, even though she didn't want to go, Christine said yes rather than hurt his feelings.

When Christine wouldn't go out with him again, the stalking began and progressed slowly, taking several years to reach the phase of violence. The stalking started with occasional telephone calls and gifts, such as flowers or candy. It slowly became more intense, until Christine's fiancé, Greg, finally spoke with the stalker when he called Christine's house.

"He said he saw it in the stars that they were meant to be together," Greg said. "That's the point where I said we're dealing with someone who is not rational. That was the start of years of hell for me and Christine."[67]

After this, the stalking began to progress rapidly toward the violence phase. The stalker, after a shouting match with Greg, reportedly told Greg that he was going to cut his and Christine's heads off and put them on posts. At Greg and Christine's wedding, Greg hired an off-duty police officer to watch for the stalker. Soon after the wedding, letters and telephone calls began pouring into the house.

"We have to live with this twenty-four hours a day," Greg said. "For the past four years, every time the phone rings, we think it's him. Every time the doorbell rings, we think it's him. Every time we hear a noise outside the house, we think it's him."[68]

Getting an unlisted phone number didn't work, as the stalker was able to obtain the new number. Greg bluntly telling the stalker several times to leave them alone also didn't work. Finally, the stalker made a threatening phone call to Christine's father, who reported it to police. Following this, the police arrested the stalker at his home in Virginia, and a judge committed the stalker to a psychiatric hospital. However, his stay there will likely be short, and Christine and Greg fear that their nightmare is simply on hold.

"He'll be back on the street and going after Christine again," Greg said, "and that's foremost on my mind."[69]

All of the anecdotes in this chapter highlight that very little interaction is needed with a potential stalker in order to trigger a long-term stalking episode. For this reason it is vitally important for potential stalking victims to watch for and recognize the warning signs of a stalker given in Chapter 2, and, if seen, to take the appropriate actions, which will be detailed in a later chapter. Attempting to appease or ignore stalkers simply won't work. Restraining and protective orders, though important and occasionally helpful, also often don't work. The stalkers' belief that they and their victims are meant for each other, or, as in the incident above, that "it is in the stars for them to be together," often overrides any fear these stalkers might have of the consequences of violating restraining or protective orders.

"Obsessive lovers truly believe—sometimes without realizing it—that their 'One Magic Person' alone can make them feel happy and fulfilled, solve all of their problems, give them the passion they've yearned for, and make them feel more wanted and loved than they've ever felt before," said psychotherapist Dr. Susan Forward. "With all of this power, the 'One Magic Person' becomes more than a lover—he or she becomes a necessity of life."[70]

How dangerous can a stalker be who only knows the victim casually? Very dangerous. According to the Bureau of Justice Statistics report *Violence against Women*, 36 percent of all aggravated assaults against women in this country are committed by acquaintances or friends, as are 53 percent of the rapes and sexual assaults and 22 percent of the homicides. Many of these women had been stalked beforehand by these acquaintances or friends.[71]

A very real danger with being stalked, as mentioned in the previous chapter, is that the victims must still work. Finding a new place to live for a while may not be difficult, but finding a new job or occupation, particularly when the victims have extensive education and training or have worked at their present job for a long time and accrued considerable seniority, just isn't easy, especially when the victims aren't sure just how dangerous the stalkers are or can be. Very few people will make such a radical life change as getting a new occupation because of threats by a casual acquaintance. Consequently, stalkers know they can go to the victims' place of employment and likely find them there.

"A stalker knows if they can't catch you at home," said Yvette Miller, a woman stalked for several years by an ex-boyfriend, "they can catch you at work."[72]

According to U.S. Labor Department figures, murder is the leading cause of death for women in the workplace, and one of the top causes of death for men. Many of these deaths are the result of stalking. A study by the Bureau of Justice Statistics found that one in every six violent crimes in America occurs in the workplace, accounting for approximately 1 million crimes a year. But multiplying the danger of this problem is the fact that the stalking of victims on the job is a fairly new problem for U.S. businesses. Consequently, many managers and supervisors don't know how to respond to the danger, and may not afford the victims the protection they need. But top executives are finally beginning to recognize the seriousness of the problem. According to the 1996 Pinkerton Security Issues survey, workplace violence was ranked as the number one concern of executives of America's Fortune 1000 companies.[73]

However, a very real danger for many stalking victims is that often fellow employees of the victims seem unaware of the dangers of stalking, particularly receptionists and others responsible for securing entry into a business. In 1994, a court convicted Army sergeant Colton Holbrook of stalking and attempting to kill his ex-girlfriend at AT&T headquarters in New Jersey. Even though the building had controlled access, Holbrook talked his way in by saying he had a surprise engagement ring for his girlfriend. For many employed stalking victims, the worry is no longer whether they will keep their jobs or be laid off, but rather whether or not they will be killed on the job by a stalker.

While it is tragic and disturbing that some people can begin their obsessive stalking on as small an initiative as the victims appearing to be kind and polite to them, this does not mean that people should stop being kind and polite to others. It does mean, however, that we should be on the lookout for the signs of potential stalkers and take action immediately if we believe we may become stalking victims.

> > > > > 5

STRANGER STALKING

"Charles Nine, take a vandalism report, 4915 East Calhoun Street."

I pulled the radio microphone off of the dashboard clip, and answered the dispatcher. "Charles Nine's clear."

As I steered the police car toward the address, I assumed this would be just another boring, routine report run about a neighborhood kid throwing a rock and breaking a window, or about a person finding damage to some property that he or she would insist had been done purposely. But this run was neither of these. Instead, it introduced me to the fear and gut-wrenching anxiety that stalkers can introduce into the lives of others, and particularly into the lives of strangers.

I turned the police car onto Calhoun Street, a neighborhood of brick and aluminum-sided ranch homes, looking for number 4915. When I spotted the address and pulled the blue Ford Custom to the curb in front of a small, aluminum-sided home with an attached one-car garage, I could see that a silver Buick parked in the driveway sat on four flat tires.

"Good afternoon, ma'am," I said to an attractive woman I guessed to be in her middle twenties who answered my knock. "It looks like you've got someone really angry at you."

She nodded, and we both walked over and looked at her car. I could see that the victim obviously took pride in her automobile, the inside spotless and the outside smelling of fresh wax.

"Do you know who did this?" I asked, expecting her to tell me a story about an angry and disgruntled ex-husband or ex-boyfriend, the most likely suspect for this type of act.

Reaching out and tapping one of the flat tires with her toe, the woman seemed to think for a few moments before answering. "Oh, I'm pretty sure who did it. I just don't know who he is."

"Excuse me?" I said.

The woman then told me that for the last year she had been receiving telephone calls from a man, but she didn't know who he was. At first, she had thought the whole thing was funny, some kind of joke. It had started when a man called her late one night a year ago. He told her he thought she was beautiful and that he had been admiring her for a long time. He wouldn't say who he was, but she said she could tell from what he knew about her that he had been watching her. At first, she thought it might be one of the guys at work, and so for a while she played along, not wanting it to appear as if she didn't have a sense of humor in case it was all just a joke.

"I didn't want to be rude since I didn't know who the guy was," she said, "but after a while, when he wouldn't tell me who he was, I told him I had to go, and I hung up."

Her hanging up didn't seem to have any effect on the caller. At first, he would call her at least once a week, and initially the calls seemed friendly. He would tell her over and over how attractive she was, and then describe what she had been wearing that day and how nice she had looked in it. Although she checked with all of her friends to see if anyone had been asking about her, she never could find out who the caller might be. Eventually, the calls started coming daily, and also quickly became an annoyance as the man continued to refuse to tell her who he was. The woman said that when she finally began firmly telling the man that his calls were not welcome, his demeanor turned ugly and mean.

"He began saying things like I was just a stuck-up bitch, and he didn't like stuck-up bitches. After that, I had my phone number changed, but then he started calling me again. It couldn't have been more than a week or so later."

"When did this kind of stuff start?" I asked, nodding at her car.

The woman looked at me for a few moments, and then let out a breath. "I know I should have reported it sooner, but I didn't. It started a couple months ago. I thought it might just stop on its own. Whoever this guy is, he must've seen me and my boyfriend together, because he called me one night after my boyfriend had been here. He started screaming and calling me a slut. The next day someone threw a brick at the side of my garage." She waved for me to follow and we walked over and she showed me a large dent in her aluminum siding.

She then said that the caller told her the following day that it could be a bullet next time rather than a brick. She also said that the calls changed after this too. Rather than mean, the man now became obscene, telling her what he would like to do to her sexually. She said that every time he started talking dirty she would hang up on him, but then he would call back right away screaming what he'd do if she kept hanging up on him. One morning, after she had let her phone ring the previous night rather than answer it, she said she smelled an awful odor and found a dead dog in her yard.

"It's getting so that I hate it anymore when my phone rings. I know it's him. Every morning I hate to go outside because I know he's done something. And every night when I get home from work I'm scared to go inside because I'm afraid he might be in there waiting on me. I just don't know what I'm going to do. I can't go on like this." The woman looked at me wide-eyed and distraught.

"Have you thought about having the phone company try to trace the calls?" I asked. This event occurred in the early 1970s, and, in those days, tracing telephone calls was not as easy as today, but still it could be done. Also, in those days the police department didn't handle harassing telephone calls, the phone company did.

"I haven't wanted to report this," she said. "I kept hoping that maybe he'd eventually get tired of me hanging up on him and start calling someone else. But also I knew if I reported it my boyfriend would find out about it. Believe me, he won't understand. I don't know what he's going to do when he finds out. But I do know he's really going to be mad when he finds out how long this has been going on. But I finally just had to call you guys. This man's really starting to scare me. He told me a couple days ago that he's watching me all the time, and he said that he could rape me anytime he wanted. The other night he told me exactly when I came home, what I was wearing, everything. I don't know what to do. This guy's got me scared to death."

In those days we had no law against stalking, and there was little I could do for her, particularly as we didn't know who the caller was. After I had gotten all of the information I needed for my vandalism report, I again advised her to contact the phone company about getting a trace put on her telephone.

Unlike many incidents a police officer responds to, this one didn't just fade away after I went home or after I had taken a couple hundred more runs. It stuck in my mind and caused me some considerable heartburn. I took a lot of pride in being able to protect the people on my district, but after this run I began to realize how powerless both the victim and I really were in this type of case. I could also imagine the fear a single woman living by herself must feel knowing that a mentally disturbed person was out there somewhere watching her and waiting. I could imagine the terror she must have felt not knowing when this stalker might suddenly decide to strike out violently at her.

In the early 1970s the Indianapolis Police Department worked rotating shifts. We would work 7:00 AM to 3:00 PM one month, 11:00 PM to 7:00 AM the next, and then 3:00 PM to 11:00 PM. Several times while on the night shift I sat a block down from the woman's house with my lights off, hoping to see someone snooping around her property. I also watched for lights and movement in nearby houses in case the stalker turned out to be a neighbor. A couple of times I also did this early on the day shift in case the stalker might be some type of early morning deliveryman. Several months before, I had used this same technique to catch a burglar who had been tearing up my district. I also advised the other officers who worked the district about the problem. I received a note in early January from one of these officers that said he had taken a report of someone breaking into her house and turning off the furnace. I also found that the woman had had the phone company attempt to find out who the caller was, but that the calls had stopped while they were trying. We never did catch anyone, even though the stalking went on for at least another year before I transferred to a new district. I've wondered many times since I began writing this book if the stalker was ever caught, and thought about checking to see, but unfortunately our computerized record system doesn't go back that far.

➤　　➤　　➤　　➤

While being stalked by someone with whom the victim has had an intimate relationship, or by someone known to the victim who has perhaps attempted unsuccessfully to establish an intimate relationship, is frightening enough, at least the victim knows who the stalker is, what he or she is capable of, and what to likely expect. When victims are targeted by stalkers seemingly unknown to them, however, the stalking takes on a much more frightening, ominous feeling. Because the stalkers are unknown to the victims, the victims have no idea who to be on the lookout for, who to be careful of or around, and who to speak to and who to avoid. Although the danger level connected with stranger stalking may not in actuality be higher, the stress level most certainly is.

"What we call the 'stranger stalker' is the most terrifying because you just don't know how to deal with it," said FBI agent James Wright.[74]

Often stranger stalkers suffer from erotomania, a mental disorder that causes the stalker to believe another person, often a stranger, is in love with him or her. Because of this disorder, stranger stalkers may fantasize either that they have had an intimate relationship with their victims or that their victims truly love them and want to have an intimate relationship with them.

"Erotomania is directed at both men and women," said Dr. Park Dietz, "but more men act on the delusion."[75]

Although erotomania is the root cause of most celebrity stalkings, no one should be stunned by this because celebrities often hire large staffs just for the purpose of making them appear alluring and attractive to the public. So naturally they're going to attract a few such unstable people. But for the ordinary person this can be both confusing and terrifying.

Victims find themselves constantly asking: could the stalker be the stranger across the street, the person standing behind them in the store, or the driver of the car that seems to be following them? The victim has no idea who the stalker is, and also no idea what might happen. This unpredictability and uncertainty can be psychologically and emotionally crippling. The victim doesn't know the stalker's propensity for violence, what the stalker wants, or, more important, what the stalker plans to do.

Victims of stranger stalking often ask themselves: why me? They search through their memories for any event that might have provoked this reaction from a stranger. But many times, as the following incident shows, the victims of stranger stalking are simply selected at random.

An Allen County (Indiana) judge in June 1996 sentenced 31-year-old Michael Osselear to a 3-year prison term, with 2 years suspended, after he pled guilty to charges of stalking, harassment, and theft. Michael reportedly had never met his victim.

The stalking began after Michael broke into the victim's car and stole her vehicle registration. From this information he obtained her telephone number. According to the court records, Michael called the woman and told her that he would kill her if she didn't give him some of her personal items, including underwear, shoes, and photographs. Calling himself "the pantyhose rapist," he also told his victim that if she didn't give him those items he would kidnap another woman, torture her, and then telephone the victim so she could hear the kidnapped woman scream. He allegedly told the victim of having stalked other women, and that, if she would do as he demanded, he would move on to a new target.

According to Allen County court records, Michael made more than 80 harassing and threatening phone calls to the victim. He told her, when asked why he was doing this, that "he was the hunter and she was his target."[76] After this incident made the newspapers, another woman who said Michael had also stalked her reported to police that he had recently called and harassed her. This stalking, she said, took place after Michael had pled guilty to the charges involving the woman whose vehicle registration he stole.

Occasionally, as in the case above, victims of stranger stalking may eventually find out who their stalkers are. Often, the stalkers are completely unknown to them, as Michael was, sometimes they are just nodding acquaintances, and sometimes, as in the incident below, they are individuals who have had chance encounters with the victims.

West Palm Beach, Florida, resident Fonda Lurye had never met Officer Louis Perez of the West Palm Beach Police Department. In September 1993, she found his police car in her parking spot at the apartment complex where she lived. He allegedly told her that he was checking the neighborhood for prowlers. Ms. Lurye didn't give the incident much more thought.

A month after this chance meeting, Officer Perez reportedly knocked on Ms. Lurye's door late one night. He told her that he had seen two boys attempting to break into cars in the apartment parking lot, and he wanted to be sure that her car was all right. Police officials later said there was no report on file about any attempted car break-ins or suspicious activity in the area that day.

In January 1994, Officer Perez allegedly called the police dispatcher, attempted to disguise his voice, and reported that there were prowlers in the apartment complex where Ms. Lurye lived. As this was his patrol district, Officer Perez would be the officer sent to check on this. The dispatcher, however, recognized Officer Perez's voice, and alerted her supervisor, who instituted an internal police department investigation of Officer Perez.

Soon after the police department internal affairs investigation of Officer Perez began, Ms. Lurye started receiving calls from an anonymous man who said he was "going to get her." After being questioned by internal affairs detectives, Officer Perez reportedly admitted making the threatening calls and also admitted going several times to Ms. Lurye's apartment under the guise of checking for prowlers. The police department notified Officer Perez that he was going to be fired. Ms. Lurye, however, said she felt he ought to be arrested for stalking her.

According to an article in *Counseling Today*, a study of the Criminal and Supreme Courts of New York City, conducted by the Forensic Psychiatry Clinic, found that of the stalkers these courts deal with, 58 percent are prior acquaintances of the victims, 21 percent prior intimate partners, and 21 percent strangers to the victims.[77] It should be pointed out, however, that because these are cases that have come to the attention of the courts, they would more likely be cases of stranger stalking than cases of intimate-partner stalking, as many victims of intimate-partner stalking regard this as a private matter, and so don't report it. Yet, even though the percentage of stranger stalking in this study probably reflects larger numbers than reality, still this leaves a large number of stalkers who have selected total strangers for their victims.

With stalking incidents involving former intimate partners or even former acquaintances, at least the victims know the identity of the person they have to deal with. This is not the case with stranger stalkers. What can you do against a stranger stalking you? You can't ask the stalker's family to intercede, you can't have a friend or intimate partner threaten the stalker, and you can't get much help from the criminal justice system.

"I couldn't get a restraining order because I didn't know who it was," said Renee Anderson, a Montana woman who was stalked by a stranger, and eventually, for her safety, forced to give up her apartment and move back in with her mother. "And [the stalker] wouldn't stay on the phone long enough for the police to trace his calls."[78]

Although stranger stalkings usually don't end with the level of violence of many intimate-partner stalkings, they are no less terrifying and disrupting. Being stalked by a stranger can affect the way a person looks at others and at life in general. Victims of stranger stalking often feel they can no longer smile at or be friendly with strangers or casual acquaintances and come to question the meaning of smiles given by others. They stop being outgoing, instead becoming standoffish and self-protective. They discover that their whole lives are changed. Fortunately, as with all other types of stalking, there are measures that can be taken that will stop stranger stalking.

➤ ➤ ➤ ➤ ➤ 6

STALKING OF JUVENILES

The stalking began when Crystal Peterson was 7 years old. Swimming in the pool in her yard, she saw a man standing on the sidewalk in front of her house staring at her. Even for someone living in the small town of Independence, Oregon, this brought goosebumps of fright. Unbeknownst to Crystal or her family, for the next 3 years the strange man on the sidewalk, 21-year-old Robert Thomas Coker, would keep Crystal under surveillance from the house across the street, where Robert rented a room.

When Crystal turned 10 years old, Robert finally stopped just watching and made his first contact. The Petersons found a note on their porch addressed to Crystal, and the next day found a second unsigned note. The notes said: "I really like you. I think you're cute. When I looked at you, my heart felt funny, like it was melting. And I had trouble breathing."

The family, thinking that some young boy had a crush on their 10-year-old daughter, didn't become overly alarmed by the notes. Crystal felt flattered by the attention and wondered who the writer could be. For the next month a note appeared nearly every morning. Sometimes, along with the notes, the family would find a stuffed animal or other gift.

But then the notes suddenly changed. A note one morning said: "I saw you down the street with that boy. You are just like other girls. Sorry, don't like sluts." Crystal's parents now became concerned, not just because of the change in the writer's attitude, but also because the note plainly showed that someone had been watching their daughter.

The content of the notes now became erratic. One day they would be filled with writings of love, and the next day with hatred and viciousness. The love notes would be signed "Robert," and the hateful, vicious notes signed "Thomas." Also, the gifts left with the notes now suddenly became expensive cameras and cassette players. Soon, the notes began containing sexual themes and allusions to marrying Crystal.

Because of the ominous change in the notes, Crystal's parents no longer allowed their daughter to see them. Now anxious and extremely concerned, Crystal's mother began canvassing their neighborhood, trying to find the "lovesick preteenager" she and her husband still believed wrote and left the notes. The family also began keeping their window shades down at night and their children under constant watch.

Finally, when the notes became even more frightening, full of rambling, disturbing writing, Crystal's mother called the police. Although the police increased their patrols around the Peterson house, they didn't spot anyone. Eventually, Crystal's mother took to staying up all night, sitting in the dark and fighting off sleep as she watched the front of their house from an upstairs window. Finally, after many sleepless nights, she at last saw the stalker put a note in their mailbox. She sat stunned for a moment when she realized it was an adult. However, by the time she ran downstairs, the man had disappeared.

Soon after this episode, the family left for vacation. Very early one morning, while they were gone, Robert broke into their home and called Crystal's grandmother, apparently finding her number written down near the telephone. Waking the elderly woman up at 3:00 AM, Robert told her that if he couldn't have Crystal, no one could, and that they would soon be in Heaven together.

When the family returned from vacation and talked with the grandmother, they again notified the police, who could do nothing because they still didn't know who the stalker was. Crystal's mother, however, wouldn't give up, and, in an attempt to identify the writer of the notes, left a letter in the mailbox for the stalker, suggesting a meeting. The stalker left a note agreeing, then another note the next day telling the Petersons that he lived across the street from them. Crystal's parents again called the police.

When the police went to the home of Robert Thomas Coker's parents, the parents told the officers that they believed their son was very disturbed. For some reason Robert could not communicate with people face-to-face, they said, and he would even leave notes for his mother when he wanted to tell her something. On arresting Robert, the police found six letters to Crystal in his pockets.

However, arresting Robert didn't stop his obsession. He soon began sending Crystal letters from jail. Robert's explanation for his actions was that he didn't believe he was doing anything wrong. "I wanted to get my foot in the door early," he explained. His plan, he said, was that after he and Crystal had written each other for several years, he hoped Crystal's parents would allow them to date.

Two months after his arrest, Robert entered into a plea agreement. He would go into treatment for his problem and would promise to leave Crystal and her family alone. In return, the charges of burglary and threatening Crystal's life would be dropped.

The very night he left jail, however, Robert sent Crystal a rambling, four-page note. In this note, besides Crystal, he also mentioned Crystal's younger sister, Brittany. The police arrested Robert again.

At his trial, Robert pled guilty to the charges and a judge sentenced him to a year in jail. However, the day after entering his guilty plea Robert sent a letter to the Peterson family from jail, saying: "When I saw Crystal I wanted to drop to my knees and ask her to marry me." Even once incarcerated in prison, Robert continued sending letters to 11-year-old Crystal. Finally, prison officials convinced him to stop.[79]

The above incident should be enough to frighten parents almost out of their senses. A disturbed 24-year-old man writing love notes to an 11-year-old girl. Yet, although the Peterson family and the law did all they could, what will happen when Robert finishes his 1-year prison sentence? Very likely, he will resume his stalking of Crystal.

Although readers might hope otherwise, the above incident is in no way an isolated one. In my research for this book I came across many cases in which adults, claiming to be in love with young children, began stalking them, sometimes going no further than frightening the children and their families, but far too often with much more serious results.

In St. Paul, Minnesota, for example, a 28-year-old man, just released from jail for stalking a 15-year-old boy, allegedly shot and murdered the boy. The stalker had once worked at a day-care center and met the boy there when the youngster was just 9 years old. The young victim, on finding that the stalker had been released from jail, fled to his grandmother's house to hide, but the stalker tracked him there.

Even in those cases in which the stalkers don't physically harm the children they stalk, they can still, through their actions, cause tremendous psychological damage. The following incident demonstrates just how frightening the stalkers of children can be.

➤   ➤   ➤   ➤

In St. Petersburg, Florida, 14-year-old Laurisa Anello received a bouquet of flowers from a secret admirer who turned out to be Bruce Raines, a man in his mid-20s who had umpired Laurisa's Little League games. Then came letters and telephone calls from Bruce begging Laurisa's parents to allow him to date her. And, as with most stalkers, he also made threats.

"It makes your skin crawl, the things he would say," said Laurisa's mother, Linda Anello. "Things like: 'I know you don't like what I'm doing. But I'll never stop. I'll never stop.'"[80]

The family also found notes tacked to their door. One note said: "I almost got your daughter last night. You're making it too easy." Other notes were slipped into the family's newspaper, notes that said: "I'm out here. No telling what I might do. I'll be watching so I can catch you."

Linda Anello said that whenever she looked in the rearview mirror of her car, she would see Bruce's gray Hyundai following them. "Like a Hitchcock movie," she said. "He was always following."[81]

Because of her fear for her daughter's safety, Linda Anello began secretly following Laurisa whenever she left the house. "Just in case he's around," Linda said. "I just know if he goes over the edge, he's capable of doing anything. That's the horror of it."[82]

Although the police arrested Bruce several times for the stalking of Laurisa, he continued the letters. "We've had no peace in our family for four years," Linda Anello said when testifying before a Florida legislative committee considering an antistalking law. "You get into a pattern of looking over your shoulder all the time. It's like being a prisoner."[83] Because of Linda's tireless efforts at the state legislature, Florida passed a tough antistalking law.

As might be supposed, many of the stalkers of juveniles are pedophiles—people who fixate sexually on children. In 1992, in Roanoke, Virginia, for example, residents urged Governor Douglas Wilder to expedite a recently passed antistalking law because they saw it as the only way to stop a man who had been stalking local schoolchildren. Known as the "Raleigh Court Stalker" for the neighborhood he haunted, the man, before moving to Virginia, had been arrested twice in Memphis, Tennessee, for abducting or attempting to abduct children. A judge in Memphis ordered the man to leave town. After moving to Roanoke, the man received a 30-day jail sentence for making obscene telephone calls to a schoolgirl.

But individuals such as this can do much worse than just make obscene telephone calls. Because these stalkers are convinced they are in love with their young victims, yet cannot have them, some decide to kill the youngsters and even themselves, as in the following incident.

Known as lovable "Grandpa Gary" to his tennis students at an exclusive girls' schools in Manhattan, 56-year-old Gary Wilensky also had a much different, darker side. Although in 1992 the U.S. Professional Tennis Registry named Wilensky "Pro of the Year" for New York, New Jersey, and Connecticut, in 1988 the police arrested him for stalking three children while wearing a black leather mask and a wig.

Wilensky's darker side apparently had plans for a former student of his, 17-year-old Jennifer Rhodes. Wearing a ski mask and wielding a cattle prod, Wilensky attacked Jennifer and her mother outside an Albany, New York, hotel. Jennifer managed to escape and run for help. A hotel employee then came to the mother's rescue and scared Wilensky away, who later killed himself.

The police said they found detailed plans indicating that Wilensky had meant to take Jennifer to an Adirondacks cabin he had outfitted with listening devices, motion detectors, night vision goggles, leather muzzles, and steel chains. Behind the hotel, police officers discovered handcuffs, masks, wigs, a police badge, two guns, cassette tapes on which Wilensky talked about Jennifer, and an X-rated video titled *Jennifer's Nightmares.*

The stalking of juveniles, as shown by the incidents so far in this chapter, can be not only exceedingly dangerous, but also very psychologically damaging. Young stalking victims find that, to be safe, they must often remain at home and avoid normal social activities. They may miss some of the most important social events of adolescence. They are afraid to go to parties, dances, fairs, or anywhere the stalker might be able to follow or find them. And even if the victims finally leave home for college, they must, out of fear for their safety, often keep the location of their college secret. There is no more happy-go-lucky youth for them.

Even more disturbing, though, often the stalkers of teenagers are other teenagers. Many times these stalkers, like their older counterparts, cannot accept that a romantic relationship is over or that a person refuses to have a romantic relationship with them. Young boys in particular tend to worry a lot about their masculinity and how they appear to other young people. To these young boys, a girl breaking up with them is a direct blow to their masculinity. Consequently, some of these boys will resort to stalking in an effort to win the girls back and reclaim their masculinity.

"We have something called teenage territorialism," said psychologist Barry Lubetkin, "where teenagers become extremely possessive of that which they believe belongs to them."[84]

As a part of the research for this book, I spoke at length with a teenage stalking victim. She told me, "I couldn't have any friends, guys or girls. Everything had to be just him and me. He'd get real upset if he saw me talking to anyone or if I ever said anything about something I had done before I met him. After a while it got really bad because any night he wasn't with me he would call me over and over. If I wanted to talk to someone else after I finished talking with him I had to use another telephone because he would call to check and see if I was on the line." One time, the young stalking victim told me, after she tried to end their relationship, he rammed his car into hers when he saw her with another guy.

What can parents do to protect their children from stalkers? Most important of all, children must be taught about personal boundaries, and about how they must tell a parent or some other adult if they find that a person is violating these boundaries. Also, parents must take action by calling the police immediately after they become aware that a person may be stalking their child. A positive result is illustrated in the incident below.

A jury in northern Indiana deliberated for only 45 minutes before convicting David S. Jones, a 27-year-old man, of intimidation and stalking. According to court records, Jones placed up to 30 calls a day to the home of a 17-year-old girl, who steadfastly refused to date him. In addition, he called her at school and at work, along with writing her dozens of letters saying that he would kill her if she didn't date him. Several witnesses also testified at his trial that they saw Jones following the girl. Only timely intervention by the criminal justice system likely kept this case from becoming a tragedy.

Unfortunately, however, along with showing what can be done, this case also reveals the unpredictability of our justice system. In another jurisdiction, or even another court in the same jurisdiction, the outcome of this case could have been very different, that is, if the case was even prosecuted. These legal problems and issues are discussed at length in Chapter 15.

The idea that a mentally disturbed individual has set his or her sights on your child is certainly the stuff of nightmares, yet it occurs everyday. Parents, however, are not powerless. As discussed in later chapters, there are direct, forceful actions parents can take that will stop the stalking.

➤ ➤ ➤ ➤ ➤ 7

CELEBRITY STALKING

On seeing the title of this chapter, many readers may believe that its contents, although perhaps interesting, won't have much relevance for them. After all, what danger could the average person face from a celebrity stalker? And, unlike the average stalking victim, don't all stars and celebrities have bodyguards and other staff who can stand between them and the stalker? With such protection, what real danger could celebrities be in from stalkers?

As the incidents in this chapter will show, average people are in great danger of being harmed or killed by celebrity stalkers. Also, many celebrities, and particularly those just on the verge of stardom, those who can't yet afford expensive protection, share with the average person a very real danger from stalkers. In addition, readers should keep in mind that individuals who stalk celebrities share many of the traits of those who stalk ordinary people.

➤ ➤ ➤ ➤

"Are you Theresa Saldana?"

The actress, best known for her role as Robert DeNiro's sister-in-law in the movie *Raging Bull*, immediately saw that the man asking the question stood much too close to her, and it sent a sickening chill of terror through her. Saldana had been concerned and watchful for the last week, ever since she had been warned that a strange man, under various guises, had been calling people she knew or worked with, and asking them for her home address. Although she hadn't reached the success level yet in her acting career where she could afford to hire a bodyguard, Saldana, because of her concern about the caller, had been playing it safe for the last week. Since the warning, she had been having her husband, Fred Feliciano, walk with her to her car, and she had been staying with friends on the nights her husband wasn't home.

However, the lack of anything untoward happening that week had made Saldana believe that perhaps her fears had been unfounded, and so that morning she left their apartment before her husband had time to get dressed and walk with her to her car. She realized now how foolish she had been as she stood defenseless, alone in the street that ran in front of the apartment building where she and her husband lived. Sizing up the situation, Saldana knew the only chance she had was to try to run back into the apartment building, and so she bolted for the door. The man, however, anticipated this and caught her before she could reach the safety of the building, his hands locking onto her with the grip of a maniac. Then, to Saldana's horror, the man reached into the bag he carried and pulled out a knife, plunging it into her chest.

"He's killing me! He's killing me!" Saldana screamed as she tried to fend off the attacker, finally able to grab onto the blade of the knife in an attempt to stop the brutal attack.[85] But her valiant efforts couldn't stop the crazed attacker, who kept plunging the knife into her over and over as she screamed and screamed for help, blood beginning to gush from her wounds and soak through her clothing, the pain becoming intense as the knife slashed open one gaping wound after another. Defenseless against her attacker's maniacal strength, Saldana feared death was near.

Fortunately, a delivery man, Jeff Fenn, heard her screams and rushed to the actress's defense, finally pulling the frenzied attacker off her. Saldana, losing blood at a deadly rate, first fell to the ground, but then, fearing the man would resume the attack, managed to get to her feet and stumble back to her apartment building, where her husband grabbed her and carried her inside. He immediately called for paramedics and the police. Deputies from the Los Angeles Sheriff's Department arrived quickly and arrested the attacker, a Scottish drifter named Arthur Jackson, who had apparently traveled thousands of miles in his obsession for Saldana.

Paramedics arrived soon afterward and, after stabilizing her as best they could, rushed Saldana to Cedars-Sinai Hospital. The surgery to save her life took 4½ hours, required several surgeons, and over a 1000 stitches. She would have to endure 3½ months of daily pain and intense care before she could return to life outside the hospital.

Saldana's attacker, the police learned after arresting him, became obsessed with her after seeing her in the movies. Besides calling her friends and the people she worked with in an attempt to find out where she lived, Jackson had hired a private investigator. The police also discovered that Jackson kept a diary that he titled "Death's Petition," in which he recorded a rambling account of his love for Saldana. He told the officers that "he was the benevolent angel of death with the divine mission of killing Saldana so that the two of them could spend eternity in Heaven together." Jackson apparently figured that after murdering Saldana he would receive the death sentence, and then join her in the hereafter.

After convicting Jackson of attempted murder, a court sentenced him to 12 years in prison. Jackson, however, never gave up on his belief that the only way he could have Saldana was by killing her, and he swore to continue this mission once he finished his sentence. In a letter to Saldana from prison, Jackson said he regretted using a knife on her because "a gun would have given me a better chance of reunion with you in Heaven."[86]

Scheduled to be paroled from prison on the attempted murder charges in April 1990, Jackson received an additional sentence of 5 years and 8 months for sending threatening letters to Saldana. In the summer of 1996, the U.S. government deported Jackson to Great Britain, where he was scheduled to stand trial for a 30-year-old murder. On 29 January 1997, an English court committed Jackson to a psychiatric hospital after he pled guilty to the murder.

Seven years after this vicious assault another rising Hollywood star would fall prey to the attack of a love-crazed stalker. In 1989, 21-year-old actress Rebecca Schaeffer seemed to have her career right on course. She was costarring with actress Pam Dawber (of *Mork and Mindy* fame) in the popular sitcom *My Sister Sam*. She had just finished a movie titled *One Point of View*, and had appeared in the movie *Scenes from the Class Struggle in Beverly Hills*. The last thing Schaeffer's fans expected was her tragic and untimely murder.

On 18 July 1989, neighbors in the Fairfax area of Los Angeles noticed a man in a yellow Polo shirt wandering through their neighborhood carrying a large manila envelope. Each time he encountered someone on the street he would pull out a glossy publicity photograph of Rebecca Schaeffer and ask the person if he or she knew where Rebecca lived. In the folder, police would later discover, the man also carried a .357 magnum revolver and a copy of *Catcher in the Rye*, the same book carried by John Hinckley, Jr. when he attempted to assassinate President Reagan. Even though people living in Los Angeles might be accustomed to strange, and even bizarre, people this man made them feel uneasy.

Later that day, neighbors said they heard a gunshot and then Rebecca scream. When several people ran to Rebecca's aid as she lay dying in the vestibule of her apartment building, the man in the yellow Polo shirt fled up the street. The next day, Tucson, Arizona, police officers, answering the call of a man acting strangely and disrupting traffic, discovered 19-year-old Robert John Bardo, an unemployed janitor, dodging cars as he walked along the ramp that led onto Interstate 10. He had apparently just stepped off the bus from Los Angeles. The police had already been advised by a friend of Bardo's that he might be the killer because the friend knew of Bardo's obsession with Schaeffer, and of his threats to kill her. After being taken into custody, Bardo reportedly confessed to the officers that he had indeed shot actress Rebecca Schaeffer.

On 29 October 1991, after a trial in Los Angeles prosecuted by Marcia Clark (of the O.J. Simpson trial), the court found Bardo guilty of first-degree murder. He received a sentence of life imprisonment without parole.

Although the split-second act of firing the bullet that ended the life of actress Rebecca Schaeffer had been driven by Bardo's fixation with her, his obsessive behavior had actually been growing and festering for years. At age 13, Bardo reportedly stole money from his mother's purse and took a bus to Maine in search of Samantha Smith, the young girl who had become famous for writing letters to then Soviet President Mikhail Gorbachev. Apparently, Smith had replied to a letter Bardo had written her. Eventually, though, the police picked up Bardo as he wandered around Maine looking for Samantha Smith, and sent him back to Arizona.

During high school Bardo would often write and send bizarre, rambling letters to his teachers, letters in which he talked about death, murder, and killing himself, signing the letters "Dirty Harry Callahan, James Bond, or Scarface." One teacher, after receiving a 10-page rambling letter from Bardo about suicide, became concerned and recommended that he receive professional care. Bardo went briefly to a mental hospital, where a psychiatrist diagnosed him as severely emotionally handicapped and coming from a pathological and dysfunctional family. After Bardo's release from the hospital, his parents, allegedly refusing to believe that their son had any sort of mental problems, would not allow him to receive any further treatment.

Although a straight-A student, Bardo eventually dropped out of high school. "A time bomb waiting to explode," was how one of his teachers described him.

"My mistake was dropping out of high school," Bardo would later say from the Los Angeles County Jail. "I was isolated. I didn't have any friends, never had a girlfriend."

Because Bardo reportedly came from an extremely dysfunctional family, he began retreating more and more into himself. "He began to live a fantasy life," said John Stalberg, a psychiatrist who interviewed Bardo three times, "to give him relief from the mental pain and torture."[87]

Bardo's fantasy life included Rebecca Schaeffer. "She just came into my life at the right time, when I was sixteen," Bardo said. "She was bright, beautiful, spunky—I was impressed with her innocence. She was like a goddess for me, an icon. I was an atheist out there. I worshipped her."[88] Bardo watched her over and over on the television series *My Sister Sam*, and eventually began writing her letters.

An employee hired by Schaeffer's fan service to handle her mail apparently made the fatal mistake of responding to one of Bardo's letters and signing it "Love, Rebecca." For someone with an obsession like Bardo's, this became absolute proof that an intimate relationship existed between them. Today, security experts warn celebrities against any such personal responses to fans. The slightest thing can be seen by obsessed stalkers who suffer from erotomania as confirmation of the love between them and the celebrity.

"It's like having a relationship with Jesus Christ," said Bardo, explaining his obsession with Schaeffer. "People don't know him, but they want a personal relationship. I identified my happiness with public figures. That was Rebecca Schaeffer."[89]

Soon after receiving what he believed to be a personal response from Schaeffer, Bardo wrote in his diary: "When I think about her I feel that I want to become famous and impress her." However, on the same page he wrote: "How do you I [sic] know if the table and paper before me is just a field of electronic pulses. How can I be sure this is reality?"[90]

In 1987, Bardo took a bus to Los Angeles, and attempted to enter Warner Bros. studio, where *My Sister Sam* was filmed. He brought along a large stuffed animal for Schaeffer. Guards at the gate, however, sent him away. Enraged, Bardo returned a month later, this time carrying a knife, but once more the guards turned him away.

Afterward, Bardo wrote to his sister: "I'm obsessed with something I can't have. So I'm going to make it so that something doesn't exist anymore."[91]

On returning to Tucson, though, Bardo forgot about Schaeffer for a while and became obsessed with singers Debbie Gibson and Tiffany. However, in 1989, the movie *Scenes from the Class Struggle in Beverly Hills*, featuring Rebecca Schaeffer, began showing in movie theaters. In one scene Schaeffer appeared in bed with an actor. When Bardo saw Schaeffer in the sexually suggestive scene he became furious and convinced that she didn't deserve his love any longer and should be punished, believing she had become just "another Hollywood whore."

Soon after this, Bardo read an article in *People* magazine about Arthur Jackson, the stalker who had stabbed and seriously injured actress Theresa Saldana. Jackson, he found, had attempted to obtain Saldana's address by hiring a private investigator. Thinking this sounded like a good idea, Bardo paid a private investigator $250 to obtain Schaeffer's address for him, telling the detective that he and Schaeffer were old friends. The detective obtained Schaeffer's address through the California Bureau of Motor Vehicles. Bardo then persuaded his brother to buy him a gun, a .357 magnum revolver (Bardo was only 19 and couldn't buy one). After this, Bardo boarded the bus again for Los Angeles.

Although given Schaeffer's address by the private detective, the apartment building she lived in just didn't look right to him somehow, and so Bardo wandered around the neighborhood for a while, asking the people he passed if Rebecca Schaeffer really lived there. Finally, convinced that she did live there, he entered and rang for her apartment.

Unlike more famous and established stars, Schaeffer didn't live in a high-security building, and couldn't afford bodyguards. Apparently, the building's intercom hadn't worked for some time, and so Schaeffer had to go down herself to see who was ringing her buzzer. When she opened the door, Bardo reportedly handed her a letter he had written to her. She took the letter and told him, "Take care. Take care."

Bardo then left the apartment building and went to have breakfast at a nearby diner. An hour later, he returned to the building, and Rebecca once more came down and opened the security door for him. This time, however, rather than giving her a letter, Bardo fired one shot from the .357 magnum revolver, striking Schaeffer in the chest. She reportedly screamed and then asked, "Why? Why?"

Actress Lynne Marta, a neighbor of Schaeffer's, heard the gunshot and called 911. "I opened the little window hatch in the door and there was a smell I will never forget as long as I live. It was the smell of gunfire and it was quiet except for this little moaning."[92]

Schaeffer died on the scene from the gunshot wound.

How common are attacks like these on celebrities, media stars, and public figures? The Los Angeles Police Department's Threat Management

Unit, which helps protect stars (and ordinary citizens) from stalking, has handled more than 1000 cases since its formation in 1990.

Gavin DeBecker, a security consultant to hundreds of celebrities, said, "It is possible to identify between 50,000 and 100,000 people who are pursuing encounters with public figures with inappropriate reasons."[93]

Dr. Park Dietz adds, "A surprisingly large number of Hollywood stars have been subject to 'strange, unwanted attention.'"[94]

According to a National Institute of Justice report, as many attacks on public figures by people with mental disorders happened between 1969 and 1989 as had occurred in the preceding 175 years.[95] The Threat Assessment Group, which conducts safety consultation for celebrities, finds that about 17 percent of the estimated 200,000 stalkers in the United States stalk celebrities. "Celebrity stalking is very much on the rise," said Threat Assessment Group founder Dr. Park Dietz.[96]

Celebrity stalkers, experts find, are many times not as much obsessed with a particular celebrity as they are obsessed with the obsession. The stalker of actor Michael J. Fox, for example, eventually moved on to actor Scott Bakula. Robert Bardo, before murdering actress Rebecca Schaeffer, had had obsessions for singers Madonna, Tiffany, and Debbie Gibson, and for actress Dyan Cannon.

"They're disturbed individuals in search of an identity," says Dr. Park Dietz. "They keep files and press clippings as psychic reward for their activity."[97] Dr. Dietz adds that these stalkers turn violent not because of their love for the celebrity, but because they cannot fulfill their romantic delusions.

Although celebrity stalkings can occasionally end in an assault or even murder, still many celebrities actually encourage and want obsessive fans, but only those with a minor obsession. The band "The Grateful Dead," before Jerry Garcia's death, had a large group of people, called "dead-heads," who, similar to stalkers, followed the band all over the country attending their concerts. Most celebrities want such fans, fans who worship them and read every story printed about them in the newspapers, tabloids, and magazines. They want fans who feel they just *have to* see the star's next movie, *have to* buy the star's latest CD, or *have to* attend the star's next concert. Celebrities also want fans who believe that everything they do is fascinating and special. This is why celebrities hire publicists. This is why there are fanzines, movie magazines, and fan clubs. The problem, of course, is that some fans carry their adulation too far. Stalkers, many unfortunate celebrities find, do not recognize or respect the appropriate boundaries for such relationships.

Celebrity security experts have discovered, however, that there is no positive way to know if a fan will cross the boundary from obsessed to dangerous. However, security experts have found that the likelihood of this increases if the stalker expresses a desire or intention to approach the celebrity, or if the stalker believes either that he or she and the celebrity share a special fate or that he or she and the celebrity have a secret love relationship (common delusions among celebrity stalkers). The danger also increases if the stalker mentions a specific time or date when something will befall the celebrity.

Because many celebrity stalkers suffer from erotomania, they often live under the delusion that there is a special love relationship between them and the celebrity, and that the celebrity is communicating this relationship to them through songs, or through things said or done in movies, television programs, and the like. One stalker, for example, believed that a star communicated his love to her by the way he would occasionally brush his cheek with his hand. This was his secret signal of love to her.

So, how does any of this affect readers? Actually, it can affect the average person very directly. These kind of stalkers, experience has shown, are dangerous not just to celebrities, but to everybody. In December 1988, for example, Nathan Trupp of New Mexico killed two security guards at Universal Studios because they wouldn't let him in to see star Michael Landon. Trupp had reportedly become convinced that Landon was a Nazi, and Trupp meant to kill him. During this incident at Universal Studios, imagine the danger to any person who had been on a tour there that day. Also, as the following two incidents show, celebrity stalkers can be extraordinarily dangerous to their own families.

➤   ➤   ➤   ➤

Michael Perry, an escaped mental patient from Louisiana, became obsessed with singer and actress Olivia Newton-John on seeing her in the movie *Xanadu*. After attending the movie, he wrote to her: "Either the dead bodies are rising or else there is a listening device under my mother and father's house. The voices I hear tell me that you are locked up beneath this town of Lake Arthur and were really a muse who was granted everlasting life."[98] This kind of letter should raise concern in even the most fearless person.

Perry, because of his obsession, soon moved to Los Angeles, living near Olivia Newton-John's estate so he could watch her. Several times he tried to break into her home. In his last attempted break-in, private security officers caught him and reportedly "escorted" him out of California. After this incident, Perry returned to Louisiana.

Once home, infuriated because of his failure with Olivia Newton-John, Perry drew up a list of 10 people he intended to kill, including Olivia Newton-John, her husband Matt Lattanzi, Supreme Court Justice Sandra Day O'Connor, his own mother and father, two cousins, and a baby nephew. Within a few weeks of returning home, Perry killed his parents, his two cousins, and his baby nephew, purposely shooting out the eyes of all his victims. Police officers arrested Perry 2 weeks later in Washington, D.C., in a motel near the Supreme Court building. In the room sat seven television sets broadcasting static. On the screen of each television set Perry had drawn a staring eye. Convicted of the murders of his family members, Perry now sits on death row in Louisiana.

Singer Olivia Newton-John has been an extremely popular target for stalkers. At the same time Michael Perry stalked her, she was also stalked by Ralph Nau.

In 1980, Ralph Nau became convinced that Olivia Newton-John was in love with him, and that all of the records and films she made were actually secret romantic messages from her to him. He had never met Olivia Newton-John, but this didn't diminish his delusion.

Before his obsession with Olivia Newton-John, Nau had been involved in writing sex-filled letters to a woman named Cindy, who would respond back to him—for a fee (much like the 900 telephone sex lines). The letters both ways were steamy, and finally, overcome with passion for Cindy, Nau traveled to Peoria, Illinois, to find her. Once there, though, he discovered that Cindy's mailing address was just a mail drop, items being forwarded from there to another mail drop in Arizona. His obsession and desire for Cindy still strong, Nau traveled to Arizona to continue his search for her, but the people at the mail service there refused to give him any information about her. Not knowing what else to do, Nau wandered around the extraordinarily hot desert in Arizona for a while. Suddenly, a vision came to him that Olivia Newton-John loved and needed him. Nau returned home and began sending her hundreds of bizarre, rambling letters.

Nau eventually moved to Los Angeles to be near Olivia Newton-John. For a while in Los Angeles he switched his fixation to singer Sheena Easton, also sending her letters by the bushel. He would often sign these letters "Shawn Newton-John," whereas his letters to Olivia Newton-John usually bore his real name. Several times during his obsession with Sheena Easton, Nau tried to get onto the stage during her performances, but each time security guards stopped him. Eventually, he became convinced that the person he saw on stage wasn't really Sheena Easton at all, but a double, and his fixation became short-lived. His obsession then switched back to Olivia Newton-John. In 1981, while working at a veterinarian's office, Nau killed a puppy, pulled out its teeth, and mailed them to Olivia Newton-John. In his letter to her, Nau wrote: "Whoever is in charge of this shit, they're going real low when they start in on a defenseless little puppy. They should all be six feet under."[99]

In 1984, Nau flew to Australia to find and be with Olivia Newton-John. He wasn't successful. Soon after this, he returned to his family's farm in Wisconsin.

Nau's return home, however, wasn't a happy event. His family knew he was odd, but now they suspected he was insane. Once home, he began behaving more erratically than ever. He would suddenly and unexpectedly begin screaming, and late at night he would jump through the bedroom windows of his family members and scare the hell out of them. Once, when a cow died, Nau reportedly gutted it and slept inside the carcass.

Soon after this, Nau returned to Australia in search of Olivia Newton-John. As before, however, he didn't find her. Instead, he wandered around the wilderness of the Outback for some time before finally returning home. When he came home this time, though, he found that his mother and father had divorced, and that his mother had married another man. Nau moved in with his mother and her new husband. Within a short time, though, when someone mysteriously murdered one of Nau's new stepbrothers with an ax blow to the head, the police arrested Nau for the crime. The prosecutor eventually dropped the charges, however, and the state instead committed Nau to a mental hospital.

➤　➤　➤　➤

These two incidents demonstrate very clearly how dangerous celebrity stalkers can be to both celebrities and ordinary people, particularly their own families. The incidents also show some of the mental problems suffered by many celebrity stalkers. "Ninety-five percent of stalkers have obvious mental disorders," said Dr. Park Dietz, talking specifically about celebrity stalkers. "Seventy-five percent are psychotics."[100]

According to Gavin DeBecker, "Studies show that more than 90 percent of the people who might deliberately cause harm to public figures are mentally ill."[101]

And yet, although many celebrity stalkers suffer from obvious mental problems, this has no effect on their persistence. "It's nothing for the average celebrity stalker to spend a decade or more chasing the unwilling object of their desire," said Lieutenant John Lane. "They're schizophrenics, manic-depressives, people with delusions."[102]

Interestingly, even though celebrity stalkers will often go to extraordinary lengths to contact and impress their idols, and even though most celebrity stalkers believe there is a special love relationship between them and the celebrities, these stalkers have usually not thought out what they really want as an end result of their pursuit. They need for their idols to recognize them and give them identity, but beyond that most haven't planned what they will do next.

"That's the way a lot of these people are," said FBI agent Jim Wright. "They plan up to the point of attaining the unattainable, and then their planning ceases."[103]

But although celebrity stalkers may not know what they would do were they to actually attain their idols' love, most superstar celebrities know they must keep these stalkers away. Their dangerousness has been demonstrated too many times. Because of this, many superstar celebrities have set up elaborate security systems and hired a large staff of bodyguards, but even this often doesn't stop the more obsessed, determined stalkers, as the following incident shows.

On 29 May 1995, a security guard at the home of pop star Madonna shot intruder Robert Dewey Hoskins, aged 37, three times in the arm and abdomen. The security guard had confronted Hoskins after he threw several bags over a wall at the Hollywood home of Madonna, as if he were moving in, then scaled the wall and took a swim in her pool. When several guards tried to restrain Hoskins, he reportedly shouted at them he was Madonna's husband and that they were fired. He then allegedly grabbed for one of the security guards' gun as the guard attempted to restrain him. According to security personnel at Madonna's home, this wasn't their first encounter with Hoskins. He had been stalking and threatening the star for some time.

Hoskins also allegedly attempted to break into Madonna's home on 8 April 1995. When stopped by security guards during this attempt, he told them that he was either going to marry Madonna or "slit her throat from ear to ear."[104]

Madonna reportedly became so upset and shaken by the stalking and break-in attempts that during the trial of Hoskins her attorney asked that the defendant be kept out of the courtroom during Madonna's testimony, or that she be allowed to testify on videotape. The judge denied both of these motions, and, following this, Madonna reportedly wanted to just drop the charges rather than confront Hoskins. The prosecutor, however, refused to drop the charges, and the judge threatened to arrest Madonna and hold her on $5 million bail if she didn't appear in court.

Although the decisions by the judge and prosecutor may have served the criminal justice system's objectives, Dr. Park Dietz warns that "hauling stars into court with their stalkers often cements their relationship." He also warns that the celebrity stalker's ultimate dream is to be eternally associated with a star victim.[105]

Eventually, Madonna did appear in court and testify, though she said she felt sick being in the same room with Hoskins. "I didn't want to be in the same room face-to-face with the man who threatened my life," she said.

During her testimony, Madonna said, "I feel incredibly disturbed that the man who threatened my life is sitting across the room from me, and we have somehow made his fantasies come true. I'm sitting in front of him and that's what he wants."[106] She told the jury that Hoskins haunted her nightmares, and "I guess I felt incredibly violated."[107] She also testified that she had been confronted by Hoskins when she returned home from riding her bicycle the day before his break-in attempt at her home in April 1995. "I saw a man who looked very strange," she said. "He had a real crazy look in his eyes."[108]

At the proceedings, a detective testified that Madonna appeared shaken and had trembled when she read a note Hoskins allegedly left for her. "I handed it to her and she took it and shuddered, and it was like a cold chill went through her body," said Detective Andrew Purdy.[109]

The jury deliberated 5 hours and returned a guilty verdict on all charges, which included felony stalking, making terrorist threats, and assaulting a security guard. The court sentenced Hoskins to 10 years in prison. After the trial, Madonna's attorney, Nicholas DeWitt, said that the star worried about copycat stalkers and planned to sell the house where the break-ins occurred because it attracted "negative energy." In September 1996, Madonna sold that home and moved to another part of Los Angeles.

"Even if her bodyguards can protect her, Madonna still feels the terror," said Joy Silverman, a stalking victim discussed in Chapter 2. "It's psychological rape."[110]

West Coast Bureau Chief for the supermarket tabloid the *Star*, Barry Levine, agrees when he says, "The stars can have security guards and security systems more sensitive than a bank's, but people can still buy a star map for $2 and haunt these people."[111]

Detective Greg Boles of the Los Angeles Police Department's Threat Management Unit adds the chilling thought, "The whole idea of stalking is becoming more well known because of cases like this. The Madonna case publicizes the ugly crime of stalking, but also fuels the imaginations of those considering such activity, particularly against celebrities."[112]

➤   ➤   ➤   ➤

According to experts who deal with and attempt to treat mentally disturbed people who stalk celebrities, it is because these people have often been unable to establish or maintain emotional relationships in the real world that they now do so through delusions about celebrities. These stalkers often form obsessions about the celebrities in an attempt to enhance and enlarge their own identities. They believe that if they can become part of the celebrities' lives, then part of the fame and notoriety that the celebrities enjoy will come to them. As an example of this, Hoskins has reportedly written on his cell wall: "The Madonna Stalker." For celebrity stalkers, even a sick relationship with the celebrity is better than no relationship at all.

Unfortunately, the news and entertainment media often inadvertently assist stalkers in forming their love-relationship delusions about celebrities. The stalkers of movie stars have often seen the celebrities nude or nearly nude in the movies, and they have heard or read about many of the celebrities' activities in Hollywood (true or not). They have also seen the inside of celebrities' homes, and have watched their favorite celebrities relaxing off-screen (on programs such as *Lifestyles of the Rich and Famous* or a Barbara Walters interview). Adding to this, the intense media coverage of celebrities in supermarket tabloids and on television programs such as *Hard Copy* and *Entertainment Tonight* often helps cement the stalkers' delusions that they have an intimate relationship with the celebrities.

"The reason [for the increasing number of celebrity stalkings] is because of how visible and personal they become," said Dr. Park Dietz. "We have...a personal interview about someone's favorite restaurant and artistic likes. And the more personal and intimate the media portrayal, the more that mentally disordered people will misinterpret this as something personal for them."[113]

The stalkers of celebrities, incidentally, besides being a danger to the celebrities, can also be a threat to the families of the celebrities. The following two incidents clearly show this danger.

Margaret Ray's stalking of late night television host David Letterman started in 1988 when she began claiming she was his wife. Since then, she has broken into his New Canaan, Connecticut, home at least eight times, one time camping out on his tennis court and another time stealing his Porsche and driving it around the town. Once, after serving 4 months in jail on harassment charges, she showed up again at his home only days after her release. She has also occasionally shown up with her young son in tow, who she claims was fathered by Letterman.

In August 1996, Margaret Ray appeared in Indianapolis, David Letterman's hometown, and where his mother still resides. On 2 August 1996, security officers arrested Ray for shoplifting at a Wal-Mart store very near where David Letterman's mother lives. When questioned about her proximity to the house, Ray insisted it was only a coincidence, but prosecutors weren't convinced. On 9 August 1996, Ray pled guilty to the shoplifting charges. She spent 34 days in jail, and on 4 September 1996 the Sheriff's Department paid for her ticket and put her on a bus back to Danbury, Connecticut. Authorities warned her that she would have to return to Indianapolis in November to answer another charge against her: resisting arrest. To no one's surprise, she didn't appear for her November court date, and no one is sure of her present location.

In another incident involving a celebrity's family, Christopher James Taylor, aged 19, pled no contest to charges that he stalked and threatened the son of late actor Michael Landon. Apparently, Taylor became obsessed with young Landon after finding a file at a modeling agency that contained a photo and Landon's personal information. Taylor reportedly called Landon over and over at home and at school. However, as often happens in stalking cases, the telephone calls soon became threatening, and Taylor told Landon he was going to kill him.

In addition to the few celebrities mentioned up to this point, others who have been stalked include singers Janet Jackson, who had a man, claiming to be her husband, attempt to break into her Encino, California, home, and Whitney Houston, who finally had to obtain a restraining order against a man who has stalked her and claimed to be the father of her child. A stalker sent actress Stephanie Zimbalist (of the television series *Remington Steele*) over 200 letters containing such threats as "You can run, but you can't hide." One time, he sent her a photograph of her house with the notation: "Here I am watching your house."[114] After his arrest, the man pled guilty to mailing threatening communications.

Actress Justine Bateman (of the television series *Family Ties*) had a man professing love and devotion for her sit down in the courtyard outside the Berkeley Repertory Theater where she was performing. He then held the police at bay for 3 hours by pressing a gun to his stomach and threatening to kill himself. The previous year this same man bluffed his way onto the set of *Family Ties* and twice came face-to-face with Bateman. "I just wanted to make sure [Justine] knew how much I still cared about her," the stalker said after being taken into custody. He suffers under the delusion that he and Justine Bateman once had an affair.[115]

Justine Bateman's costar in *Family Ties*, actor Michael J. Fox, received over 6000 letters from stalker Tina Marie Ledbetter during a 2-year period, many of them threatening. She signed the letters to Fox "Your Number-One Fan." Along with letters she also sent him boxes of rabbit droppings. After being convicted of threatening Fox, Ledbetter changed targets and began sending letters to actor Scott Bakula (of the TV series *Quantum Leap*). (Besides rabbit droppings, stalkers have sent other strange items to celebrities. A few of these include vials of blood, containers of urine and semen, animal body parts, and mutilated photos of either the stalker or the celebrity.)

Leigh Penn, an obsessed fan of actress Sharon Gless (of the television series *Cagney and Lacy*), broke into Gless's home in 1990, and then, when she found Gless wasn't there, barricaded herself in a bathroom with a semiautomatic rifle and 500 rounds of ammunition, holding the police at bay for several hours. A year earlier, Gless had obtained a restraining order against Penn. Penn later told the police that her plan had been to sexually assault Gless, murder her, and then commit suicide.

Authorities recently charged a police volunteer in Los Angeles with stalking after he allegedly went to the home of actor Richard Lee Jackson (of the television series *Saved by the Bell*), claiming he was a police officer investigating a fight at a Hollywood nightclub. He said he needed to interrogate Jackson about the fight.

I have only given a few, but the names of all the well-known celebrities who have been stalked would be incredibly long. Adding to the list of the ones I have already mentioned are actor Sylvester Stallone, attorney Melvin Belli, singer Tanya Tucker, television personalities Kathie Lee Gifford and Leslie Stahl, comedian Jerry Lewis, singer-turned-politician Sonny Bono, and Senator Dianne Feinstein, the former mayor of San Francisco.

Actually, as in the last two examples above, politicians are almost as likely as movie stars to have stalkers. Threats to members of Congress, for example, soared to 566 in 1991, up over 200 a year since 1987. In reality, it would be more accurate to say that very few people who have attained celebrity or public figure status haven't attracted a stalker at some time. It seems to come with the territory.

A celebrity, however, doesn't have to be a superstar in order to attract a stalker. Even lesser levels of celebrity status can attract them. In Columbia, South Carolina, the police charged a New York man with stalking former Miss America Kimberly Aiken. A court recently convicted Harry Veltman of sending obscene and threatening material to Olympic skater Katarina Witt, and police charged another man, who has tried to make personal contact several times, with trespassing at the family home of Olympic swimmer Summer Sanders. A court in Milwaukee County (Wisconsin) convicted a man who stalked Catholic Archbishop Rembert Weakland. Fashion designer Todd Oldham asked the New York City courts for a restraining order against a man who has stalked him because of the mistaken belief that Oldham had him arrested on child molestation charges. In Golden Valley, Minnesota, police charged a man with stalking a reporter at a local television station. The man had previously been charged with trespassing when he tried to get inside the station to see the reporter. After this, the station sent the stalker a certified letter ordering him to stay away from the reporter and the station. Police caught him on the station property trying to see the reporter give the evening weather forecast. The police found an assortment of photographs of the reporter in the stalker's car.

Although most celebrities realize the danger that stalkers represent to them, average people should never believe they have nothing to fear from celebrity stalkers. As several incidents in this chapter have shown, family members of the stalkers are very much in danger, as is anyone standing in the way of the stalker's obsession. In addition, when celebrity stalkers decide they are going to kill the object of their obsession, they often don't care who's near or what kind of danger they put other people in. Stalkers, no matter what type, are dangerous to everyone.

CAUSE STALKING

When people fervently and absolutely believe in a cause they will many times go to great lengths to promote it. History is replete with examples of individuals and groups who have been willing to go to these great lengths, even willing to die or to kill for a cause, particularly when they believe their cause is morally or religiously just. In recent years, a number of groups and individuals, in an effort to promote and further their cause, have begun to use stalking to intimidate their opposition.

In one of America's most volatile causes during the last decade—abortion—often even members of the same family hold opposing views as to whether it is right or wrong and whether it should be allowed in certain cases or stopped totally. I have seen this division in my own family. Before going on, therefore, I want to say that nothing in this chapter is meant or intended to imply that in any cause, one side is right and the other side wrong. That is not my intention. Readers should not assume that this chapter is taking one side or the other in the abortion question, or in any other political, moral, or religious question. Instead, this chapter will only consider how stalking is often used by those promoting a cause, as demonstrated in the following incident.

➤ ➤ ➤ ➤

Wichita (Kansas) Family Planning had been the site of virulent abortion protests for some time. The protests had become so intense that one of the doctors working there had taken to wearing a mask when traveling to and from the clinic to avoid being identified by the protesters.

"His employer doesn't want it known [that he performs abortions]," said Raymond Sharon, leader of a group named Godarchy, which led the abortion protests in Wichita. Boasting that his group had tactics for learning identities that would make the CIA look like amateurs, Sharon added, "We exposed him. We would be happy if he would just promise never to do this again." If the doctor didn't see things Godarchy's way, Sharon told reporters, steps would be taken to make his life miserable. The group reportedly sent a letter to the doctor showing how much it had learned about him. The letter included the doctor's address, birthplace, real estate holdings, and his girlfriend's name.

"You have forsaken the healing arts for that of a circuit rider vampire, preying on innocent women and children," the letter said. "You cannot smoke enough Benson & Hedges Menthol, or drink enough Budweiser to endure the local and national exposure that awaits you." The group, Godarchy, enclosed in the letter a photograph they had taken of the doctor standing in the yard at his house.

In addition, antiabortion activists placed a sign in the doctor's front yard identifying him as a "baby killer," and then passed out fliers about him throughout his neighborhood. Soon after this, Wichita Family Planning began receiving death threats against the doctor.

"It sounds criminal," said District Attorney Nola Foulston. "I certainly support the right of all those individuals to peacefully protest. But when individuals consider committing criminal acts or threaten or harass other people, it's beyond free speech and into criminal actions."

However, the antiabortion activists didn't see it that way. "What I did was in no way, shape, or form stalking," said one of the antiabortion intelligence gatherers.[116]

Clinic operators, however, disagreed, and became so concerned about the threats that they purchased a bulletproof vest for the doctor targeted by the group. They did this because in August 1993 an antiabortion activist shot a doctor outside the Wichita clinic.

In August 1993, the police arrested Rachelle Shannon of Grants Pass, Oregon, and charged her with shooting Dr. George Teller. Police say Shannon shot Dr. Teller as he sat in his car at the Wichita clinic, and then fled from the scene in a car driven by another person. Authorities later found that Shannon had been writing to a man who was being held by the police in Florida for the murder of a doctor at an abortion clinic there.

"I know you did the right thing," Shannon said in one of her letters to the Florida prisoner. "It was not murder. You shot a murderer. It was more like anti-murder. I believe in what you did, and really want to help if possible. I wish I could trade places with you."[117]

The members of Godarchy, however, didn't agree with Shannon's feelings about taking action this drastic. Denise Billings of the group said of the shooting, "I was absolutely shocked to hear he'd been shot. I don't know how to respond to that except to say that the pro-lifers I know are responsible people and they stand for the sanctity of life."[118]

On 25 March 1994, a court convicted Shannon of attempted murder for her attack on Dr. Teller, and also convicted her of aggravated assault because she had pointed a gun at a nurse. A judge sentenced Shannon to 11 years, which included 10 years in prison for the two charges above and 1 year in jail for contempt because Shannon refused to tell where she had obtained the gun she used.

In October 1994, federal grand juries in Sacramento (California) and Portland (Oregon) returned indictments against Shannon charging her with 30 felony counts involving attacks on abortion clinics in California, Oregon, Nevada, and Idaho. The indictments accused Shannon of arson, interference with commerce by force, and interstate travel in aid of racketeering.

Although many antiabortion activists, who obviously believe fervently in their cause, deny that their actions constitute stalking—actions that often include such things as protesting in front of doctors' homes, publishing and displaying posters and leaflets about abortion doctors, following the doctors and their families, and threatening the doctors with unfavorable publicity if they continue performing abortions—courts across the country have disagreed. A number of antiabortion activists have been convicted of stalking.

In February 1994, a jury in Charleston, South Carolina, convicted antiabortion activist Cathy Rider of stalking the Charleston Women's Medical Center director Lorraine Maguire. Rider reportedly encouraged people to rip off Maguire's daughter's arms so she would know how a fetus feels when it's aborted. She also allegedly told Maguire to wear a bulletproof vest because "you might be next" (referring to the murder of an abortion doctor outside a Pensacola, Florida, clinic). The court sentenced Rider to 5 years on probation, with the stipulation that she stay at least 500 feet away from Maguire.

In Youngstown, Ohio, a judge found Alan M. Smith guilty of stalking an abortion doctor. Dr. Gerald Applegate claimed Smith ran him off the road, sent him nasty letters, and threatened him and his family. Mr. Smith received 6 months in jail and a $1000 fine.

A court found an antiabortion activist in Pensacola, Florida, a man already on probation for stalking the administrator of a family planning clinic there, guilty of continuing the stalking. As part of his probation on the original stalking conviction, Jack Hinesley had been ordered to stay away from the Pensacola clinic and its administrator. Hinesley, however, reportedly followed and photographed the administrator and made a threatening gesture and comment.

In 1995, a Dallas jury of six women and one man awarded a doctor and his wife $8.6 million in damages. The court ordered three antiabortion organizations and seven individuals to pay these damages. The jury awarded $5 million to Dr. Norman Thompkins and his wife Carolyn for invasion of privacy and intentionally inflicted emotional distress. They awarded the other $3.6 million as punitive damages (juries can award punitive damages when they feel the actions of the defendants are so grievous as to warrant punishment). The Thompkinses had reportedly been the targets of picketing at the doctor's office and hospital, the couple's home and church, and the wife's workplace. The couple also received threatening telephone calls and mail. (This case shows a different approach that victims can use when confronting stalkers: suing for monetary damages in a civil court rather than prosecuting in a criminal court. Unfortunately, this option only becomes feasible in a very small number of cases because most stalkers don't have the assets that would make suing them worthwhile.)

A judge in Portland, Oregon, in May 1996, used Oregon's recently passed antistalking law to order one of the leaders of the Advocates for Life Ministries, Paul deParrie, to stay away from the head of a Portland clinic. Mr. deParrie had reportedly called the head of the clinic on the telephone, sent her a threatening postcard, and led demonstrations in front of her house. Mr. deParrie said he would obey the terms of the court's order.

As anyone who follows the news knows, most antiabortion activists believe totally and absolutely in the rightness of their cause, and feel they are only doing what must be done to stop abortions and save the lives of unborn children. To further this end, in Melbourne, Florida, antiabortion activists sponsored a boot camp for protesters. They reportedly taught the recruits how to jam telephone lines, how to trace the license plate numbers of women coming to the clinics so they can be sent antiabortion mail, and how to harass abortion doctors at home and at work. One antiabortion activist even proposed following doctors' wives to their hairdressers and standing outside with picket signs saying "This hairdo is paid for by blood money." In 1995, Operation Rescue planned a new campaign against abortion doctors called "No Place to Hide." This campaign planned to target abortion providers at any location they could be found.

In Melbourne, Florida, antiabortion activists even went so far as to print up "wanted" posters against a doctor who performed abortions, offering a $1000 reward for information leading to his arrest or to the revocation of his medical license. The poster also listed the doctor's mother's address and telephone number, and the license plate numbers of two of the doctor's ex-girlfriends. The children of one of these ex-girlfriends reported being taunted by antiabortion activists at a school bus stop. And although most activists will deny that their actions are stalking, unfortunately, as the cases above demonstrate, their behavior often fits the description of the laws against stalking.

On the other side, abortion providers counter antiabortion arguments by saying that the law supports them and what they are doing, whether the antiabortion groups like it or not. These protest groups, however, abortion providers claim, rather than peacefully protesting an act they believe is morally wrong, instead often resort to criminal activity to stress their opposition to abortion.

"We have been confronted and attacked more violently than ever," said Susan Hill, president of the National Women's Health Organization, in testimony before a Congressional Subcommittee on Crime and Criminal Justice. "Protesters stalk our physicians, staff, and patients, slash their tires, vandalize their cars, write and call in death threats."[119] Supporting this claim of intimidation, in Tallahassee, Florida, the House of Representatives Healthcare chairman felt it necessary to request police protection for himself and his committee while they discussed a controversial abortion bill.

Not all antiabortion activists, however, support this type of protest. Helen Alvare, spokeswoman for the National Conference of Catholic Bishops, said, "We are opposed to following clinic employees or their children, or any activity that is not explicitly peaceful public witness. Such efforts may seek a good end—such as stopping abortion—but you can't use a bad means to get there."[120]

As a police officer, I always find it interesting how normally law-abiding people, when involved in a cause they truly believe in, feel morally correct in resorting to what could be considered criminal activities to support and further their cause. Incidentally, this doesn't involve just abortion protests. Often, for example, people involved in bitter labor strikes will resort to acts defined by law as stalking to further their side in the strike, as I discovered very early in my police career.

➤   ➤   ➤   ➤

When I was a new officer on the Indianapolis Police Department in the late 1960s I worked as what was known as a "floating officer." A floating officer didn't have an assigned beat yet, but simply floated around the city filling in for officers marked off sick, on vacation, and so forth. Once while serving as a floating officer the lieutenant assigned me and another floating officer to a factory that had been the scene of a bitter strike for almost a year. The lieutenant told us that our job was simply to stay at the factory and be visible for our 8-hour shift in order to prevent any acts of vandalism or violence.

Apparently, when the strike began the year before, not all of the employees had joined the walkout. The workers who did had demonstrated in front of the factory in a perfectly legal form of protest (as is most protesting at abortion clinics). However, as the strike wore on with no resolution, some of the strikers became bitter. Soon threats came over the telephone and through the mail against those employees who hadn't joined the others in the strike. Following this came vandalism to the cars of the employees not supporting the strike. Finally, the homes of these employees became the targets of vandalism, and their families the targets of threats.

After a month or so on the detail, the two sides settled the strike, and the lieutenant pulled me and the other officer off. I suppose the striking workers went back to their jobs and became ordinary, law-abiding citizens once more. And I assume they began working again alongside the people they had stalked.

As another example, during a strike in Detroit in early 1996, members of the newspaper union announced plans to follow carriers as they delivered the *Detroit Free Press* and the *Detroit News*. The carriers complained that this amounted to stalking.

"If I were one of those carriers, I would consider it somewhat harassing to have picketers following me," said a subscriber to the *Detroit News*. "It also smacks of being stalked."

Dearborn, Michigan, police chief Ronald Deziel said, "The ambulatory picketing activity...would constitute stalking under [the] statute. I foresee a lot of calls to the police department from citizens demanding a stop to the activity."[121]

The unions, however, contended that the picketers have a right to follow the carriers. Whether they do or not, though, will probably have to be decided in court.

> > > >

Interestingly, like stalking in domestic situations and love obsession cases, when the stalking by those involved in a cause doesn't accomplish what the stalkers had hoped it would, the intensity of the stalking often increases. As shown above, this happens many times in long, bitter labor strikes, and has occurred during abortion protests. A large number of medical clinics, both those involved in performing abortions and those simply advocating planned parenthood, have been the targets of violence. A study of abortion clinics in 1994 found that 51.9 percent had experienced death threats, stalking, chemical attacks, arson, bomb threats, or blockades. As the following incidents show, this movement upward in intensity, along with leading to worse and worse violence, can occasionally lead even to murder.

> > > >

On Wednesday, 10 March 1993, Dr. David Gunn, a physician who performed abortions at a Pensacola, Florida, clinic, entered the back door of the clinic in an attempt to avoid the protesters who had been demonstrating regularly at the clinic. A protester later identified as Michael Griffin, a 31-year-old chemical plant worker from Pensacola, who witnesses said shouted, "Don't kill any more babies!" raced up behind Dr. Gunn, brandished a .38-caliber revolver, and shot the doctor three times in the back. A few minutes after this, Griffin walked up to the responding police officers and said, "I've just shot Dr. Gunn."[122] Dr. Gunn died later at the hospital.

Almost a year later, a jury deliberated only 3 hours before finding Griffin guilty of first-degree murder. A judge sentenced him to life in prison, with a minimum of 25 years to be served before becoming eligible for parole. Although at one time Griffin had said he wanted to act as his own attorney and that he would use the Bible as his defense, he did not testify at his trial, saying he no longer remembered what happened that day at the clinic.

The next year, also in Pensacola, Florida, Paul Hill, a right-to-life crusader, used a shotgun to murder Dr. John B. Britton and clinic escort James H. Barrett outside an abortion clinic. Hill received two death sentences for the killings after a jury took only 20 minutes to find him guilty. Witnesses said Hill had been protesting at the clinic for about 6 months prior to the murders, and that he had been seen carrying a sign saying: "Execute Abortionists." Hill reportedly hid the shotgun in some bushes, and then grabbed it when the victims pulled into the parking lot.

In imposing the death sentences on Hill, Judge Frank L. Bell said, "Dr. Britton was still alive after the first volley of fire and was able to see what was happening. He could see the defendant stalking across from him, reloading the gun. Dr. Britton had twenty to thirty seconds to contemplate his death. He was able to watch the defendant prepare his execution and see it unfold before him."[123]

Hill doesn't deny that he killed the two men. He maintains, however, that what he did was "justifiable homicide" to protect unborn children.

Authorities reportedly recovered from Hill a "justifiable homicide" statement signed by 30 antiabortion activists. The document said, "We, the undersigned, declare the justice of taking all godly action necessary to defend innocent human life including the use of force. We proclaim that whatever force is legitimate to defend the life of a born child is legitimate to defend the life of an unborn child.

"We assert that if Michael Griffin did in fact kill David Gunn [the slain abortion clinic doctor in the preceding incident] his use of lethal force was justifiable provided it was carried out for the purpose of defending the lives of unborn children. Therefore, he ought to be acquitted of the charges against him."[124]

In another violent and deadly incident, in December 1994, in Brookline, Massachusetts, a suburb of Boston, John C. Salvi, an apprentice hairdresser, walked into the Planned Parenthood clinic and opened fire with a .22 caliber semiautomatic rifle. He then drove to a second clinic nearby, where he murdered two receptionists and wounded five other people. Following this, Salvi drove to Virginia, where he fired more shots at another clinic.

The authorities probably should have seen this violence coming. A year earlier, John Salvi had angrily confronted the leader of Operation Rescue in Massachusetts when she said she thought that anyone who would kill (speaking of Michael Griffin's murder of Dr. David Gunn) for the cause of abortion could not really be pro-life, and that they should pray for Griffin. Salvi angrily told her that he thought Griffin was a hero. The leader of Operation Rescue, concerned about the intensity of Salvi's reaction, alerted the police that Salvi did not appear stable. However, what the police did with this information is unclear.

Found guilty of the two murders, Salvi received two life sentences. On 30 November 1996, prison authorities in Walpole, Massachusetts, found Salvi dead under the bed in his prison cell. He had tied a plastic bag over his head and committed suicide.

The murders in these incidents are, of course, drastic overreactions by a few people frustrated and disillusioned because they didn't see their protests as being effective in stopping something that they felt was wrong. Unlike the individuals in the incidents above, most abortion protesters show their opposition to abortion through perfectly legal forms of protest. No legitimate antiabortion group I am aware of approves of taking this type of drastic action, and instead most caution their members to refrain from any type of violence.

John Heithaus, director of CALL (Collegiates Activated to Liberate Life), an organization of college students opposed to abortion, said of his group's purpose, "Our goal...is to prevent abortions from happening, and to do it in a nonviolent and passive way. We want to stop murder, not create more murders."[125]

Rabbi Norman Lipson of Temple Beth El in Hollywood, Florida, speaking of a murder at an abortion clinic, said, "We're not dealing with religion. We're dealing with vigilantes, with sloppy theology and with fanaticism."[126]

A recent decision by the U.S. Supreme Court, however, will likely not have much of a calming effect on future abortion protests. In February 1997, the court, in an eight-to-one decision, held that "in-your-face" protesting, such as that done by antiabortion activists who confront women and doctors en route to abortion clinics, attempting to verbally dissuade them from having or performing an abortion, is protected speech under the First Amendment.

"There is no generalized right to be left alone on a public street or sidewalk," said Chief Justice William A. Rehnquist.[127]

The court, however, did recognize the right to prohibit such activities on private property. The justices also said that sidewalk protesters had no right to grab, push, or stand in the way of persons heading to an abortion clinic.

Abortion and labor strikes, however, aren't the only causes in which stalking is used by some of the cause's proponents. In Miami, Florida, in 1995, the police arrested Manuel Gonzalez-Goenaga for stalking and threatening the life of Miami City Manager Cesar Odio. Mr. Gonzalez-Goenaga has been arrested a number of times for what he calls his "political activism." On 31 May 1995, the police arrested him again, alleging that he walked around Miami City Hall screaming, "Tell Emperor Odio that if they continue to arrest me, I'm going to blow his head off!"[128]

Most people who believe fervently in a cause also believe that for justice and right to be done, their side must prevail. Often, though, those deeply committed to a cause see the end results as more crucial than the path to get there, a path that many times includes stalking. This type of stalking, though, no matter how worthy the perpetrator may believe its motivation is, can be just as devastating to the victims as any other type.

> > > > > **9**

REVENGE STALKING

In Fort Lauderdale, Florida, several female customers of a cable television company got a bit less than what could be considered good customer service. One of the company's employees stalked them. After disagreements with the employee, the customers began receiving threatening telephone calls and disturbing letters that graphically described how they were going to be tortured and sexually assaulted. Sometimes the letters contained pornographic pictures. None of the victims, however, connected the stalking to the disagreement with the cable company employee because it had seemed so minor at the time.

When a woman complained to the Fort Lauderdale Police Department about the stalking, Detective Mark Shotwell recalled three other women who had described similar cases of stalking. Detective Shotwell had the four women fill out a detailed questionnaire about their activities just prior to the stalking. On analyzing these, the detective found that all four women had had a telephone squabble with the same employee of the cable company.

When the police brought the employee in for questioning, he reportedly confessed to being the stalker, and the police charged him with four counts of aggravated stalking. The employee told the officers that whenever he had a disagreement with a cable company customer he would get a printout of the customer's file and then use this information to begin sending them the threatening letters. Concerned that his phone number could be traced, he had a friend in New York make most of the telephone calls.

"[The employee] felt these people he'd spoken to on the phone had treated him badly," said Detective Shotwell, "so he wanted them to see what it felt like."

If the employee meant to strike fear in the women through the stalking, he certainly accomplished what he set out to do. One victim became so fearful she moved out of her house, another almost got fired because she thought a fellow employee was the stalker and consequently had refused to go to work, while another spent over $100 on pepper spray.

"It doesn't surprise me because he was very vindictive," said a former friend of the stalking suspect. "If someone made him mad, he would get very angry and say 'I'll never forget!' I thought it was just talk."[129]

In Denver, Colorado, when television cable installer Tamera Krizman received a promotion and her own cable company truck, it incensed fellow employee Robin Tally so much that he began stalking her. Soon after her promotion, Krizman complained to company officials that Tally followed her to an installation job, where an angry confrontation took place. She also said that she suspected he made a series of harassing telephone calls to her home.

On 24 August 1995, Tally reportedly grabbed a 9mm handgun and drove to the site where Krizman was working, then waited for her to return to her truck. When Krizman did return, Tally later told police, he shot her in the upper body several times. After she fell to the ground bleeding, he stood over her and pumped several more shots into her. Tally then drove to a Lakewood, Colorado, police station and turned himself in. Tally, who is being held on first-degree murder charges, told the officers he had been contemplating the murder of Krizman for several weeks.

Stalking, as seen in the above two incidents, can be an extraordinarily effective tool for terrorizing someone. Abusers involved in disintegrating and unsuccessful domestic and intimate-partner relationships often know this very well, and will use this effect of stalking in an attempt to force the victims to either stay in or resume the relationship. Love-obsession and celebrity stalkers also realize stalking's effect on its victims and use it to accomplish their goal of becoming attached to the target of their affection, even if only as an object of fear. However, stalking, as the two incidents above demonstrate, can also be used as a weapon by people seeking revenge against others who may not be involved in any domestic, intimate-partner, or fantasy love relationship with them, but have only, at least in the stalkers' minds, wronged them. These stalkers often find they can very effectively use the terrorizing aspects of stalking to gain the revenge they seek.

Revenge stalkers, however, don't pick only victims who appear weak and helpless, or victims who don't know who the stalkers are. Sometimes, as the following two incidents show, the victims targeted by revenge stalkers can be powerful members of society.

Ramsey County (Minnesota) District Judge Joanne Smith has been the victim of a stalker since 1985. The stalker is John Patrick Murphy, who she sentenced once for assaulting a woman.

"I'm a victim because I am a judge," she told a Minnesota House of Representatives criminal justice subcommittee. "[A stalker] can undermine the very integrity of the legal system by making powerful people afraid to do their duty."

Judge Smith's stalking began after she sentenced Murphy to 90 days in jail for assaulting a woman. The light sentence shocked the jury, she said, but it was the maximum the law provided. Soon after Murphy's release, the judge, the assault victim in the case, and a witness who had testified for the victim all became targets of stalking. Judge Smith had the tires of her car slashed, mutilated animals dumped on her property, and her house spray-painted with obscenities. Another judge, who had revoked Murphy's probation, also had his house vandalized, as did Murphy's probation officer. Overall, Murphy's victims have included three judges, three prosecutors, two probation officers, two halfway house workers, and two correctional workers.

Because at the time Minnesota had no stalking law, and no one had actually witnessed the vandalism, there was little the police could do. The stalking, though, had a strong effect on its victims.

"[I'm] aware of judges who have not done what they should have done because of intimidation and fear," said Judge Smith. "There have been prosecutors who have not wanted to touch various of their cases because they don't want to be the next victim."

Eventually, Murphy received a 2½-year prison sentence in an unrelated case. Yet, the stalking of Judge Smith continued, even from prison. "I've had other inmates call my home saying 'Is this Joanne? I heard maybe you like to have a good time.'"[130]

Once Minnesota finally did pass an antistalking law, a court tried and convicted Murphy for his continued stalking of various members of the criminal justice system. Before receiving his sentence, Murphy told the court he was sorry and that he accepted responsibility for his actions, which he said was "to get even for a perceived wrong in the past." The court sentenced him to 4 years in prison, followed by 37½ years of probation, during which time the court banned him from Wisconsin and Minnesota. The court also ordered him to pay $30,000 restitution.

In another incident, this one in Fort Wayne, Indiana, the local police department asked the state police to revoke the gun permits of three admitted gang members who had allegedly stalked and plotted to kill a Fort Wayne police officer who had investigated them for several drive-by shootings. Two of the men have previous felony convictions, which should void their gun permits.

"These subjects should not be licensed to carry handguns," said the threatened police officer in a report. "They are admitted drug dealers and gang members and have threatened [my] life."[131]

The gang members reportedly kept the officer under surveillance while he was at his precinct house, while he was off-duty and teaching a karate class, and have been seen following the officer and cruising by crime scenes where the officer was working. The gang members have bragged that they listen to a police scanner to keep up on the officer's whereabouts.

➤   ➤   ➤   ➤

Although revenge stalkers can obviously strike at anyone they feel has wronged them, no matter who or how powerful, they can also strike anywhere. Revenge stalking can occur in poor, inner-city areas, and, as the following incident demonstrates, in some of our country's richest neighborhoods.

➤   ➤   ➤   ➤

The financial firm Kidder, Peabody Group has its headquarters at Hanover Square near Wall Street in New York City. In April 1993, the firm fired bond salesman John Kliebert for allegedly inflating the sales commission on a trade. The trouble for the Kidder, Peabody Group then began.

In a complaint filed in New York City Criminal Court, Joel McKoan, Kliebert's former boss at the Kidder, Peabody Group, alleged that Kliebert stopped him in front of the company headquarters and jabbed a finger at him, saying "his shirt would look good with a red splotch in the chest area." Also, according to the complaint, Kliebert reportedly telephoned a Kidder, Peabody Group trader and threatened "to get even" with four former co-workers, including McKoan. He told the trader he had a list of people he wanted to get even with and that he had purchased a shotgun. In addition, employees complained that Kliebert sent them dolls with pins stuck in the hearts. Kliebert's attorney, however, said that the incident with McKoan was "just a misinterpretation stemming from Mr. Kliebert's unusual sense of humor."[132]

The other Kidder, Peabody Group employees and the police, however, obviously didn't appreciate Kliebert's sense of humor either. The police arrested Kliebert for third-degree menacing. A police search of Kliebert's apartment uncovered two rifles and a crossbow. The Kidder, Peabody Group has taken the threat of Kliebert so seriously that they have spent more than $1 million on private investigators to trace Kliebert's movements.

Revenge stalking, however, is not used just by people wanting to get even with others who they believe have wronged them. Revenge stalking can also be used as a means of racial hatred. The following incident graphically illustrates this.

Forty-seven-year-old Howard University art professor Winnie Owens-Hart built what she describes as her dream house in Prince William County, Virginia. Owens-Hart, who is black, also purchased the bungalow next door, which in April 1995 she leased to a white couple. In December 1995, a court convicted the man she had leased the bungalow to of stalking her. Even though the court eventually sentenced the man for stalking, he has so terrified Owens-Hart that she is too frightened to return to her own home, and has instead begun living with friends and relatives, and at hotels.

The trouble began for Owens-Hart when, soon after leasing the house to the couple, she learned they had hung a swastika up in the window. Owens-Hart also said that she saw a number of what appeared to be skinheads coming and going at the bungalow, and that she witnessed the couple she had leased the bungalow to brandishing semiautomatic weapons. In addition, the man allegedly yelled racial slurs at Owens-Hart, gave Nazi salutes, screamed "white power," and made threats against blacks and Jews.

In response to the complaint against him, the man convicted of stalking Owens-Hart admitted to hanging up the Nazi flag and to making Nazi salutes on the bungalow property. He also admitted to making Nazi salutes in the courtroom and to shouting "white power." However, he denies that any of this was directed toward Owens-Hart. The court obviously disagreed.

"I don't have a house anymore," said Owens-Hart. "I'll never take my daughter back there. I fear for her life, and I need to be around to raise her. I don't need to be dead."[133]

➤   ➤   ➤   ➤

Finally, revenge stalking can also originate from incidents in which ordinary people simply do their job or duty. Some individuals, however, feeling wronged by this job or duty, stalk the person doing it in an attempt to get even, as in the following case.

➤   ➤   ➤   ➤

In Tallahassee, Florida, the police arrested Florida State University College of Law student Jo Ann Plachy, who officers say stalked a Florida State University College of Law secretary after the secretary accused Plachy of cheating. The police also allege that, in addition to stalking the secretary, Plachy attempted to hire a hitman to kill her.

According to the Florida Department of Law Enforcement file on the case, Plachy tried several times, using various ruses, to obtain the secretary's address. She called the secretary's mother, claiming to be another person, and said she needed her daughter's address and telephone number. The mother refused to give these. The police also say Plachy followed the secretary. When stopped by Tallahassee Community College security officers during her tailing and surveillance of the secretary, Plachy claimed to be the secretary's mother, and said that she was just there to check on the welfare of her daughter, who attended classes at the community college.

Finally, the police accused Plachy of calling a friend in Key West, Florida, and asking if the friend knew of a hitman who would kill the secretary for her. The friend became concerned and called police, who sent an undercover officer to meet with Plachy.

In a tape of the meeting between Plachy and the undercover officer, Plachy reportedly said, "I cannot emphasize how very important it is, it must look like a total accident. I'm talking about a situation like, say something like there's a one-car accident. The car leaves the road and hits a tree or whatever, and the driver has a broken neck."[134]

Plachy allegedly gave the undercover officer $1000 for the murder. Police later arrested Plachy at her home, and charged her with attempted murder. Plachy awaits trial in the Leon County Jail.

As revealed by the incidents in this chapter, stalking can be a potent weapon, and not just in the hands of people involved in disintegrating domestic situations, or those in fantasy love relationships. It can also be a potent weapon when wielded by someone bent on revenge. But no matter who uses stalking, or for what purpose, it is a terrifying experience for the victims.

➤ ➤ ➤ ➤ ➤ 10

ELECTRONIC STALKING

In 1974, Susan Billig's 17-year-old daughter, Amy, disappeared while on her way to her parents' art gallery in the Coconut Grove section of Miami. Soon afterward, the telephone calls began. "I have her....I've cut out Amy's tongue....Amy will be sold off at a livestock auction....I want to have sex with both you and Amy....You'll be abducted like your daughter and sold into a slave trade."[135]

For 21 years an unknown man repeatedly phoned Susan and hinted that he knew where Amy was. This possibility, unfortunately, became the glue that kept Susan listening, even when the talk degenerated to filth, because Susan had dedicated her life to finding Amy.

The moment she realized that Amy had disappeared in 1974, Susan began a two-decade-long quest to find her daughter. She immediately notified police and the press, and supplied them with all of the information she had. She then bought additional telephones and put paper and pencil by each, so that she and her husband could be ready if a call with information came. In the following years, Susan and her husband would travel back and forth across the country checking lead after lead about Amy's whereabouts, visiting biker bars because of a tip that Amy had been kidnapped by bikers, and talking to convicts in prison, hoping they might have some information about Amy's fate. Susan even persuaded the television series *Unsolved Mysteries* to do a segment on Amy's disappearance. To finance the search for their missing daughter, Susan and her husband sold their art gallery and their Bentley.

Because Susan so desperately wanted any information at all about Amy, she was willing to listen to whatever the man who telephoned her said. The caller quickly realized he had a ready, even if reluctant, audience for his sexually explicit talk. For 21 years the caller tortured Susan with hints that maybe her daughter was alive, and that maybe he knew where she was. For 21 years, Susan clung to the desperate hope that she might be able to find her daughter. For the caller, though, the talk about Amy was simply a ruse that allowed him to have an audience for his pornographic talk.

"He was obsessed with me," Susan said. "He hurt me. I went into therapy because of him."[136]

In November 1995, the police traced one of the calls made to Susan, and found that it came from a cellular telephone owned by 48-year-old Henry Johnson Blair, a 24-year veteran of the U.S. Customs Service. His arrest soon afterward stunned everyone who knew him. Married with two daughters, Blair supervised 17 agents in drug interdiction activities for the Customs Service. Blair, held in high esteem by practically everyone he knew, had once received Spain's highest civilian honor for his participation in the recovery of a Peter Paul Rubens painting stolen from a Spanish museum.

"Hank is one of the most down-to-earth, common-sensical, likeable people you would ever meet," said a customs agent in Miami, where Blair worked.[137]

There was another side to Blair, though, a side that no one had ever seen: a dark, deeply evil side. Blair eventually confessed to being the caller who had tormented Susan for so long, but claimed he wasn't responsible for his actions because he suffered from paraphilia—a psychiatric disorder characterized by intense sexual urges, which can include making obscene telephone calls.

"I felt like I was going insane," Blair told the court during a pretrial session. "It seemed like it got harder and harder to control....It was such a secret thing. How do you tell your co-workers, wife, children that you are torn apart by these thoughts?"[138] Blair claimed that family stress and alcohol brought on the overpowering "urges" to make these repeated obscene calls to Susan.

The judge in Blair's case, however, would not allow the defense to use Blair's claim of paraphilia, and would not throw out Blair's confession to police. Eventually, a jury convicted Blair on two counts involving the stalking, but could not come to a decision on the third count. However, rather than face another trial, Blair entered into a plea bargain and pled guilty to the third count. The judge then sentenced Blair to 2 years in prison (the maximum sentence possible) and 5 years of probation, with the stipulation he never again contact Susan. At the sentencing, Blair's attorney requested that his client be allowed to serve the 2 years in a work release program. However, the judge said that, considering the torment Blair had put Susan through, he could not grant the request, and sent Blair to prison. The fate of Amy Billig remains unknown.

Interestingly, but not surprising, Susan may not have been Blair's only target. As part of the investigation of the Blair case, an assistant state attorney reviewed Blair's telephone bills. Noticing several calls made to one number, he called it, and found it to be a woman whose daughter had been murdered. The story of the murder had appeared in the *Miami Herald*. When asked if she had received any lewd or harassing telephone calls, the woman said she had.

"He was just bragging that my daughter had got killed," the woman said about the calls. "Just tried to scare me, which he did." The second time the man called her, the woman told the assistant state attorney, he left a message on her answering machine. "You have a sexy voice," the man said. "I'll be watching you."

The assistant state attorney also found another number called several times by Blair. This number belonged to the mother of a crack addict whose story had also appeared in the *Miami Herald*. Again, when asked whether she had received any lewd or harassing telephone calls, the woman said she had.

"He talked about penises, all kind of nasty stuff," the mother of the crack addict said about the calls. "He wanted to go out with my daughter. He asked me where she was at and told me what he would do to her. I thought by my daughter being a street person, it was somebody she met in the street and gave my number to, so I didn't think anything of it."[139]

When asked about making such calls, Blair said, "The *Miami Herald*, the Local Section, was my soft porn."[140] Apparently, Blair combed the newspaper for stories about tragic victims, and then would target the victims' families for his obscene telephone calls.

As with most stalkers, Blair refuses to take full responsibility for his actions. Amazingly, he even blames his victim, Susan Billig, for what happened.

"She just chatted along," Blair said. "I never told her anything that was true. We're just two obsessive people bouncing off each other. Maybe we both should be locked up together. Mrs. Billig has become obsessed."[141]

Mrs. Billig was only obsessed with getting her daughter back safely. Blair was obsessed with talking filthy to her. Blair used Susan's obsession with finding her daughter, hinting that he knew where Amy was, for his own purposes. He baited Susan into listening to his filth by hints that he knew where her daughter was. The fact that Susan pleaded with him many times for information about where Amy was didn't seem to figure into his reasoning of why she stayed on the line. In May 1996, 2 months after Blair's sentencing, Susan filed a civil lawsuit against him, seeking damages for the years of mental torture.

> ➤   ➤   ➤   ➤

As seen in the above incident, stalking need not involve someone following and confronting a victim, someone standing outside a victim's home, or someone vandalizing property. Without ever seeing his victim, Blair inflicted as much emotional and psychological damage on Susan as a stalker who follows, confronts, and threatens a victim. Feeding off her tragedy, Blair stole two decades of her life. Through his incessant stalking, and his continual hinting that her daughter was alive, Blair robbed Susan of any peace she might have known. This, unfortunately, is not an isolated case.

In Englewood, Colorado, a court sentenced Donald Allen Davis to 5 years in prison for the obscene telephone calls he made to child abuse reporting hotlines. Making thousands of such calls, Davis horrified listeners by describing in lurid detail how he was about to rape his daughter (he had no daughter).

"There was a good deal of community outrage," said Arapahoe County prosecutor John Hower. "It was such disgusting behavior, and he was very deliberate in choosing targets that would have a severe reaction."[142]

Electronic stalking, however, besides being used by sadists, can also be used as another means of intimidation by love-obsession and "refuse to believe it's over" stalkers. Many of these individuals use electronic stalking as a means of keeping the fear going in their stalking relationship. "If you looked up 'fear' in the dictionary, it doesn't begin to describe how these women feel," said C. L. Barker of the Las Vegas-based Cease Stalking Now group, speaking about victims stalked electronically. Electronic stalking, however, doesn't involve just using the telephone, as shown in the following incident.

> ➤   ➤   ➤   ➤

Kevin McLaren of Pembroke Pines, Florida, simply couldn't accept it when the woman he had been living with told him she wanted to end their relationship. Fuming about the breakup, McLaren allegedly began sending his ex-girlfriend threatening faxes a few weeks after they parted ways. The ex-girlfriend promptly got a restraining order against McLaren, which ordered him not to have any contact with her.

However, even though served with the restraining order, McLaren reportedly continued sending the threatening faxes, both to his ex-girlfriend and to her new boyfriend. The police arrested McLaren for aggravated stalking.

"He was pretty much surprised when he was arrested," said Pembroke Pines police sergeant Ray Raimondi. "It's the first case we know of where a fax machine was used to stalk."

Fort Lauderdale detective Sonya Friedmann, who investigates stalking cases, adds, "Anything that causes substantial emotional distress and serves no legitimate purpose is considered stalking. We're in an electronic age and people are finding new ways to harass each other."[143]

Detective Friedmann is certainly correct. Whenever scientists invent something to make humankind's existence a little easier, someone always finds a way to subvert the invention to criminal purposes. The computer is a good example of this, as the following incident demonstrates.

Andrew Archambeau, a 32-year-old sign painter from Dearborn Heights, Michigan, met someone he believed to be the woman of his dreams through a video dating service. The woman said she picked Archambeau from the 1500 possibilities the video dating service offered because she found he shared her interest in computers.

The couple met face-to-face for the first time at a social gathering sponsored by the video dating service. A few days later, they went out on a casual date. The woman, though, said she soon became both concerned and alarmed because Archambeau immediately talked about the two of them getting married and having children. She decided she needed to end the relationship, and so she sent him a computer E-mail message saying so.

Like many people who become involved in stalking, Archambeau simply couldn't take "no" for an answer. He began sending lovesick, pleading messages to her through E-mail. The woman responded in very clear terms that she did not want a romantic relationship with him, and also wished no further communication of any kind with him. However, in a 2-month period, Archambeau sent the woman over 20 E-mail messages and 10 letters and packages through the regular mail. In one message he told her that he sometimes watched her at the school where she worked as a teacher. He also once parked near the school and waved at her as she walked to her car.

The final blow for the victim, though, came when Archambeau left a message on her telephone answering machine. On it he said, "I stalked you today."

"I was scared out of my mind when I got that message," the woman said.[144]

The victim took all of the messages she had received from Archambeau to the local prosecutor. On reviewing the evidence, the prosecutor filed charges against Archambeau under Michigan's stalking law, which at the time was one of the broadest, most comprehensive stalking laws in the country, and was the first law to include provisions for E-mail stalking.

"After speaking with the victim, all of those qualifications [to prove stalking] were present," said assistant prosecutor Kelly Chard. "The victim became very upset, as anyone would be, knowing that someone was watching you leave work after you had told him not to contact you anymore."[145]

The police spoke with Archambeau and instructed him not to contact the woman anymore. That same night, however, he reportedly sent another E-mail message to the woman. "This letter is the LEAST of the many things I could do to annoy you," Archambeau wrote. He then allegedly threatened to discuss the woman's behavior on an open computer chat line, and with her co-workers, family, and a former boyfriend.

"It was a case of love gone bad," said Detective Brian DeGrande, the officer who investigated the case. "She was trying to be nice, let him down easy, and he kept calling her and sending her E-mail. Mr. Archambeau just couldn't take 'no' for an answer."[146]

Oakland County (Michigan) Assistant Prosecutor Neil Rockind added, "The traditional way we think of stalking is that there is some man hiding in the bushes in front of your house, following you to work. But if you think about it, if I start dropping off letters to your house—sliding them under the door and sticking them in your mailbox—and you feel harassed, molested, frightened or intimidated, you would feel stalked. The computer is the same thing. When you fly these E-mails to my house, it's no different than if you put them under my door."[147]

Mr. Archambeau and his attorney both said they were looking forward to the upcoming trial. The attorney said he would challenge the constitutionality of Michigan's stalking law. Archambeau, in a thought pattern typical of stalkers, said he looked forward to seeing the victim again face-to-face, and perhaps being able to explain his actions. However, on 24 January 1996, Archambeau pled no contest to the stalking charge. The court sentenced him to a year of probation, ordered him to undergo a psychiatric evaluation, and also instructed him to stay away from the victim.

The above, unfortunately, is not an isolated incident. A woman in Maryland who posted a warning on the Internet about a company that tried to charge an exorbitant fee to review a book she had written received more than 200 harassing E-mail messages. Someone also posted her name, address, and home telephone number with several Internet sex newsgroups, inviting people to call or stop by her home anytime.

In Dallas, Texas, a judge issued a restraining order against a man who reportedly used the Internet to harass a Texas family. The alleged stalker had apparently been involved in a dispute with a family who operated an Internet access service, and had been posting vulgar and obscene electronic messages about the family.

Another person became an electronic stalking victim after she became involved in an argument during an online discussion about advertising. Soon afterward, the victim began receiving nasty E-mail messages from the man she had argued with. Following this, she discovered that a photograph of a nude woman had been posted on the Internet, giving her E-mail address.

➤　　➤　　➤　　➤

Computer E-mail, as in the above incidents, is estimated to be used by 35 million people daily. With such a large volume of users, it is to be expected that it would be abused by those inclined to stalk others. Actually, as discussed earlier, E-mail harassment is no different than a stalking victim who receives unwanted, harassing, and threatening telephone calls and letters. Only the medium of communication is different.

"Generally, it's guys with old girlfriends," said University of Utah computer programmer John Halleck, who sets up Internet accounts for students. "They ought to learn some social skills and go play somewhere else. This is not a joke to the women being harassed."[148]

Because modern communication techniques can now allow a person to reach dozens of other people quickly and easily, electronic stalkers can often have many victims. The Internet, presently unpoliced, has become a perfect arena for stalkers who don't want to be identified or held accountable for their actions. Because much of this stalking is done anonymously from behind a computer screen, the identity of the stalkers can often prove difficult to uncover, as in the following incident.

A woman put a notice on a computer bulletin board asking for tips on raising children who are confined to wheelchairs. Instead of advice, the woman received a message from a man who identified himself as "Vito" that contained a graphic description of how he would like to sexually molest these handicapped children. This woman, though, authorities discovered, was just one of hundreds of computer users harassed by Vito, who once threatened a woman by telling her he was coming to her state "for a human hunt." Vito also reportedly attempted to use the computer to ruin other people's credit, and he once sent a fax to a man's boss, falsely accusing the man of being a child molester and a convicted rapist. Reportedly, Vito would often begin the relationship with his victims by carrying on innocent computer conversations with them, and then suddenly and unexpectedly turn vicious and threatening.

Officials believe Vito managed to carry out his computer stalking undetected for so long because he set up dozens of bogus accounts using several large Internet providers' offers of free trial hours on-line. Using these offers, a person can get on-line without having to supply proof of identity. Also, because some of these Internet providers have millions of customers, Vito could hide behind the computer screen and have his pick of victims.

In 1995, authorities arrested a 40-year-old, part-time school teacher from Fresno, California, who they believed to be "Vito," and charged him with 112 counts of computer fraud. A search of the man's home turned up over 180 subscriptions to on-line services. A federal magistrate ordered the suspect to stay off the Internet until his trial.

One estimate places the number of obscene and threatening telephone calls made each year in this country at between 30 and 50 million. As related in this chapter, with the advent of new technology for communications, it was only a matter of time before this new technology would be used for harassment and stalking. In the future, scientists will undoubtedly invent even more ways for people to communicate quickly and easily with each other, but which likewise will be subverted and used to stalk others. This is an unfortunate aspect of human nature, one that flies in the face of the commonly held belief that every person has the right to live his or her life in peace, without having to be the victim of threats and harassment.

> > > > > **11**

SERIAL STALKING

On 5 January 1994, 32-year-old David DeGennaro pled guilty in a Bucks County (Pennsylvania) court to more than 100 counts involving the stalking and sexual harassment of 35 women since 1990. According to court records, he targeted women who worked at or patronized two exercise spas in the Oxford Valley area just north of Philadelphia. The allegations against DeGennaro included nine cases in which the prosecutor charged that DeGennaro sprayed women's cars with semen, scratched the word "slut" into the paint of their automobiles, and left threatening, sexual messages on Post-it notes attached to their windshields. The prosecutor also accused DeGennaro of leaving a videotape outside one of the exercise spas. On the tape a man is shown masturbating while wearing a woman's one-piece bathing suit and a mask. At the time of the videotape drop-off, police were still attempting to identify the person responsible for the many acts of stalking.

The police finally cracked the case when they lifted a partial fingerprint from one of the threatening Post-it notes and matched the fingerprint to DeGennaro. After his arrest, a police search of his home produced the bathing suit worn in the videotape. DeGennaro, a married man with four children, used his and his father's house as security and posted the $800,000 bond a judge set.

At DeGennaro's trial, many of the women who testified against him said they feared he would receive only probation and then be free to stalk them again. "I constantly look over my shoulder," said one of the victims, who moved because of her fear of DeGennaro.[149]

On 18 March 1994, the women's fears nearly came true. DeGennaro received a prison sentence of 1½ to 3 years, an exceedingly light sentence considering that he could have received as much as 100 years in prison.

At the conclusion of the trial, as officers led DeGennaro handcuffed from the courtroom, he turned and grinned at the victims. He reportedly said, "See you all down the road."[150] Unfortunately, for most stalking victims this is a very likely possibility.

In August 1995, after serving only 17 months of his sentence, DeGennaro received from a Bucks County judge, over the objection of the District Attorney's Office, approval to be moved to a work release program, which meant he would be free during the day and only locked up at night. Along with the objection of the District Attorney's Office, officials at the Bucks County Men's Correctional Center, where DeGennaro served most of his sentence, also opposed this move. The latter officials said that DeGennaro had continuously minimized the seriousness of his crimes.

"That's crazy," said one of DeGennaro's victims. "I believe he's not cured in this short of time. The only time I felt safe was when he was put away. It really haunted me for a long time."[151]

Along with being granted this move to a work release program, DeGennaro, the victims found, would also be eligible for parole in September 1995. In December 1995, however, the Board of Probation and Parole denied DeGennaro's request for parole, and stated he wouldn't be eligible to apply again until September 1996, a welcome reprieve for his many victims.

Although many victims of stalking may feel that their stalkers have chosen them because they represent something unique and desirable, and that the stalker is fixated on and possessed with only them, this often isn't the case. Detectives find that with many stalkers, if a thorough investigation is made into their past, often other cases of stalking, and occasionally a large number of them, turn up. Recently, for example, police in Westminster, California, investigating a man who has stalked a woman for 17 years, discovered him to be a serial stalker with numerous victims, and who had an unusual reason for picking them. They all bear a resemblance to the woman he has stalked for 17 years.

"[He] is a serial stalker," said one of the detectives who investigated the case. "In his case, all of his victims have physical features similar to [the victim stalked for 17 years]."[152]

What percentage of stalkers are serial stalkers? Experts say that more than half of the stalkers in America have been involved in prior incidents of stalking. "Psychiatrists cannot accurately predict when the behavior will stop or recur," said Dr. Maurice Rappaport, "but they know that about two-thirds of those showing obsessive behavior have had prior episodes."[153]

Stalking for some people is simply the way they deal with the frustrations of life. When frustration strikes, they fixate on another person as the one, and the only one (at least at that moment), who can solve the problems that have brought on the frustration, or they may fixate on the person as the one who has caused the problems and frustration, and who should therefore be punished. Far too often, as in the following incident, a look into the past actions of a stalker can be a frightening glimpse into how the present stalking will end.

➤ ➤ ➤ ➤

On 3 November 1995, Rosa Leveritt's worst nightmare became reality. Even though obtaining a restraining order, she still lived in constant fear that her ex-boyfriend, Eartha Carr, would carry out his continuous threats to kill her. That day, Carr entered the West Columbia (South Carolina) Chicken Plant, where Leveritt worked and, until a few weeks before, Carr had worked. He walked up to Leveritt, said a few words to her, then pulled out a handgun and killed her.

"We were wrapping up the day and he come out of nowhere," a fellow worker of Leveritt's said. "I saw him fire the first shot then I shouted to my co-workers, 'He's got a gun—run!'"

Police officers investigating the murder discovered that Leveritt and Carr had dated for 4 years before Leveritt decided in April 1995 to break off the relationship. Following this decision by Leveritt, Carr threatened and harassed her almost daily, one time even assaulting her while she waited at a bus stop.

Investigators found, however, that this wasn't the first incident of stalking and violence in Carr's life. In 1984, Carr, a former Tennessee police sergeant, stalked a girlfriend with whom he had lived for 6 years. He apparently became enraged when she ended their relationship and soon after began a new relationship with an inmate at the state prison. Carr allegedly followed her and found her sitting in the prison picnic area with her new boyfriend. Now even more enraged, Carr grabbed a shotgun from his car and fired at the couple through a chain link fence, seriously wounding the ex-girlfriend and her new boyfriend.

"I shot her and I meant to kill her," Carr told the police after his arrest. "I loved the ground she walked on, but she did me wrong. I just flipped out."

Carr received two consecutive 10-year prison sentences after pleading guilty to two counts of assault and battery with intent to kill. However, as often happens in these types of cases, he didn't serve much of the time, and in 1989 was already free and arrested once again, this time for simple assault and battery.

"He was charming at first—bought her a lot of gifts," said Leveritt's daughter. "Then he got mean. That's why she broke it off—she was scared."[154]

After murdering Leveritt at the chicken plant, Carr attempted to flee from the scene. However, police arrived just as he ran out of the plant. Carr, finding himself cornered, sat down and placed the gun against his temple, shooting and killing himself.

For many stalkers, as the above incident shows, stalking is a way of dealing with relationships that don't go exactly as the stalker wants, a way of trying to force both people and relationships to fit the scripts and scenarios stalkers have often meticulously drawn up for them. Unfortunately, the reason these people use stalking is because they so often find that it accomplishes just what they want: stalking many times convinces the victims to return to the relationship. Victims seldom do this because they believe the relationship will now work, but more often because of their intense fear of the stalkers. Victims often very realistically fear for their lives.

However, unlike the above incident, frustrated serial stalkers don't have to have had an intimate relationship before they begin stalking their victims, and they may even stalk more than one victim of the same household at the same time. The incident below demonstrates this.

For over 8 months two women who shared an apartment in Akron, Ohio, had found blood smeared on their automobiles, sanitary napkins tossed into their cars, their mail stolen, and letters and cards with sexual connotations sent to their friends in their names. One of the women also discovered sexually oriented items charged to her credit card.

The police eventually arrested Mark A. Goddard, a professor of mathematics at the University of Akron, and charged him with menacing by stalking, forgery, and aggravated burglary. According to the police, Goddard confessed to the crimes.

. "He said they were attractive and he was infatuated with them," said Detective Michael Brown of the Akron Police Department.

The stalking apparently began after both women turned down Goddard when he asked them out on a date. Although neither woman connected the date refusal with the stalking incidents, Detective Brown found a connection when both women mentioned that Goddard had asked them out at about the same time the stalking began. Detective Brown then checked the handwriting on some of the forged letters and cards sent to the women's friends with samples of Goddard's handwriting and got a match.

According to Detective Brown, Goddard found a key that one of the women had left in her apartment mailbox and used it to steal the women's mail, including the credit card on which he charged the sexually oriented items. Also, the detective alleges, Goddard broke into the women's apartment, and rummaged through their things.

"He went through our trash," said one of the victims. "He knew our prescriptions, who our doctors are. He knew every little detail about us."[155]

Officers took Goddard to the Summit County jail. He is being held under $50,000 bail.

Unfortunately, as discussed in Chapter 6, some stalkers target children. As with other types of stalkers, a close investigation into a juvenile stalker's background will usually turn up other incidents involving the stalking of children, as the incident below shows.

On 14 July 1996, Los Altos, California, police arrested James Alan Stiritz, known locally as "Grandpa Jim." The police charged Stiritz with harassing and kidnapping a 9-year-old girl. While Stiritz sat in jail under

a $100,000 bond, the local prosecutor added new charges of committing lewd and lascivious acts and having substantial sexual contact with two 4-year-old girls. Because of the new charges, a judge denied Stiritz bail, saying he considered Stiritz a danger to the community.

After the prosecutor added the new charges, police detectives began looking into Stiritz's conduct over the past 10 years, and eventually compiled a 2-inch-thick file on him. According to court records made public, Stiritz has allegedly been stalking and harassing one woman, now 20 years old, since she was 10. The woman's family over the past decade has obtained several restraining orders against Stiritz, which the police have jailed him several times for violating.

"I'm afraid of this man," the victim said. "I don't know what he's going to do next."[156]

Investigators discovered that certain times of the year seem to invigorate Stiritz's desire to stalk the victim, particularly Valentine's Day and the victim's birthday. On one Valentine's Day, Stiritz allegedly sent the woman a blank marriage license, a blank premarital health certificate, and brochures on housing in the Los Altos area.

Detectives in Los Altos, during their investigation, also began contacting other nearby law enforcement agencies to see if they had had any contact with Stiritz. Reportedly, a large number of stalking incidents involving Stiritz came pouring in, all involving girls aged 4 to 9.

Although stalking victims may desperately want to know why they were chosen as victims, what they might have done to trigger a stalker's obsession with them, often, they find, the answer is nothing. They are just one of a serial stalker's many victims. These stalkers are simply following a pattern of behavior they have practiced for years. But no matter what the reason or cause for the stalking, victims should be cautioned that serial stalkers in particular are very disturbed individuals. However, as will be detailed in later chapters, they can be deterred.

UNINTENTIONAL AND THIRD-PARTY VICTIMS OF STALKING

Richard Wade Farley first met Laura Black in July 1984 when he stopped in her department at ESL, Inc., a defense contractor in Sunnydale, California, to talk with a friend. The chance meeting became the starting point of a 4-year campaign of stalking and harassment that eventually ended in a shooting rampage at ESL, Inc. The rampage left seven people murdered and four injured, all but one of whom had nothing at all to do with the stalking.

Soon after their chance meeting at ESL, Inc., Farley and Black, along with Farley's friend, had a casual lunch at the Eat-Your-Heart-Out Deli. Everyone paid for their own meal, and Laura Black thought this was nothing more than just a brief break from work. For Richard Farley, though, it was the beginning of a deadly obsession.

"I think I fell instantly in love with her," he would say later at his trial for the mass murder at ESL, Inc. "I thought she was attractive. It was just one of those things, I guess."[157] At ESL, Inc. Farley had a government top-secret clearance and worked as a software engineer, test technician, and computer programmer. Although no one knew it, Farley also collected guns and had an extensive library of books, journals, and magazines about violence.

Farley's colleagues at ESL, Inc. thought his fixation on Black was silly and foolish. She was 22 years old, pretty, athletic, popular, and had a dazzling smile. In contrast, Farley was 36 years old, overweight, and had few friends. High school classmates of Farley described him as "nerdie" and a "wimp."

"I don't think girls were attracted to him," said a female classmate of Farley's from high school. "And I don't think he had the guts to go after a girl." Another classmate commented, "He was one of those faceless people."[158] Farley's mother said her son never had a high school sweetheart, and she didn't know of him ever having a girlfriend in his adult life.

Yet, despite his background of emotional poverty, Farley asked Black out for a date, to go see a tractor pull. She politely refused. He asked her out again and again. She still refused. For 7 weeks in 1985, Farley baked blueberry cakes, and every Monday morning he would put one on Black's desk. Farley also began buying her gifts and asking for her telephone number and address, and then finally demanding them. When at last it became apparent that the months of polite refusals weren't working, and that Farley wasn't going to quit asking her out, Black finally very bluntly told him she wouldn't go out with him if he was "the last man on Earth."

"I had the right to ask her out," Farley said. "She had the right to refuse. When she did not refuse in a cordial way, I felt I had the right to bother her."[159]

Part of Farley's method of bothering Black included dozens of letters, some of which he agonized over for 8 hours or more to be certain of his wording. "She told me to stop writing the letters," he said later in court. "I tried. But when I stopped, she started ignoring me. By that time I was hooked on her. I had fallen madly in love with her and I had to see her, even if I had to make her mad."[160] For Farley, even angry contact with Black was better than no contact at all.

In one of his letters, Farley wrote: "It is my option to make your life miserable." And he tried. Farley began following Black to the company softball games she played in, he joined her health club to be in her aerobics class, he hung around the parking lot of a convenience store where she shopped, and he copied down the license plate numbers of the men he saw her with. He also called her over and over on the telephone. At Farley's trial, Black told jurors that Farley would show up everywhere she was. No matter where she went, Black said, she would see him there.

Similar to most stalkers, Farley began gathering personal information about Black. He went through her computer files. He pried into her personnel file, and one time, when rifling through her desk, he found an application for a security clearance, which contained a gold mine of information, including family addresses and telephone numbers. Like most stalkers, having this type of information about a victim gave Farley a feeling of intimacy with Black.

Farley's obsession with Black finally became so great and his harassment of her so open that his employers at ESL, Inc. warned him to leave her alone or else he would be fired. They also told him he could no longer attend any of the company-sponsored activities where Black would be, such as company softball games. Farley promised he would leave her alone. But he didn't. He had become so obsessed that he began believing the two of them actually had an intimate relationship. Farley fantasized that he and Black had gone on a skiing trip together to Vail, Colorado. To support this fantasy, he doctored a photograph taken of Black in an aerobics class to make it look like a ski picture. He also later claimed to an attorney hired by Black that he had in his possession (but never produced) a tape recording of loving conversations between them, credit card slips from dinner dates they had gone out on, and a key to her house (which he had secretly copied when he found a set of keys Black had left lying on her desk).

Finally, in May 1986, ESL, Inc. fired Farley because of his continued stalking and harassment of Black. When this occurred, thoughts of violence apparently began forming inside Farley's head.

"Once I'm fired, you won't be able to control me ever again," he wrote her. "Pretty soon I'll crack under the pressure and run amok and destroy everything in my path."

Even though out of work and forbidden to enter ESL, Inc. property, Farley continued stalking and harassing Black. His letters became even more threatening. In one of them he wrote: "I feel capable of killing to protect myself, and to hell with the consequences. I do own guns, and I'm good with them. I'm really not insane, but I'm calculating. I might just scare us both with what I might do if I'm pushed into it."[161] Paradoxically, but common with stalkers, even though Farley's letters to Black often contained threats, he felt that as long as she was reading his letters the two of them still had a relationship. Farley became so gripped by and tied up in the fantasy that he and Black had an intimate relationship that at the bottom of one of his letters he wrote "Call me Saturday morning," a comment individuals might write to a person they actually had an intimate relationship with, not someone who had been rejecting them for several years.

Eventually, Farley, deep in debt and in trouble about back taxes, landed another job. Interestingly, even though fired from ESL, Inc. because of his harassment of Black, he still retained his government top secret clearance. Farley also found a girlfriend. Yet, he still couldn't get over his obsession with Black, and he continued to stalk and harass her. In January

1988, Black found a letter from Farley stuck in her door. Along with the letter was a key to her house, apparently to warn Black how vulnerable she was. (Farley had also purchased a control for her type of garage door opener, and had spent hours sitting in front of Black's house running through combination after combination until he finally found hers.)

On 2 February 1988, realizing she could no longer feel safe, Black and her attorney went to court and obtained a temporary restraining order against Farley. The court ordered Farley to stay at least 300 yards away from Black's house, workplace, and health club. The court also set 17 February 1988 as the date it would hear evidence on making the restraining order permanent.

Farley apparently completely snapped after being served with the restraining order. It meant that the woman of his obsession would be denied to him forever. Farley would later say that being near Black in any way he could was what he lived for. On 16 February 1988, one day before the hearing to make the restraining order permanent, Farley received a letter from Black's attorney reminding him of the court hearing the next day. The thought that he would be banned forever from seeing the object of his obsession apparently was too much for him to take. Farley rented a motor home, filled it with guns, ammunition, gasoline, and handcuffs, and then headed for ESL, Inc., where he knew Black would be working. His plan, he testified at his trial, was to show Black he wasn't a wimp by shooting up the computers at ESL, Inc., and then killing himself in front of her.

"I just felt she had to see the end result of what I felt she had done to me," he said. "It was important that she see it and not just read about it."[162]

At 3:00 PM, after parking the motor home at the entrance to Building M5 at ESL, Inc., Farley loaded himself down with 98 pounds of guns and ammunition. When he left the motor home, looking like an overweight Rambo, Farley apparently forgot about his plan to just shoot up the computer equipment, and in the parking lot he instead shot and killed a former co-worker, Lawrence Kane. A shotgun blast tore away Kane's jaw and went through his neck and into his left lung. Farley left him lying dead on the parking lot pavement as he stormed into Building M5. Once inside, Farley began shooting his way through the first floor as he headed for the stairway that led up to the second floor office where he knew Black would be. "Some people popped out from around corners," Farley would later tell police, "and I just shot them."[163] He also fired through the door of an office and killed a worker inside, then shot and killed another person on the stairway going up to the second floor. In addition, Farley shot and wounded a man attempting to drag a wounded colleague to safety.

By this time, the people on the second floor, hearing the shooting and screaming, began running and hiding in panic. The evacuation siren began wailing. Black, however, still sat behind her desk when Farley shoved open the door to her office. From the hallway he shot her once with a shotgun, and she fell to the floor, bleeding profusely from a gaping wound to her shoulder. Somehow, from the floor, Black managed to push the door shut with her foot. Farley would later say that he hadn't come there to kill her, and so, instead of forcing his way back into the office, he walked down the hallway, randomly shooting at the computers and any fleeing employees, eventually destroying $300,000 worth of equipment and killing seven people.

Black, though seriously wounded, managed to stumble down to a computer assembly room, where she found three other women hiding, who tried as best they could to stop the bleeding from her gaping wound. The people in the building said it was a war zone. There were bodies lying everywhere. People hid anywhere they could, one man even hiding in a heating duct. A wife of one of the shooting victims said her husband, who had gone through two tours in Vietnam, called this worse than anything he had experienced over there. And yet, even though it was extremely dangerous to move about and expose herself, Black managed to escape from the building.

After the shooting started, calls poured into the police department. The police responded immediately. Because of the number of dead and wounded, and the possibility of there being hostages, the Sunnydale Police Department SWAT team also responded to the scene and set up a command post and security perimeters outside the building. A police hostage negotiator made telephone contact with Farley, and, as is a police hostage negotiator's most important initial task, he tried to calm Farley down in order to forestall any more killings.

"I'm not ready to come out yet," Farley told the negotiator when they first began talking. "I want to gloat for a while." He told the negotiator that he had stopped shooting because it wasn't fun anymore.[164]

Police negotiators often hear this kind of bravado talk from individuals who have committed grave crimes, but the negotiators also know that after enough time passes the feelings of power and euphoria wear off and the perpetrators begin to worry about the consequences of what they have done. The negotiator at this incident, however, found that Farley seemed rational and lucid, and that he already realized the magnitude of what he had done. As expected, Farley soon expressed concern about going to prison.

"I never wanted to hurt her," Farley told the negotiator. "All she had to do was go out with me."[165]

Unable to persuade Farley to surrender right away, and wanting to forestall thoughts of suicide, the negotiator began talking to Farley about his future, such as the possibility of teaching computer classes in prison. Negotiators do this to make a person see beyond the immediate situation, and to forestall any thoughts of ending the situation by self-destruction, which can often include killing others first. Finally at 8:30 PM, Farley asked for a diet Pepsi and a number 26 sandwich from a local delicatessen: a ham, turkey, and cheese. Soon after this, he came out and surrendered to police.

"It was her smile," the police negotiator told reporters. "He knew she wasn't attracted to him, but he told her it wouldn't end until either she went out with him or he died."[166]

Even after his arrest, Farley continued writing to Black. In one of his letters, he said: "I'll smile for the camera on my way to the gas chamber."

Three and a half years later, the case finally went to trial. The police negotiator who had persuaded Farley to surrender testified in court that, "He knew what he had done, but he had to make a point. When he arrived at the parking lot, he almost changed his mind. But it had to be done. He didn't want Laura Black to think he was a wimp."[167]

Farley appeared very calm and almost unconcerned during much of the trial. However, he became totally absorbed in the case when Black took the stand, seeming to hang on her every word. To demonstrate to the jury part of what Farley had done, Black showed them the still very visible scars of the injury to her shoulder, an injury that caused her to lose 50 percent of the mobility in her left arm. She told the jury about having to go through seven operations to repair the damage, and of having to use bone from her leg and muscle from her back to reconstruct the shoulder.

The jury found Farley guilty of seven counts of first-degree murder, five counts of attempted murder, and one count each of assault with a firearm, burglary, and felony vandalism. The jury recommended that Farley receive the death penalty. The judge agreed and sentenced Farley to death. He presently awaits execution on death row at San Quentin prison.

Several years after the incident at ESL, Inc., a studio made a television movie titled *I Can Make You Love Me: The Stalking of Laura Black*. Unfortunately, as stated in Chapter 1, although much of the public obviously finds such incidents interesting, and some apparently find them riveting, this kind of publicity brings with it the extreme danger of firing up the imagination and motivation of unstable people who have thought about committing such acts. To these unstable people, movies such as this can make the perpetrator appear almost heroic.

Clearly, 10 people who worked at ESL, Inc., who had no part in the stalking, nevertheless became the unintentional and third-party victims of Richard Farley's obsession with and stalking of Laura Black. These individuals hadn't even attempted to prevent Farley from reaching Black. They just happened to be in the same area when the stalker went on a rampage. Unfortunately, this is not a rare occurrence.

Many times, though, third-party victims of stalking become involved unintentionally, not because they are in the same area, as in the incident above, but because the stalkers believe that injuring or killing them will somehow benefit the stalking victims, and consequently make the stalkers more attractive in the victims' eyes, or that by injuring or killing them the stalkers will look heroic to the victims. For example, on 30 April 1993, a man obsessed with tennis star Steffi Graf, who had converted his mother's attic into a shrine to Graf, attacked tennis star Monica Seles with a 9-inch boning knife during a tennis match in Hamburg, Germany. The man believed that by eliminating Seles he would advance the tennis fortunes of Graf.

In another incident, John Hinckley, Jr., with no apparent concern for unintentional victims, attempted to assassinate President Ronald Reagan, and in the process permanently injured press secretary James Brady. He didn't do this for any political or ideological purpose, but rather to impress actress Jodie Foster, whom he had been stalking. Hinckley had become obsessed with Ms. Foster after seeing her performance in the movie *Taxi Driver*.

Some unintentional and third-party victims of stalking become victims because of society's lack of knowledge about the phenomenon of stalking, or about its dangers. For example, supervisors and managers at places of employment may believe that a stalking victim is overreacting, or that the problem is personal, and thus do not get involved. Through this indifference and consequent lack of security, supervisors and managers can inadvertently help the stalker, many times to their own peril, for by being in the workplace, they are often in just as much danger as the victim.

Although working at a location where a person is being stalked can certainly be dangerous, as the incident at ESL, Inc. confirms, individuals in even more danger are those who maintain close relationships with stalking victims, such as friends and family members. Stalkers have been known to break into these friends' and relatives' homes searching for information about the whereabouts of the victims. The stalker may also believe that a victim is hiding at the house of a friend or family member, or that a friend or family member is assisting the victim in avoiding the stalker. This belief can occasionally lead to a deadly assault, as the following incident reveals.

➤   ➤   ➤   ➤

In November 1996, in Indianapolis, a judge sentenced Charles Barker to death for murdering the grandparents of his ex-girlfriend. On 3 August 1993, looking for his ex-girlfriend, Candice Benefiel, whom he had been stalking for some time, Barker broke into the home of Benefiel's grandparents, where she was staying. Benefiel's grandfather attempted to stop Barker, but Barker shot him through the heart, killing him instantly. Benefiel's grandmother tried to hide in a bathroom with a 1-year-old child that Barker had fathered with Benefiel. Barker kicked in the bathroom door and shot the grandmother through the head as she held the infant in her arms.

Afterward, Barker kidnapped Benefiel and the infant and drove to a former wife's house. There, he kidnapped his former wife and forced the three of them to accompany him to Tennessee, where police finally arrested him.

"He never intended to hurt anyone," said a relative of Barker at his trial. This is a typical response of many close family members. Even people like Barker, who murdered several people in cold blood, often receive sympathy from relatives, who many times see stalkers as simply lovesick individuals.

"It was calculated and premeditated conduct carried out after hours of deliberation," said Deputy Prosecutor Larry Sells. "He's placed the blame everywhere but where it belongs, which is squarely on his shoulders."[168]

➤   ➤   ➤   ➤

As shown above, being a family member or close friend of a stalking victim can be extremely dangerous. This creates a dilemma for individuals close to the victims—not wanting to abandon the stalking victims but knowing that it would be much safer not to be involved at all. It also causes a dilemma for stalking victims. They may not want to endanger others, but to survive, both physically and emotionally, they need the support and help of family members and close friends.

Stalking victims are individuals facing a crisis. They are being followed, harassed, and threatened by a person possibly capable of extreme violence. Stalking victims often live every moment of every day in fear and terror. They need someone to be an emotional anchor for them. They need the support and reassurance of family members and close friends who will listen, understand, support, and, if necessary, help them stay safe. This, of course, is not without its risks, and so family members and close friends should be just as interested as the victims in the tips and safety precautions I give in later chapters.

It must never be forgotten that most stalkers have mental problems, and many of them have *severe* mental problems. These types of individuals are often capable of extreme violence when carrying out their stalking plans. Also, most stalkers have no social conscience and no remorse for the harm they do to others, including harm to completely innocent people.

In the small, quiet town of Harrodsburg, Kentucky, a community of 7000 people, the unthinkable occurred. A man committed a triple murder, and then killed himself.

"People walk around at 11 o'clock here," said a local resident. "You just don't expect it to happen here. It's a tragic kind of thing."[169]

The murderer apparently saw his wife, who had recently left him, and whom he was stalking, in a car with five other people reportedly en route to get something to eat. The husband began following the car in his truck. When the estranged wife saw her husband following them, she knew that trouble was near. She instructed the driver to stop at the Harrodsburg Fire Department, believing that the police department was still located in the same building (unbeknownst to her the police department had recently moved to a new location). Before anyone could get out of the car, though, the estranged husband pulled up and opened fire on the six people with a .357 magnum revolver, killing three, including his estranged wife.

The killer then fled to the Pleasant Retreat Shopping Center in nearby Lancaster, Kentucky. Lancaster police, however, had already been alerted to be on the lookout for the truck. When a police officer spotted and stopped the truck, the murderer put the .357 magnum revolver up to his own head and killed himself.

In another incident, this one in Miami, Florida, Micheline Telfort had filed several complaints with police about her ex-boyfriend stalking her. On 19 March 1995, she called North Miami police and filed another complaint. She told the officers that her ex-boyfriend had harassed her that day at the store where she worked and had struck her. Because the stalking had been going on for a long time, Telfort's roommate would often wait in front of their apartment building for Micheline to get home from work and walk with her up to their apartment.

On the night of 19 March 1995, Telfort called her roommate and told her about the most recent confrontation with her ex-boyfriend. The roommate made certain to be waiting for Telfort in front of their apartment building that night. The two women walked together up to their third-floor apartment. As they opened the door, Telfort's ex-boyfriend, apparently hiding, surprised them in the hallway and began firing a handgun at them. The roommate died from the gunfire as she tried to protect Telfort. The ex-boyfriend then shot Telfort twice, beat her severely, and tossed her off the third floor balcony. Telfort landed on a car below with such force that she dented the top, but, amazingly, she got up and ran for help. Physicians treated and released her that night from the hospital.

The police arrested Telfort's ex-boyfriend. They charged him with first-degree and attempted first-degree murder, and armed burglary.

Besides being dangerous and deadly to their victims, and just as dangerous and deadly to the families, friends, and even co-workers of stalking victims, stalkers can also be extraordinarily dangerous to the police officers who attempt to intercede and arrest them. Often, stalkers can be dangerous because they have just committed a grave crime and know they now face serious punishment, and occasionally stalkers can be so mentally unbalanced that they become dangerous over what appear to be minor matters. Every once in a while, stalkers can strike at police officers for no apparent reason.

In October 1996, in New York City, police lieutenant Federico Narvaez, a supervisor at the 70th Precinct, stopped when a woman flagged

him down. She told him she was being stalked, and then pointed out Harvey Richardson as the stalker, a man on parole for assaulting the aunt of the stalking victim. Lt. Narvaez got out of his police car and walked over to talk with Richardson. However, as he approached the alleged stalker, Richardson turned and fired a handgun at him, killing the police officer instantly.

Richardson then attempted to flee from the scene, but two blocks away two other police officers spotted him. After an exchange of gunfire, the officers killed Richardson.

"This is human garbage," said New York Mayor Rudolph Giuliani, who held up for reporters a 6-foot-long criminal record that showed Richardson had many arrests and seven major felony convictions, including convictions for rape, attempted rape, assault, and stalking. "When he was not in jail he would rape, stalk, and assault people. That's all he did. All he did was harm people."[170]

As previously mentioned, every year more than one-fourth of all Americans suffer from some kind of diagnosable mental disorder. Yet only one in five of these individuals receives any kind of treatment. Most stalkers fit into this category of troubled people not receiving help. Stalkers can often suffer from mild to severe mental problems, yet few receive any serious psychiatric care. Obviously, people such as this can be extremely dangerous for police officers to confront and arrest, as the above and following incidents show.

In Eastchester, New York, a suburb of New York City, Richard Sacchi had agreed to surrender to authorities on stalking charges involving his estranged wife. He had previously been convicted of aggravated harassment, and the recent charges came from him showing up at her apartment with a shotgun. However, on the day before he was to surrender, he unleashed a barrage of gunfire at residents in his neighborhood.

Like the residents of Harrodsburg, Kentucky, in the incident related earlier in this chapter, the residents of Eastchester also believed that this sort of incident didn't happen in their quiet little community. "I've lived here for thirty-five years," said a neighbor of Sacchi. "This is a quiet town. It's strange, it's weird that this is happening."[171]

Apparently, before the random shooting began, Sacchi made a call to the Eastchester Police Department, requesting that they send an officer out to assist him. When Officer Michael Frey and his partner arrived, Sacchi, hidden in the attic of his house, shot Frey in the chest and both arms, killing him. He also wounded Frey's partner.

Responding to the assault on the officers and the random firing at neighbors, local police assessed the situation and then called in the New York City Police Department, as they have much more experience in dealing with armed, barricaded subjects. Police negotiators attempted to contact Sacchi via loudspeakers, but Sacchi responded with blasts of rock music. At last, after a 15-hour standoff, police forced entry into Sacchi's home, where they found his grandmother murdered and the family dog killed. After a room-by-room search of the house, police officers discovered Sacchi in the attic, dead from a self-inflicted gunshot wound. On the walls of the attic Sacchi had scrawled: "Jesus, forgive me for my sins." He had also left out a gray-black suit with the message: "Clothes for my funeral."[172]

In another incident, this one in New Albany, Indiana, a community along the Ohio River, Deborah Ingle had recently obtained a restraining order against her estranged husband, John Ingle, who she said had been stalking her and who she feared would harm her. The two had been having domestic problems that had intensified to the point where Deborah now felt her life was in danger.

On 27 July 1996, John walked into the bar area of the Tommy Lancaster Restaurant in New Albany, where Deborah worked. Seeing her estranged husband come into the bar, and knowing there would be trouble, Deborah attempted to get away. However, before she could escape, John allegedly fired several shots at Deborah with a handgun, striking her in the head and body and killing her. He then fled the building.

"We were sitting in the last booth," said a customer at the restaurant. "We heard the first shot and ducked. Then we heard the second shot and got the hell out of there. The shots went off real fast, and we heard four or five shots."[173]

Local police officers sped to the scene of the shooting and immediately put out a description of the suspect. A few minutes later, Detective-Sergeant Russell Witt radioed that he had the suspect. However, the next radio call came out as "officer down" (police jargon for an officer seriously wounded or killed).

When police officers converged on the scene they found Sergeant Witt lying on the sidewalk, shot four times. Although he wore a Kelvar (bulletproof) vest, which had stopped several of the bullets, one had passed through the arm hole of the vest and into his chest. An ambulance transported him to a nearby hospital, where doctors listed him as critical, but stable.

A short while later, John Ingle surrendered to police near the site where the shooting of Sergeant Witt had occurred. He told officers he had hidden along the riverbank after the shooting. Police recovered a handgun and charged John Ingle with murder and attempted murder. His criminal record, police report, includes a hostage incident and at least one other shooting.

Occasionally, individuals who do not even know the stalkers or their targets can become victims of acts meant to harm the stalking victims. For example, recently in Newark, New Jersey, Continental Airlines filed suit against the ex-wife of one of their pilots. Reportedly, the ex-wife admitted under oath that, in an effort to get back at her ex-husband, she baked him a loaf of rye bread into which she added marijuana. She knew that her husband, a 10-year veteran, would be flying for the airlines and consequently be subject to drug testing. Continental Airlines fired him when their drug testing showed evidence of marijuana in his system, though he was later vindicated and reinstated. Of course, the real concern here is not necessarily the career of the pilot, but rather the extreme danger the passengers flying with this pilot were unknowingly put in. Flying a commercial jetliner requires total concentration and alertness, not someone under the influence of marijuana. Unfortunately, this lack of concern for the welfare of others is a common trait among stalkers.

In October 1996, in Duluth, Minnesota, as the police talked to a stalking victim, she suddenly spotted the four stalking suspects and pointed them out to police. The four fled in a car and for 21 minutes the car raced at high speeds through the streets of Duluth, before the police finally managed to stop it. As someone who has been involved in a number of high-speed pursuits, I can attest to the extreme danger these create, not just to the police and those in the pursued car, but also to any person who happens to stray into the path of the pursuit. A high-speed pursuit ending in a fiery crash with another vehicle is a much too common occurrence.

All of the facts and anecdotes in this chapter are meant to emphasize that everyone should be concerned about the crime of stalking. As we have seen, not only are the stalking victims often in grave danger from the stalkers, but so are the victims' family members, friends, and co-workers. And, although it would be safer for these people to completely avoid the stalking victims, the latter need family members, friends, and co-workers to be close by and supportive during their ordeal. Therefore, it is imperative that everyone close to a stalking victim read carefully the suggestions provided in later chapters for dealing with stalkers. It could mean saving not only the life of the victim but also their own lives.

> ➤   ➤   ➤   ➤   ➤   **13**

PHYSIOLOGICAL AND PSYCHOLOGICAL EFFECTS OF STALKING

Kathleen Baty hardly knew Larry Stagner when they were classmates during high school. She couldn't remember ever speaking to him. Yet, he would eventually become a focal point of her life.

The nightmare for Baty began on Thanksgiving Day 1982. Then a junior at UCLA, Baty was spending the holiday with her parents at their home in Redwood City, California. The telephone rang and her brother, Rob, answered it and then said to Baty, "It's for you, and he sounds weird."

Baty took the telephone, and the caller said he was John Riley. She didn't know a John Riley, but to be polite Baty stayed on the line and talked, knowing, however, that she had heard the strange speech impediment of the caller, an almost baby-talk voice, somewhere before. Suddenly, it came to her. She recognized the voice to be that of Larry Stagner, a former student and fellow track team member from her high school. (As a very young child, Stagner had had a hearing defect that interfered with his normal speech development, and consequently he talked in short, clipped sentences.) But why would he be calling her? Baty wondered. She couldn't remember ever having any kind of interaction with him before.

"I think you must have mistaken me with somebody else," Baty finally told him. "I have to go."

The next day the hang-up calls started. For 4 hours the phone rang every 5 minutes, but no one would say anything when Baty picked up the phone. Finally, she said, "I know who you are!"

"Why are you talking to me now?" the caller finally said. "You never used to talk to me before."[174]

She hung up, but it wasn't the last of Stagner. That night, at a stoplight, he pulled up next to her in a truck. In the back of the truck, Baty noticed with a stomach-clutching apprehension, hung a gun rack.

Later that evening, as Baty returned home with her boyfriend, Stagner stepped out from some bushes near her house, where he had been hiding. After a confrontation with Baty's boyfriend, Stagner got into his truck and sped away. But later that night he called Baty and told her he had 180 rounds of ammunition and was going to kill her boyfriend.

Baty called 911, and the police spotted Stagner in her neighborhood. When they tried to stop him, Stagner sped away, and the police gave chase. When they finally managed to stop him, the police found that Stagner did have 180 of ammunition in the truck, along with a rifle and a hunting knife. Because this turned out to be Stagner's first arrest, he could only be held for 48 hours. A psychiatrist who examined him during this 48-hour hold noted that Stagner had a "sadomasochistic element to his personality with a quality of revenge." The psychiatrist also described him as "a borderline personality with paranoid schizoid features."

Three months later, the stalking began again. Stagner appeared at Baty's parents' door and asked for her. Baty's father, not knowing Stagner, told him she wasn't there. Later, when friends of Baty's parents, who had been visiting them, left, they saw Stagner duck down in the seat of his truck, which he had parked in front of Baty's parents' house. Concerned, the friends called Baty's parents as soon as they got home and told them about the incident. Baty's parents called the police, but Stagner left before they arrived.

When Baty arrived home, her parents told her what had happened. They said they had been so frightened of being shot that they had stayed away from the windows. Soon afterward, Stagner telephoned and asked Baty why her parents had called the police. Baty quickly hung up and called the police.

Officers responded immediately and found Stagner in the neighborhood near Baty's parents' home. When they took him to the police station, Stagner opened up to the detectives and told them about his fixation on Baty. The officers learned that Stagner's obsession was so deep he had quit his job several months before so he could devote his whole time to stalking Baty. He told the officers that he had broken into her parents' home near San Francisco to get her address in Los Angeles, where she attended college. Stagner said he then drove to Los Angeles in an attempt to find her, only to discover that she had already left to visit her parents, and so he turned around and drove back (a 14-hour round trip).

On further questioning, the detectives found that Stagner had planned to kidnap Baty and take her to the wilderness of the Trinity Mountains in northern California. The police also discovered that he had made detailed plans for this abduction, even equipping his truck with police scanners so he could track police movements as he raced with his hostage to the mountains. Stagner told the detectives that he realized the police would eventually catch up with him, and he expected to be killed in a blazing and glorious gun battle with them. A psychiatrist who later examined him would say that Stagner had difficulty distinguishing fantasy from reality, and that his obsession with Baty was untreatable.

Baty, now in real fear of what Stagner might do, immediately obtained a restraining order against him. This proved unnecessary at that time, however, because, as stalkers often do, Stagner inexplicably left Baty alone for a while—3 years—only to then unexpectedly start the stalking again. During the 3 years of quiet, Baty graduated from UCLA and moved into an apartment with two girlfriends in the Marina del Rey section of Los Angeles. She became one of the L.A. Gear girls, promoting L.A. Gear products at trade shows.

In May 1987, after Baty returned home from an L.A. Gear road trip, neighbors told her they had chased off a man trying to break into her apartment. When she showed the neighbors a picture of Stagner, they said, yes, that was the man. Baty called Stagner's probation officer, but discovered he wasn't on probation any longer. The probation officer warned her, though, that Stagner's father had called him recently and said that his son seemed deeply depressed and had disappeared.

The next afternoon, returning with a roommate from the beach, Baty saw Stagner on the street in front of her apartment building. The two women raced into their apartment and called police. From her apartment, Baty saw Stagner get a handgun from his vehicle and put it in a paper bag, then start toward her building. In panic, Baty and her roommate decided to jump from their sun deck to a neighboring deck to escape Stagner. The roommate did it safely, but Baty seriously injured her leg in the jump. During all of the screaming and shouting following Baty's injury, the police arrived, but in the confusion Stagner escaped.

The following day, Baty obtained another restraining order against Stagner, and, as she suspected, Stagner came back to her apartment in violation of it. The police arrested him for the violation and a judge sentenced him to 60 days in jail and another 3 years of probation.

Baty left the Los Angeles area soon afterward, and went touring for L.A. Gear. Eventually, she and her future husband, Greg, moved to Menlo

Park, California. As both the house they lived in and their telephone were put in Greg's name, Baty felt relatively safe. She believed Stagner wouldn't be able to find her. But in July 1989, fate and coincidence intervened.

One night, Baty ordered a pizza, and when she went to the door she didn't look right away at the deliveryman as she searched through her purse for money. When she did look up, though, she felt as though a live wire had been touched to her chest. The deliveryman was Stagner.

When Baty called Stagner's probation officer the next day she found that he had already called about the incident. Even though a coincidence, Stagner reported it because he feared it might be a violation of his probation. Baty also learned that Stagner would be off probation in a few months. With a sickening queasiness, she realized that her earlier feelings of safety had been simply an illusion.

On Thanksgiving Day 1989, 7 years after her first call from Stagner, he called her again. The voice on the telephone asked for "Dave," but she knew who it was. The terror was beginning again. With trembling hands, she hung up. Several times in the days following the call she would catch glimpses of Stagner driving away as she pulled up to her house in Menlo Park.

Baty now became so frightened she would peek out doors before leaving, and would drive around the block several times, checking for Stagner, before parking at her house. On New Year's Eve 1989, during one of Baty's neighborhood sweeps, she saw Stagner trying to duck down in the front seat of a car. She called police, and Stagner, in violation of a restraining order, received 4 months in jail and 3 years of probation.

Released from jail at the beginning of May 1990, Stagner kept the first appointment with his probation officer, and appeared very cooperative. However, when he didn't show up for his second meeting, the probation officer checked and found that Stagner had given the probation department a phony address. An alert went out to the police to pick Stagner up because authorities knew he almost certainly would head toward Baty's house.

The stress of all the years of stalking was now beginning to catch up with Baty. When she could sleep, she had nightmares about Stagner, and if she heard a noise in the middle of the night she would crawl around the house on her stomach, terrified it was him.

"The anticipation was killing me," Baty said. "I almost wanted him to make a move, to get it over with."[175]

On 17 May 1990, Baty walked into her house, and a few moments later the nightmare she'd been having about Stagner came true: she found herself standing face-to-face with him. He had broken into her house and was waiting for her with a knife and a gun. Later, she would say she almost felt relieved that he had finally committed a serious crime that would merit a long incarceration.

Stagner told her he knew his life was over, but that before it was over he was going to take her with him to the mountains in northern California. He said he had tried to be good and stay away from her, but he just couldn't. Before they could leave the house, though, the telephone rang. Stagner, apparently not wanting to cause concern if someone knew Baty was supposed to be home, allowed her to answer it. The caller turned out to be Baty's mother, who quickly realized something wasn't right. She asked her daughter if Stagner was there, and Baty said yes as cheerfully as she could, hoping Stagner wouldn't realize what she was doing.

On hanging up, Baty's mother immediately called police, who were well aware of Stagner's obsession with Baty. They responded immediately and surrounded the house, but stayed out of sight. Inside the house, Stagner, unaware that police had arrived and were waiting for him, tied Baty's hands and led her out a side door. He then took her around to the front of the house, but as he put a key into the car door a half dozen police SWAT team members suddenly confronted him, weapons out and ready. In the confusion of the confrontation, one of the officers motioned for Baty to run, which she did, safely getting away from Stagner.

Although now trapped in a hopeless situation, Stagner refused to surrender. No longer having a hostage to threaten, and apparently forgetting about his earlier boast of engaging the police in a blazing and glorious gun battle, Stagner put a gun to his own stomach and threatened to kill himself. For the next 11 hours he held the officers at bay with his threats of suicide.

He managed to do this because the SWAT team commander decided that, with Stagner now mostly just a danger to himself, they would let time and the cold night air break down his resolve. And it did. At 4 o'clock in the morning Stagner finally agreed to put the gun down if the officers would allow him to go into the Baty garage to get warm. When Stagner got to the garage, though, two SWAT officers hidden inside kicked open the door and tossed out two flashbangs (grenades that do little damage but explode with a brilliant flash and a tremendous explosion, the combination of which overloads a person's sensory system and causes disorientation). One of the flashbangs, though, exploded in Stagner's face, injuring his left eye.

While the police charged Stagner with kidnapping, burglary, false imprisonment, attempted auto theft, and violation of a restraining order, the judge threw out the most serious charge—kidnapping—because Stagner had only taken Baty a little over 240 feet before police confronted and stopped him, not far enough to constitute kidnapping. Stagner originally pled not guilty by reason of insanity, but eventually changed his mind and pled no contest. And yet, even though he pled no contest, a shocked Baty discovered that Stagner, because of the reduced charges, would likely spend only 4 years in prison, less than half of the time he had been stalking her.

"I am so angry and so disappointed in our system," Baty said. "It's a joke. It blows me away how [the judge] could sentence a man without hearing from the victim. It's scary to think that one man read the case on pieces of paper. I'm in counseling twice a week. My life will never be the same. You can't read that on a piece of paper."[176]

Baty attempted, without success, to convince the judge to impose a stiffer sentence. She knew that if she couldn't, then once the state released him in 4 years the stalking would almost certainly resume.

"When that release occurs," Baty said, "Larry Stagner's sentence is over. And that is when my sentence begins. Each year that Larry Stagner is in custody is another year that I can live normally, without fear."

The 8 years of stalking have changed Baty's life from one of being happy and carefree to one of constant fear and apprehension. "I turn and see him standing behind me everyday," said Baty. "Nighttime alone is absolute hell."

Because of the circumstances of her last confrontation with Stagner, Baty can no longer just come home. Now she steps into her house cautiously, leaving the door wide open so she can flee if necessary, and not closing the door until she is positive Stagner is not there. "It's like part of me is dead," Baty said, "a part I can't get back."

As to her future involvement with Stagner, Baty is not optimistic. "He's going to come back. Each time, it has been more violent—and the next time it will be even more violent."

Stagner's probation officer agrees. "He's probably going to haunt her."

Even Stagner's attorney agrees. "He has a history of being unable to avoid contact with the victim. It seems like an irresistible impulse."[177]

As Baty feared, after Stagner served just 4 years in prison the state paroled him on 19 December 1994. He checked into a halfway house, but on 18 January 1995 Stagner left for an appointment and didn't return. Authorities arrested him a week later in Truckee, California. For violating his parole, Stagner received another year in prison.

On 26 January 1996, the state again paroled Stagner. As for a continuation of his stalking of Baty, Stagner said, "I don't have nothing to do with her. I'm a total stranger. I've affected her life in a very negative way. I have no reason to talk to her."

The police, however, aren't convinced. "He's a liar," said Menlo Park Chief of Police Bruce Cumming. "He's obsessed with Kathleen Baty...there's no question in my mind that he's going to work his way back to Menlo Park. The question is when and where and how soon."[178]

As a police officer, even though I have seen it often enough, I have never really sat down and thought about what a stalking victim's life of constant fear and apprehension must be like. I have many times responded to radio runs where victims have had an encounter with stalkers. I've listened to their stories of fear, and tried to be sympathetic, but it's hard for someone not experiencing it to know what living with this kind of terror every minute of every day must be like. The victims almost always appear just on the edge of hysteria.

The victims of stalking tell stories of always checking their rearview mirror when driving, knowing that the stalker is following them, of always examining every crowd, knowing they will see the stalker's face, of dreading it when the doorbell or the telephone rings, certain it is the stalker. This would be bad enough, but stalking victims say that one of the worst parts of stalking is its unpredictability. A victim never knows what the stalker will do. Stalkers may stop their pursuit for long or short periods, only to suddenly and unexpectedly begin the stalking again. Sometimes stalkers will call dozens or even hundreds of times a day, and then months will go by with no contact with the victims, giving these victims hope that perhaps the nightmare is finally over, only to have the stalking suddenly begin again. And even more frightening, nuisance-level stalkers may abruptly change their tactics, suddenly becoming aggressive and dangerous, then inexplicably changing back to nuisance level, and all at once aggressive and dangerous again. But the absolute worst part, say stalking victims, is never knowing how deranged and violent a stalker is. Will the stalking remain just a constant annoyance, or will it suddenly and unexpectedly explode into mindless violence? The uncertainty is agony.

"It's always on my mind," said a stalking victim. "You never know what might happen. You get paranoid. I'm not really as friendly as I used to be and really not that trusting."[179]

Victims of stalking find that because of their victimization their entire lifestyle and outlook on dealing with others change. They become extraordinarily cautious of anyone who rings their doorbell or telephones them. They no longer feel safe going out for social activities. And especially those victims stalked by strangers, they no longer feel comfortable making new acquaintances. Victims of stalking say that they jump at the slightest noise, are always looking behind them, and find themselves checking the street outside their home a hundred times a day. Stalking can transform a happy, outgoing person into a paranoid recluse.

"It affected my whole lifestyle," said a stalking victim. "I was afraid to do anything alone. I was losing all of my friends. I had bad dreams. I thought he was always outside my window. I was going paranoid. He was driving me nuts."[180]

A stalking victim I interviewed told me, "You don't eat right. You don't sleep right. You have heartburn, ulcers, headaches. You are not yourself mentally. You see him when he's really not there."

Most victims also discover that once the stalkers have gained a hold on them, few of the stalkers will ever let go. The victims may often feel overwhelmed because many times they have done nothing to initiate the stalking, and yet nothing they do will stop it. Victims ask themselves: Is there ever going to be an end to this? And even for the strongest people, those who will not allow stalkers to break them down physically or psychologically, still the experience taints their lives by making them see how extraordinarily vulnerable they are, and how the trusting of other people can be dangerous. Regardless of personal strength, stalking will make anyone a bit less outgoing than before the experience.

"Nobody knows how traumatic and devastating it is to have a life where you never know what will happen," said Peggy Gusz, executive director of the Crime Victims Center of Chester County (Pennsylvania). "The trauma encompasses everything."[181]

Many times in police work I have experienced fear, and occasionally even terror. Going into a business on a holdup alarm, never certain if the alarm is good or not, is scary. Going into a large, dark warehouse at night looking for burglars is frightening. Once, I became involved in a gun battle with a robbery suspect, and, although police officers on television and in the movies may appear fearless, I found the experience terrifying.

All of my experiences, however, have been short-term fear, not the weeks, months, and years of fear experienced by stalking victims. The closest I have come to this experience happened when I first became a police officer in the late 1960s. We had a race riot in Indianapolis. For almost 16 hours, I patrolled one of the city's worst housing projects, the spot where the violence had begun, jumping and feeling my stomach crawling up my throat every time I heard gunfire.

Although a huge crowd of rioting people, who had been occupying the streets when police first arrived on the scene of the disturbance, eventually retreated, under police pressure, back into the buildings of the housing project, this gave them a safe place from which to snipe at the police. It was truly a frightening 16 hours, an eternity of constant fear because the housing project was large, and we were easy targets for anyone hiding with a firearm in one of the hundreds of apartments. For 16 hours, my heart stopped every time I heard gunfire, and the three or four times I heard a bullet ricochet close to me my blood turned to ice.

When the disturbance finally ended, I went home totally exhausted, my body drained of energy. But it wasn't so much the physical exertion as the mental exhaustion of living with intense fear for 16 hours. My mind felt mushy. I can hardly imagine what living for weeks, months, or even years with this kind of fear would do to a person, both physically and psychologically, but I suspect, as in the following incident, it could cause a person to do drastic and irrational things.

➤   ➤   ➤   ➤

Michelle Grist briefly dated Robert Kahles in 1992. Although Grist soon wanted to end the relationship, Kahles didn't, and reportedly called her on the telephone and threatened her, harassed her while she rode her bicycle, and through his actions kept her constantly terrorized. Grist filed a complaint, and the police arrested Kahles, but he soon got out of jail on bond.

A couple of weeks later, while out on bond, Kahles allegedly broke into Grist's house, handcuffed and gagged her, and then forced her to go with him to a field near where she lived. Fortunately, Grist managed to escape when a car suddenly passed by the field. Police again arrested Kahles.

While waiting for the trial, Grist lived in daily fear that Kahles would be freed on bond again, and this fear seemed to consume her life. She worried constantly about it. The apprehension only got worse as the trial day drew nearer because she then became even more terrified that Kahles would be set free by the court or receive just a short sentence, and consequently soon come after her again. Her fear was certainly well founded based on many other stalking cases.

"What she was fearful about was that he either would beat the charges or that, since he has already spent more than a year [in jail] awaiting trial, the time served would lessen his sentence and it wouldn't be long before he would be back out on the streets coming after her again," said Ott Cefkin, a spokesman for the Broward County (Florida) Sheriff's Department.[182]

As the trial day drew nearer, Grist began to worry more and more about it. She dreaded the thought both of Kahles being released and of her having to confront him in court. Finally, the anxiety and worry became too much.

On 11 January 1994, Grist walked out and stood in the middle of a railroad track. "I'm waiting for a train," she told a friend who tried to stop her. Unable to move her, the friend went to get help. Before the friend could return, a train struck and killed Grist.

When a person remains in a constant state of fear and stress, as a stalking victim does, the body doesn't get a chance to recover from the adrenaline surge, and return its systems to normal. Eventually, the body's systems begin to fray, and physical and psychological problems develop.

A few of the physical and psychological problems stalking victims suffer include loss of appetite, inability to sleep, nightmares when they do sleep, inability to concentrate, loss of self-esteem, isolation, thoughts of death or suicide, and panic attacks. All of these, incidentally, are symptoms of clinical depression. Some experts have suggested that stalking victims can also suffer from posttraumatic stress disorder (PTSD), described as an exposure to a stressor or event outside the range of usual human experience. War veterans, natural disaster victims, and others who have experienced something so horrible that their mind cannot accept it have been known to develop this disorder. The symptoms of PTSD include panic, grief, despair, traumatic nightmares, avoidance behavior, emotional numbing, and generalized anxiety disorder. Anyone who deals with stalking victims can see that this indeed describes both their experience, which is certainly outside the range of usual human experience, and their symptoms. Yet, even worse than the symptoms is the fact that once a stalker has driven a victim to this condition, the victim becomes even easier to control and intimidate. The victim will do anything to make the fear and anxiety stop.

"I knew I was turning into a raving lunatic," said a stalking victim. "I couldn't answer the phone. I couldn't read my mail. I couldn't prove the connection, but I started getting sick, for the first time in my life—depression, intestinal problems, all sorts of things."[183]

The effects of unrelenting fear and anxiety can sometimes cause a person to snap psychologically and do things the person would perhaps not normally do otherwise. It can cause even people who most would consider stable and reliable to behave unexpectedly and out-of-character, as shown below.

➤   ➤   ➤   ➤

Willington is a sleepy town of 6000 residents in northeastern Connecticut. Traditionally, people feel safe and comfortable in small rural towns like Willington. Few people would have expected it to become the site of a stalking, or of a scandal, yet it became the site of both.

For 2 years, Brian Philbrick, a former student of fifth-grade teacher Kathy Gerardi, allegedly stalked her. He would reportedly call her over and over late at night, vandalize her car, and send her threats through the mail. When police arrested Philbrick, they said he told them how sexually aroused he became whenever he watched Gerardi's house or peered at her through the classroom window.

Philbrick received a short jail term and probation for his harassment of Gerardi. Soon after Philbrick's release from jail, Gerardi began receiving more threatening letters. One said: "OK, Bitch, drop it all now or we shoot the kids. Bang. Bang. No more teacher, no more kids. DOA." Another note, made of letters and words cut from magazines, said: "I mean what I say and I know where to find you. One...Two...Three... POW! So long Sweetie."

The town of Willington mobilized behind their beloved teacher. The town leaders called emergency town meetings, and the residents packed the school gym. They discussed what they should do about the threats, including closing down the school. Because of the possible danger, officials canceled several sporting activities, as they did the traditional end-of-the-year ice cream social, and they moved other activities away from the school. Some parents wouldn't allow their children to go to school for fear of violence if the stalker should appear.

But then the case cracked. State police noticed that two of the threatening letters to the teacher had come in envelopes with an embossed rose on them. They remembered that Gerardi had sent them a thank-you note after they arrested Philbrick for the first incident of stalking. The thank-you note had come in an envelope with an embossed rose on it. Forensic experts then closely examined the threatening letters and found one of Gerardi's fingerprints on the sticky side of the tape used to attach some of the cut-out magazine letters.

Confronted with this evidence, Gerardi, who had dwindled down to a sickly 90 pounds during the ordeal, admitted she had written and sent the threatening letters to herself. She tearfully told of how she just couldn't cope with the constant fear since Philbrick's release from jail. She apparently would only feel safe when the authorities locked him up again, and so she attempted to fabricate evidence against him.

"I was terrified and I knew that this was not going to end," Gerardi said. "I felt like Brian was everywhere I went and I could not feel safe, physically or emotionally. I felt my condition was deteriorating."

The revelation about the origin of the threatening letters divided the residents of Willington over their feelings about Gerardi. Some felt bitter because she had duped them, but others were more understanding.

"Who knows what she went through," said a neighbor of Gerardi. "Fear is such an incredible emotion. It inspires people to do things they wouldn't normally dream of doing. We can't judge what went on in her mind."[184]

➤   ➤   ➤   ➤

"Some psychologists believe that stalking is a throwback to the instinctive predatory behavior of prehistoric man," said Jane McAllister, president of the grass-roots group Citizens Against Stalking. "Others explain it as a form of psychiatric illness. Still others describe it as the action of an emotionally and spiritually bankrupt person. Whatever theory you choose to accept, one thing is certain. It is devastating to the victim."[185]

When and where will it all end? That is the question many stalking victims find themselves asking every day. This question, though, is much too important to be left up to anyone but the victims to answer. It could mean the difference between life and death. Because so much is at stake, victims simply can't afford to sit back and hope that someone else will do something. Victims must act on their own to stop the stalking. As I will show in later chapters, there are many things victims can and must do that will stop the stalking. Victims are not defenseless.

> > > > > **14**

HOW STALKERS GET THEIR INFORMATION AND HOW TO STOP THEM

A stalking victim, identified only by the pseudonym Anne, told *San Jose Mercury* reporters that the stalking of her by a man she had met only once became so distressing she wanted her life to end. Because of the stalking, Anne said, she stayed locked in her home so much she felt like a prisoner. She would leave only when she absolutely had to, shopping just once a month for groceries because of her fear of him confronting her.

"Stalking is the worst because it is the loss of your freedom," Anne said.

The stalking began a short time after she had been introduced to the man. Wherever she went she would see him nearby watching her, or find notes on her windshield letting her know that he was always around. At first, she said, when he would approach her, he would pretend that their meeting was just a coincidence, and suggest that since they were together they should have lunch.

Anne told him no again and again, but with little effect. She also begged him to stop tailing her, but again with little effect. The stalking eventually became so intense and took up so many hours of the day that the man lost his job, and then, unemployed, he began spending all day in his pursuit of her. Several times, Anne found him sleeping on her doorstep.

As often happens, when Anne continued refusing his requests for dates, the stalking turned ugly. He would call her, saying that he was going to kill himself, and threaten to leave her a bloody package. He also began telling her that he was going to kill her. Now beyond just fear, and living in real terror of him, Anne obtained a restraining order. The stalker ignored it.

Once during the stalking, Anne went outside and found that the stalker had taken her trash. "I can't tell you what I felt like when I went out and my trash was gone," she said. "Everything about you is in your trash—who you call, where you shop....."[186]

Finally, Anne returned home one day and found that her stalker had taken the final step in his obsession for her. He had broken into her apartment, and was waiting for her. As if that wasn't terrifying enough, Anne saw with unbelieving horror that he had brought a number of instruments to make her death a truly horrible one.

After all of the months of living a nightmare, Anne just couldn't stand it any longer. She began screaming hysterically and kept screaming until finally the stalker, apparently fearing someone would hear her and call the police, fled her apartment. The police caught up with the stalker and arrested him. Months later, a court convicted him and sentenced him to prison.

The reader is by now aware that the above stalking incident, with the exception of the intended mode of murder, is a fairly typical one. The obsession with a victim begins, seems to grow despite constant rebuffs and rejections, and eventually turns ugly. Threats and often violence follow.

In many of the stalking incidents related so far in this book, readers have seen stalkers who are totally fixated. They devote every ounce of their energy to the focus of their obsession: to have an intimate relationship with their victims. People who study or deal regularly with stalkers have found that the gathering of personal information about their victims, as the stalker in the incident above did by going through the victim's trash, is both a path to this end and an end in itself. It is a path to this end because often the information gathered on the victims gives the stalkers more access to them, particularly when the information contains telephone numbers or addresses of family members and friends, locations of jobs, or even places the victims shop. With this information, the stalkers know where they can gather more information and where they can lie in wait for their victims. This gathering of personal information, however, is also an end in itself. Because the stalkers are not having, and are not likely ever going to have, the intimate relationship they desire, obtaining personal information about their victims gives them a feeling of intimacy with the victims. Obtaining extremely personal information known only to them and their victims can give stalkers a feeling of intimacy almost as powerful as an embrace.

Stalking victims are often amazed, stunned, and disturbed by how much a stalker, who may be a stranger, appears to know about them. The stalker seems to have access to their innermost secrets. How?

Although household trash can certainly be used to track a person's life, as in the incident above, what personal information goes into the trash is under the complete control of that person. Many public and private agencies, however, store reams and reams of personal information that the individuals whom this information is about seemingly have no control over. This information can be a gold mine to a stalker. According to Jeffrey Rothfeder, in his book *Privacy For Sale*, there are billions of records about American citizens in computer databases all over the country, but more disturbing, these records move from one computer to another on the average of five times a day.[187] They are moved because other agencies and organizations want access to them. Every time a move is made, a little more control over this information is lost. This information is both stored and used by credit bureaus, credit card companies, direct mail retailers, magazine and newspaper subscription departments, and many government agencies. And although some people may believe that personal information kept by government agencies such as the Internal Revenue Service (IRS) is strictly confidential and therefore unavailable to a stalker, this is simply not the case. The following incident clearly shows this.

Lee and Meredith had lived together for 7 months. Meredith, however, decided she wanted to end the relationship, but when she told Lee, he refused to accept her decision and began a 16-month campaign of stalking in a effort to get her to resume their relationship. Because of her fear of Lee, Meredith moved twice, and finally ended up in a secured apartment building in Alexandria, Virginia, where she felt relatively safe and anonymous. She thought she had erased all leads to her new address, but just to be safe, she distributed pictures of Lee to everyone she knew so they wouldn't inadvertently give out information about her to him. Lee, on the other hand, unwilling to give up even though he couldn't initially find her, posted fliers on bulletin boards in an attempt to locate Meredith.

Although Lee didn't have much luck through the fliers, like most stalkers, he was persistent. Lee worked for the IRS, which of course maintains a wealth of personal information about taxpayers, including their addresses. Lee initially faced a minor problem, however, in that, even though working for the IRS, he didn't have access to the computers that contained the personal information he needed. So he simply persuaded a co-worker at the IRS, who did have this access, to find out Meredith's new address for him.

With this information, Lee went to Meredith's new home in the secured apartment building and left a note on her apartment door. When Meredith saw Lee's familiar handwriting, her feelings of security and anonymity dissolved instantly. The note suggested that he take her out for her birthday. It ended with: "I'm looking forward to seeing you again." As hot acid spilled into her stomach, Meredith knew the stalking had begun again.

"It's possible I have been more upset in my life," Meredith said, "but I don't remember it."

Meredith learned later that Lee had entered the secured apartment building by continuously pressing the buzzers until one of the residents finally let him in. Meredith immediately called the Alexandria Police Department and reported the incident. In the next few days she received several letters from Lee through the mail. In one, he said: "For some reason, I feel the need to tell you face-to-face that I'm not a lunatic. So I guess I'll see you soon, though I haven't decided where our paths will cross."[188]

Regardless of the fact that Meredith didn't want to have any contact with him, Lee would later insist that what he was doing was not stalking. He had obtained a copy of Virginia's stalking law, and kept it with him. The law stated that, in Virginia, a stalker had to have the intent to place a person in fear of death or bodily injury. Lee insisted that wasn't what he intended, and wasn't what he was doing. Of course, Meredith didn't feel this way. Knowing Lee, she feared this very much.

After receiving Meredith's complaint, a detective from the Alexandria Police Department called Lee and warned him that he was risking arrest with his actions. Lee paid no attention and continued stalking Meredith.

Soon after this, Meredith returned to her apartment and found two holes in her front windows. She called police again, and the same detective once more telephoned Lee. This time, the detective asked Lee to please come down to the police department.

Once Lee arrived at the police department, the detective placed him under arrest for stalking. On searching Lee's car, the detective found a stun gun, rope, duct tape, a knife, and a pair of latex gloves. Lee insisted he had an explanation for all of these items.

Two days after being released on his own recognizance (which means no bond, but simply a promise to appear in court) for the stalking charge, Lee was arrested by the detective again. This time he arrested Lee for "throwing missiles at an occupied building." Apparently, Lee used a slingshot to put the holes in Meredith's windows. A judge set Lee's bond at $50,000, and Lee remained in jail until his trial.

Lee eventually pled guilty to the stalking charge. He said he did this, not because he thought he was guilty, but because his attorney told him he would almost certainly be convicted if he went to trial. Lee entered an "Alford plea" on the missile throwing charge. An "Alford plea" is a plea in Virginia that allows a person to maintain he or she is not guilty of a crime, but at the same time concede that the prosecutor has enough evidence for a conviction. Lee received a sentence of 3 years on probation, with an order to stay away from Meredith. He also lost his job at the IRS.

In another incident, this one in San Francisco, a similar situation occurred. A woman sued the San Francisco Police Department, claiming that one of their officers used the police department's computer to obtain address information about her that he then passed along to a stalker. Nicole Abagnaro, who had fled the Bay Area because of intense stalking by a man she had broken up with 5 years before, claims that her ex-boyfriend, Edward Khoury, persuaded a San Francisco police officer to use the police department's computer to locate her new address.

Once Khoury had her new address, he allegedly went to her home and threatened to kill both her and her new boyfriend if they continued their relationship. The police arrested Khoury for stalking. He eventually pled no contest to the stalking charge, and received a 1-year jail sentence.

On hearing of the allegations, San Francisco Police Chief Tony Ribera ordered an internal investigation into the incident. He also said he planned to institute a new password system for the police department's computer to prevent any further abuse of this type.

Of course, often the problem is not so much the confidential information held by government agencies like the IRS as it is the many government files considered public record and open for public inspection that may contain personal information stalkers could use. Some states, because of this problem, have added provisions to their laws that allow stalking victims to have personal information about them in open records withheld from public view. But the difficulty with this solution is that you must know *all* of the places that have some type of record about you. Unfortunately, it would not be possible for me to list all of these places, as they often depend on the particulars of a person's life. For example, if you have been divorced there is a court record, if you own a dog there is a dog license record, if you own property there is a property assessment record, if you fly an airplane there is a pilot's license record, and so on. If you overlook even one of these places, a determined stalker will find it. Some of these records are also put into computer databases, which then make them even more accessible.

Unfortunately, incidents like those above involving computer databases occur quite often in stalking cases. However, although hundreds and hundreds of computer databases all over the country may contain information about us, still the most personal and intimate information about us is often held by family members and friends. Stalkers pursuing information about their victims will often go to these family members and friends with a number of pretexts and excuses about why they need to know the whereabouts of the individuals, or other personal information about them. Because stalkers can many times sound very sincere and convincing, far too often family members and friends will give out this information. In their search for personal data about their victims, stalkers will also call landlords, neighbors, organizations the victims belong to, merchants the victims deal with, and fellow employees of the victims.

A situation of this type occurred when I first arrived at my job as a district field captain on Indianapolis' west side. A policewoman came to me to complain that her ex-husband, a construction worker, continuously stalked her while she worked. This only became possible, the policewoman said, because another police officer on the district would call the ex-husband and tell him her location whenever she went on a radio run, and then the ex-husband would show up there and stalk and threaten her. I called the other officer in and asked him about the policewoman's allegations. Although he admitted doing it, he also insisted that the ex-husband wasn't a stalker, but really a nice guy he had known for a long time. The officer felt certain the ex-husband didn't mean any harm, but only wanted to get back with his ex-wife. I put an immediate stop to this leak of information.

When stalkers can't persuade others to give them personal information about their victims, they will often go to bizarre extremes in an effort to obtain the information they want. Some stalkers have been known to take jobs for the sole purpose that the jobs will give them access to personal information about their victims, such as jobs at telephone companies or at public utilities. One stalker even signed up for a private detective course in order to learn how to track down a stalking victim. In another case, a stalker knew that his victim had rented a car, and so he broke into the rental car company office to look at the personal information on the victim's rental contract. Stalkers have also been known to break into the homes of friends and relatives of stalking victims in search of information about the victims. In the Kathleen Baty/Larry Stagner incident discussed in Chapter 13, Stagner broke into Baty's parents' home searching for information about where she might be living. In the Laura Black/Richard Farley incident discussed in Chapter 12, Farley broke into Black's desk in search of information about her.

In a stalking case reported in *Cosmopolitan*, a woman began receiving telephone calls from a stalker. She didn't have any idea who the stalker might be, or how he got her name and telephone number. Eventually, the victim learned that the stalker was the friend of a girlfriend's boyfriend, a man she had met only once. The stalker, she discovered, had obtained her telephone number by secretly snooping through his friend's personal phone book.[189]

The truth is there is nothing stalkers will not do to obtain more and more personal information about their victims. This information is the fuel that keeps their obsession going. With it they can call their victims on the telephone, show up where their victims work or shop, or show up at relatives' homes when their victims are there. It gives the stalkers the contact with their victims they feel they must have. Also, the larger the store of personal information the stalkers gather on their victims, the closer and more intimate they feel with them. In this relentless pursuit of knowledge about their victims, there is no place or person sacred to stalkers, no confidence or trust they won't violate.

Stalkers become so desperate because they quickly realize that to succeed in their efforts, they must be able to accumulate considerable amounts of information on their victims. The stalkers must know where the victims live, where they work, where they shop, what kind of car they drive, their telephone numbers, what their interests are, and where their relatives live. If stalkers can't find or contact their victims, their stalking really isn't much of a threat or likely to be very successful. If the victims can successfully isolate themselves from their stalkers, the ability of the stalkers to intimidate them becomes negligible and the stalking a failure.

Stalkers must know their victims better than a spouse. Unfortunately for most victims, the information that stalkers need is already compiled and waiting in a computer database or record somewhere, or held by family members and friends. The stalkers only need to know where to look, and be a bit devious and ingenious about getting the information.

Interestingly, a trait common to many stalkers often helps them in this information gathering process. As discussed in earlier chapters, most stalkers suffer personality problems, some suffer emotional problems, and some even suffer serious psychiatric illnesses. Yet, they also often share another trait just as threatening to their victims. "Many abusers, and particularly stalkers, have above average intelligence," said David Beatty, public affairs director of the National Victim Center.[190] This is an important point to stress in this chapter: Even though they have mental problems, because of their intelligence, stalkers can often find ingenious ways to get around sophisticated and elaborate security arrangements. Stalkers will pose as parents, doctors, lawyers, police officers, employment supervisors, and anyone else they need to be to gain access to extra information. Stalkers seldom worry about legalities.

Also, being above average in intelligence, stalkers can often frustrate their victims' attempts to escape them. Stalkers many times are able to find new unlisted telephone numbers within hours of the victims obtaining them, and they can discover new addresses before the victims can move in all of their furniture. Victims should never forget that although stalkers may appear to be mentally unbalanced, they are still often smart enough to know where to look to find the records or information they want. And being obsessed, stalkers will violate any trust, disregard any rule, and break any law in their search for personal information about their victims.

Where would stalkers look to gather this personal information on their victims? The locations are too numerous to list in their entirety, but keep in mind that, as previously mentioned, every major event and change in your life is recorded somewhere: your birth, your attendance at school, your driver's license and driving record, your marriage and divorce, ownership of property, court cases, and so on. Therefore, besides the obvious places stalkers look for personal information, such as telephone books and reverse directories, there are hundreds of others, including business licenses, voter registration, dog license applications, credit bureaus, and utility records. I recently received an interesting offer through the mail. For $49.00, the ad said, I would be sent seven CD-ROMs on which had been recorded every business and residential telephone listing in the United States. Also, according to the ad, I could search these CD-ROMs 10 different ways, including by name, address, zip code, business type, and so on. Unfortunately, in addition to all of the many possible sources of personal information listed above, companies seldom give their personnel records the protection they deserve. All stalkers need is a bit of ingenuity and persistence, and they can get the information they want.

For beginning stalkers, those who have not yet "learned" how to find or gain access to the records they want, there is, of course, always the option of hiring a private detective, who, for a fee, will find out this personal information for them. One stalker reportedly paid a private detective over $9000 for information about a victim. Naturally, stalkers don't tell these detectives that they are stalkers. When Robert Bardo hired a private detective to find actress Rebecca Schaeffer's address in the incident discussed in Chapter 7, he told the detective he was an old friend of hers. In addition to private detectives, though, a number of firms have also sprung up around the country that claim to be able to obtain, usually for clients such as tabloids and television news magazines, information that includes unlisted telephone numbers and addresses of celebrities and other newsworthy individuals. However, if a stalker is willing to pay for this service, he or she can get the same information. An ad in 1993 listed the following prices to obtain certain "confidential" information: an unlisted telephone number, $69; a credit report, $24; a medical record, $299; a personal bank account, $249; an employment history and earnings, $99.

Station KCBS-TV in Los Angeles recently demonstrated just how easy it is to obtain personal information. It ordered from Metromail, the nation's largest distributor of lists, a list of the names, addresses, and telephone numbers of 5000 children in Los Angeles. They ordered the list in the name of Richard Allen Davis, the kidnapper and murderer of 12-year-old Polly Klaas. The television station provided Metromail with a mailing address and a disconnected telephone number. The list came the next day. The cost? Only $277.[191]

Although all of this may sound daunting to potential stalking victims, they are not defenseless in the battle to safeguard their personal information and their lives. There are ways to protect unlisted telephone numbers and the location of a new residence if they feel the need, and are able, to move in order to escape a stalker. To learn how to protect personal information and keep new addresses and telephone numbers confidential, I consulted someone who makes her living getting this personal information and finding people who have disappeared.

When I first met Leigh Hearon several years ago, she didn't fit my stereotype of a private detective at all. A slender, attractive woman with hazel eyes and auburn hair, Leigh didn't look to me like what a topnotch private detective should look like. Yet, she is one of the best private detectives I've ever met. She operates Leigh Hearon Investigative Services in Seattle, and makes her living obtaining hard-to-get information and finding people who don't want to be found.

I met Leigh when she came to Indianapolis to work on a multiple murder case in which I was one of the arresting officers. The defendant, convicted of four murders, escaped from prison and turned up a year and a half later on Staten Island running a homeless shelter. Leigh's skill as a detective and her knowledge of investigative techniques impressed me, and we have remained in contact ever since. For the readers of this book, I posed to Leigh the following two questions:

1   What advice would you give to stalking victims who don't want stalkers to find them?
2   How can victims stop stalkers from obtaining personal information about them?

"First off," Leigh told me, "unless you're a certified member of the Federal Witness Protection Program, it's incredibly hard when moving residences to ensure you're not leaving any kind of paper trail that will allow the person you want to avoid to find you. I know this because in my business I find people all the time, and no matter how much, say, a deadbeat dad doesn't want to be found, there's nearly always something he's overlooked. If a stalker, however, relies on his own skills, and doesn't employ the services of an expert, the steps below can be of value. If the stalker hires a disreputable private investigator, though, the chances of remaining hidden decrease considerably.

"Before I start, though, I want to say that whenever people call me and ask if I can find someone, I always inquire about the reason why. Most private investigators do. If it's someone who wants to know what an ex is up to, I decline the job immediately. If the reason seems legitimate, I either ask to look at the court paperwork substantiating the claim (such as a judgment) or tell clients that if I do find the person, I'll give him or her the option of contacting them. This latter approach turns off a lot of people, and I undoubtedly lose a lot of money by using it. But the fact remains that no matter how convincing a story you hear, your clients may intend to use the information you give them on a person's present location to go there with an Uzi and blow the person away. And aside from not wanting to contribute to any violent act, providing information that leads to such an act—no matter how reasonable the story seemed to me at the time—could make me partially liable, which is bad news to my insurance company, the status of my state license, and to my professional reputation.

"That out of the way, the first piece of advice I'd give to potential stalking victims is to **zealously safeguard their Social Security number**. This is by far the most superior way of finding someone. The primary reason for this is that it's on many, many public documents, and it's attached to virtually every form of credit you apply for. Creditors need to know your home address so they can send you your bills, therefore, once a stalker uses your Social Security number to get your credit record, he then also has your address. Because of the wide use of Social Security numbers in records, there are many computer programs that use your Social Security number to find your most current address—within days of moving—with just a few quick searches.

"In order to do this, the database takes a Social Security number and a previous address—usually any address will do as long as it's within the past 7 years—and searches through records from the three major credit bureaus. What comes up is that Social Security number owner's address history. These addresses are called "header" information on a credit report. While the Fair Credit Reporting Act clearly makes it illegal to obtain a credit report without written authorization from the person the report is on, it's perfectly legal to obtain everything else on the report *except* credit history—such as the header information.

"Since the credit bureaus update new address information on their records as soon as a person fills in the new address section of their latest credit card bill, there's virtually no delay in getting this information. I once got the current address of someone before he had even had the phone installed in his new home out-of-state. He had simply been too diligent, and had provided his creditors with his new address the month before he actually moved.

"**Sometimes you can locate people merely by using a name**. There are computer database searches that comb every single public record available in the United States and provide address histories for everyone with that name. Also, if you've ever put your home telephone number on some public record, this will show up too. So will the name of your spouse, and lots of other personal information.

"To stop the computer databases from reporting your new address, the simplest method I've found is to **open a private mailbox at someplace a fair distance from your new residence, and give this mailbox as your new address**. I said **private** mailbox, such as the kind you can get at Pony

Express, Mail Boxes Etc., and other retail mailbox outlets. A box at a United States post office is no good. Although years ago the U.S. Congress outlawed the ability of private citizens to obtain forwarding addresses from local post offices, there are still ways to obtain the address you provide on the card you must fill out when you open a mailbox at a U.S. post office. Trust me on this. It's my job.

"Speaking of mail, the **only** mail a stalking victim should receive at a new residence are personal letters from individuals the victim trusts absolutely. All other mail should go to the private mailbox. This includes utility bills, newspaper bills, and magazine subscriptions. When I moved this past summer, I told all of the utility companies that I was a private investigator who worked out of a building on my property, and that I wanted to keep my residential address confidential. (Often, when a private investigator is too successful and too thorough, she can make a lot of people angry.) Everyone at the utility companies was very understanding and helpful. I'm sure they would be even more understanding and helpful to someone being stalked. Of course, you will still have to give them your residential address, but your bill can be sent anywhere you want.

"I can't emphasize enough the importance of not receiving any mail other than personal letters at your new home. I thought I was well protected after I moved, and I regularly checked the address computer databases to ensure so. But then a well-meaning relative sent me a magazine subscription for Christmas. Bingo! My new address showed up on an address database the next month.

"**Tell the utility companies you want to encode your account with a password.** A lot of private investigators are masters at pretext games (as are stalkers), and can ferret out personal information over the telephone, especially if they have your Social Security number, date of birth, and mother's maiden name. If you have a password assigned to your account, they can't get into it, or the information in it (such as your address). I speak from experience.

"However, don't use an obvious password, such as the name of a pet or one of your children. Use a random word out of the dictionary. A week or two after you've provided the password, test its efficiency—call the utility company and ask about a charge on your account. If they don't ask for your password, speak to a supervisor, follow up with a letter stating the importance of maintaining your privacy, and keep checking it until you're sure they've got the message. Then change your password every 6 months.

"Many people think getting an unlisted (or unpublished) telephone number will keep them immune from harassing calls. Not so. These phone numbers are incredibly easy to get. They're called "difficult numbers" in our trade. Every private investigator knows who to call to get a difficult number—sometimes with as little information as a name and the city in which the person resides—and get positive results within 24 hours or less.

"Encoding your phone account, and having the bill sent to the retail mailbox will help. But instead of getting an unlisted number, I suggest to clients who want anonymity to **put their phone in a different name, and tell the phone company to omit their address from the White Pages**. Most people assume your phone, whether listed or not, will be in your name. If it isn't, a stalker doesn't know where to look. The phone company should have no problem with this arrangement. If you want phone service, and agree to pay for it, you can have the phone in any name you please.

"These measures should keep a stalker from finding your phone number and address. But you have to be careful about incoming long-distance phone calls. If your mother calls you every Sunday night, and the stalker knows your mother calls you regularly, he can hire a private investigator to get a list of the long-distance calls made on your mother's telephone for the past 3 months. (After 3 months all phone records are either destroyed or go into deep storage.) **So tell your loved ones to call you from pay phones.** Admittedly, this is a hassle, but it's a step worth taking.

"Cellular phone records are equally as easy to get. These records have the advantage of listing all the numbers both called to and from your cellular phone. **You can protect your cellular phone number in the same way as your residential phone—have the bill sent elsewhere, put it in a different name, and place a password on the account.**

"It's also possible to get the name and address of the person who owns a pager, if that pager number is known. The same precautionary steps as above apply here. I do not know of any way for a person to track the numbers actually received by a pager—yet.

"As for other sources of personal information, in most states all it takes is a call to the county assessor's office to obtain the residential address of a property owner. So, if you own property, **it's probably a good idea to transfer the title to someone else—someone you trust, of course!** It's getting harder to obtain residential information from voter records, but in 10 or more states it's still possible, and, in fact, this information is in several public databases. While I would not wish anyone to forego their civic privilege of voting, it's not a good idea to transfer voter registration to the area where you've moved to. Not voting in a couple of elections is better than being found.

"Also, most states allow civilians full access to court files pertaining to civil, criminal, and domestic cases. Civil cases almost always list residential or business addresses. Domestic cases also often include Social Security numbers, because people who are divorcing are required to submit parenting plans that include their income tax records. Criminal cases always include Social Security numbers and dates of birth, because they include the arresting document (officer's arrest report). **If you have any of these records in your past, my advice is to retain an attorney and get the records sealed**. It's a fairly simple procedure and not terribly costly; all the attorney has to do is show the court why the personal information in the file would be detrimental to you. Sealing a court record doesn't make it go away entirely, but it does limit the information available for viewing to just an abbreviated court docket, which lists only your name, dates of court appearances, and actions taken. If you have any small misdemeanors in your past, it's sometimes possible to get these files entirely deleted. Again, an attorney's services will be required.

"Another common method of obtaining personal information is through state records of vehicles and driver's licenses. These may or may not be public information, depending on your state, but in any case they're readily available to any enterprising stalker. California, which has become rigidly restrictive about releasing this information following the deaths of several people at the hands of stalkers who used this information source, still hasn't made the system foolproof. I receive flyers every month from investigative firms offering vehicle and driver's license information for a nominal fee and a quick turnaround time. Again, **the way to insulate yourself is to change your vehicle registration address and driver's license address to the remote retail post office**.

"It's always struck me as somewhat absurd that whenever we write a check, we give away valuable information about ourselves: our name, address, phone number, often our driver's license number for ID purposes, and, of course, our bank and account number. There's nothing we can do about the last two pieces of information, but **stalking victims can at least change the personal information on their checks to the retail post office, omit the phone number (or give a fictitious one), and not give out any other personal identifiers**.

"Speaking of personal identifiers, it would of course be ideal if stalking victims could change their Social Security numbers, or at least not have to provide them on so many commercial documents. Since that's not the case, the only way to protect yourself if you're a stalking victim is to make sure that every contact you have in the commercial world does not use your residential address to correspond with you, but rather your retail post office address.

"I'll end my advice to stalking victims by saying that the only time I couldn't find someone based on a Social Security number was when I was hired by the ex-wife of a deadbeat dad. The ex-wife had the deadbeat dad's Social Security number, date of birth, and last known address, but when I ran him I discovered his girlfriend had apparently reported him to the Social Security Administration as deceased. The trail stopped at his last address, and as long as he didn't open up any new accounts, there was no way I could find him. This alternative, of course, is fraudulent, not to mention a felony."

If victims decide to follow Leigh Hearon's advice of obtaining a retail mail box and having their telephone service put in another name, they should also sign up for Caller ID and Complete Blocking telephone service. With Caller ID, victims will know who is calling them, and, with Complete Blocking, when victims call out, their telephone number will be blocked from someone else with Caller ID. If someone calls them, and the caller has Complete Blocking, the obvious solution is to not answer the telephone. Family, friends, and others the victims want to hear from should know better. And if victims want to call someone they know and trust who has Caller ID, they can selectively unblock their call. Once at their new residence, if they must call an 800 or 900 telephone number, victims should do it from a pay phone, because their telephone number will be captured and recorded by the owners of the 800 or 900 lines, regardless of having Complete Blocking.

Another bit of advice about protecting privacy and personal information is that it is particularly important to be cautious when using cordless or cellular telephones. These are essentially radio transmitters. The cordless telephone transmits to the base set, and a cellular telephone transmits to a transmitting tower. Because they are radio transmitters, the radio waves can be picked up by anyone with equipment that can be purchased at an electronic store. The obvious advice is to never discuss any personal information when talking on cellular or cordless telephones.

This source of information for stalkers, however, may soon be stopped. On 30 July 1997, Congressman Billy Tauzin introduced a bill into Congress titled the "Wireless Privacy Enhancement Act of 1997." This bill, if enacted into law, would clarify and tighten existing laws and ban the manufacture, modification, sale, and use of electronic equipment that can illegally intercept private conversations over cellular and cordless telephones.

As Leigh points out in her excellent and thorough advice above, the key to obtaining large amounts of personal information about someone is that person's Social Security number. Because people can have the same names and even the same birth dates, many records keepers find that Social Security numbers are an excellent way to make everyone's record unique. And so, to prevent access to these many records, you must also keep access to your Social Security number restricted. Also, protect the Social Security numbers of your children, as Social Security numbers are now required by the IRS for all dependents over 1 year old.

But doing this is not as easy as I thought. Just a quick look through my wallet and the documents in my desk at home demonstrated that my Social Security number shows up on many documents. For example, I found it on my driver's license, my wallet-sized copy of my DD-214 (military discharge), my police identification card, and as the account number on a student loan for my daughter. If I were a stalking victim, I would have to track down and close to public view or change a large number of records, but, as Leigh points out, I believe it would be worth it.

The best advice, therefore, is to never give out your Social Security number unless you are totally convinced the person requesting it has a legitimate and definite need for it. Also, don't allow its use on any document open to public viewing. If, however, a company or individual insists on having your Social Security number, even though there is no legal requirement for you to give it, but not giving it will cause problems you'd rather not have, you might consider using the number 078-05-1120. The Social Security Administration used this number in the 1940s and 1950s as a sample number, and it does not belong to anyone. Also available for use, and not belonging to anyone, are the numbers 987-65-4320 through 4329. Remember, only use one of these numbers with someone who demands but cannot legally require you to give your Social Security number.

But most important, it is imperative for people to realize that whenever they give out personal information to anyone who doesn't have a legal right to demand it, such as to a pollster, the personal information requested on those little warranty cards that ask about lifestyles, or those sweepstakes entry forms that want to know a lot about you, assume that the information will not be held in confidence, but instead will be sent out to many other interested parties (and likely kept in many computer databases). Therefore, answer these at your peril. Likewise, if someone comes to your door carrying a clipboard, don't answer the door.

What can happen if you do fill out the personal information requested on a warranty card or respond to a survey? A recent *New York Times* article tells of a woman named Beverly Dennis, who received a 12-page letter at her home from a stranger who seemed to know all sorts of personal things about her. He knew her marital status, her birthday, the magazines she read, and the soap she used. In the letter the man described the various sexual perversions he planned to force on her.

Ms. Dennis eventually discovered that the letter came from a burglar and rapist incarcerated in a Texas prison. He had gotten the personal information on Ms. Dennis from a product questionnaire she had filled out on the promise of coupons and free samples. The company handling the information taken from the questionnaires, Metromail, used prison inmates to enter the information into a computer database. Ms. Dennis eventually filed a lawsuit because of this misuse of her personal information, and because of this lawsuit Texas is presently considering discontinuing the practice of using prison inmates for computer data entry. Still, 27 other states use inmates for the computer data entry of various public records, including motor vehicle registrations. Federal prisoners perform data entry for the IRS.

As Ms. Dennis certainly is, Louis Harris polls in 1994 and 1995 found that 80 percent of Americans are concerned about threats to their personal privacy. They should be because many people in control of personal information certainly aren't.

"We lost some damn good programmers—pedophiles [sexual abusers of children]," said John Benestante, director of state prison industries for Texas, talking about the plans to stop the use of prison labor for data entry. "Some of our best computer operatives were sex offenders."

"Is the government going to sacrifice the money that can be made for a little bit of privacy?" asked another supervisor of an inmate data entry program.[192]

Besides warranty cards and surveys, another way we give away information about ourselves, though few people are aware of it, is whenever we call an 800 or 900 telephone number. A device called Automatic Number Identification identifies and adds the caller's name and telephone number to their computer database, which, of course, is then available to anyone who has access to that database. In addition, the owners of 800 and 900 telephone lines also run the telephone number through various other computer databases to obtain the caller's address, which then becomes part of their database. The key, therefore, to safety for a stalking victim or potential victim is to withhold personal information from those who have no need for it or right to have it.

For most readers, however, the problem is not so much giving out personal information in the future as it is the information that has already been given out in the past and now sits in various public records, waiting to be found. Of course, what records are open for public inspection varies from state to state. What a stalker may be denied access to in one state can be an open record in another. When Leigh Hearon and I worked together, she said Indiana had one of the toughest privacy laws she'd ever run into, and that in most states she could gain access to almost any information. Readers worried about access to their personal information in public records should consult their state Attorney General's office about the privacy laws in their state. For those readers connected to the Internet, web address *http://www.epic.org/privacy/consumer/legal.html* will bring up a screen that allows users to key in their state and find out what the privacy laws are there.

The latest estimate says that 24 million people in the United States and Canada presently have access to the Internet. This means that millions of computers are hooked together every day, sending and receiving information. Anyone who believes that there is any privacy on the Internet really doesn't understand the system. Information sent over the Internet can often pass through dozens of computers, each of which may be able to capture and store the information, before it reaches its final destination. One time, while on the Internet looking into devices that claim they will keep Internet interactions private, I happened onto a site that sold equipment to do this. As a demonstration of the equipment's need, the site told me my Internet provider, where I was located, my type of computer, and the other Internet sites I had visited that night. The obvious advice is to never believe that any transaction on the Internet is really private.

The Internet, incidentally, although an amazingly powerful tool for researchers, can also be a powerful source of information for stalkers. Anyone with just a bit of knowledge on how to use the Internet can quickly find a tremendous amount of information about people on it. A number of websites give access to telephone books from across the United States. Other websites give E-mail addresses, and some give access to mailing lists. When I was doing research for this book, I found an interesting, and disturbing, item on the Internet. For $6.45, the ad claimed, an individual could obtain the name and address of the person using a certain Social Security number. As you can imagine, a stalker who has someone's Social Security number (from a record, a check stub, a W-2, and the like) could very easily find out where that person lives. Other items available on the Internet include property assessment information, the FAA Aircraft Registration Database, and a military locator service. The obvious advice here is to not be listed in any of these sources. Moving to another address to escape a stalker and then listing your new address and telephone number in some type of record makes it much too easy to find you. Also, if you believe your name and address may be on a mailing list somewhere, you should write the owner of this list and tell them you want your name taken off.

Recently, the Lexis-Nexis company caused a huge furor when they announced that users of their P-Trak service could, for a fee, obtain the address, birth date, and telephone number of individuals Lexis-Nexis had on their system. Lexis-Nexis obtains its information from Trans Union, a credit reporting bureau. Credit reports contain a wealth of personal information. They contain names and name variations, addresses, Social Security numbers, information about employment, and a list of the places a person has had credit. After the announcement of the information availability, so many calls came into the Lexis-Nexis headquarters in Dayton, Ohio, from people demanding that they be taken off the list, that the calls clogged the customer service lines.

Summarizing the advice for readers concerned about protecting their personal information from stalkers:

1   Safeguard your Social Security number.
2   Keep as much personal information as possible out of public records.
3   Open a private mailbox a fair distance from your new residence, and then use this mailbox as your new address.
4   Encode accounts at utility companies with a password.
5   Put your phone in a different name, omit your information from the White Pages, and have the bill sent to the retail post office.
6   Use the same safety procedures with cellular phones as with regular phones.
7   Have loved ones call you long-distance only from pay phones.
8   Transfer real property to another person.
9   Have any court records sealed.
10 Give vehicle registration and driver's license address as the retail post office.
11 Use retail post office address on personal checks.
12 Call 800 and 900 telephone numbers only from pay phones.
13 Use caution talking about personal information when using cellular or cordless phones.
14 Never give out personal information to anyone who doesn't have a legitimate need for it.

As should by now be obvious, it is seldom in an individual's best interest to freely give out personal information. This can seldom help as much as it can do harm. Keeping personal information away from stalkers can often make the difference as to whether or not the stalkers will continue their pursuit or move on. Without knowledge of where the victims live, work, or shop, and without knowledge of the telephone numbers through which they can reach the victims, the stalkers' chances of success decrease, as does their enthusiasm to continue the stalking.

➤ ➤ ➤ ➤ ➤ **15**

THE CRIMINAL JUSTICE SYSTEM AND STALKING

When a fellow captain on the Indianapolis Police Department learned I was writing a book on stalking, he told me about his own experience with a man who had stalked his daughter. He told me about discovering firsthand just how frightening this can be to the victims and their families. Because this experience occurred before Indiana had a stalking law, he also discovered how defenseless and powerless victims were before the legislature finally gave law enforcement a tool to fight back with.

The stalking began soon after his daughter, who had just received her undergraduate college degree, moved back home temporarily with him and his wife. During the time of this move his daughter also broke up with a boyfriend she had been dating for 2 years. Soon after this breakup, the ex-boyfriend appeared at the captain's house and said he needed to talk with the captain and his wife. The ex-boyfriend told them their daughter was heavily involved in drugs, and it was imperative that he and their daughter stay together as he was the only one who could save her. The captain and his wife listened politely, but knew the man was lying, and finally ushered him out of their house.

Soon after this, the former boyfriend began phoning their home over and over. He would beg and plead and cry for their daughter to go back with him. He also began showing up *everywhere* the family went, at shopping centers, at movie theaters, and even at church. In addition, the man did something bizarre that made the captain feel very edgy and uneasy: He purchased a car exactly like the new one their daughter had purchased—the same model, same year, and same color.

Within a few months, the captain's daughter met another man and began to date him. One time, while the daughter and her new boyfriend stood talking to some friends in a neighbor's driveway, the stalker drove up, jumped out of his car, and verbally threatened the daughter and her new boyfriend.

. The captain, incensed by this incident, knew he would lose his cool if he got personally involved, so he reported the incident to the sheriff's department, who sent deputies out to talk with the ex-boyfriend. Despite this, the captain and his family continued seeing the stalker every time they left home, even at places where the stalker couldn't have "just accidentally bumped into them," as he claimed. One time, the stalker called the daughter late at night, stated he was going to kill himself, and said he needed her to come to his place and talk him out of it. The captain immediately called the sheriff's department again, who sent deputies to the stalker's apartment. The deputies discovered that the stalker was indeed very despondent, and that he had purchased a handgun.

Eventually, the daughter moved away from home and into an apartment. Although the family made this move secretly and late at night, hoping that this would stop the stalking, the ex-boyfriend quickly learned the daughter's new address. He would sit for hours in his car in front of her apartment. Whenever the daughter left the apartment, the stalker would honk and flash his lights to be certain she knew he was there.

Finally, the captain's daughter hired an attorney and went to court to obtain a restraining order. On finding out about this, the stalker retained a lawyer of his own and tried to get a restraining order against the daughter, claiming she was stalking him. The judge, however, approved her order and denied his, saying there was no evidence she had stalked him. As with many stalkers, the former boyfriend paid no attention to the restraining order. The daughter and her parents would still run into him continually, and on each encounter he would usually begin crying and pleading for the daughter to take him back.

At last, angry that nothing seemed to work, and in fear for his daughter's safety, the captain confronted the stalker and told him bluntly and forcefully that they were tired of his behavior. He told the stalker that if he ever hurt his daughter he would kill him. The stalker blustered a bit about how a police officer couldn't get away with threatening him, but the stalking stopped.

"We had done everything by the book," the captain told me. "Here I am a police officer, but I was powerless to stop him. The last thing you want to do is react violently against the stalker, but you become so frustrated you don't know what else to do."

As the incident above demonstrates, before antistalking laws came into being even police officers were frustrated by their lack of options when dealing with stalkers. Even those sworn to uphold the law considered breaking it to protect themselves or their loved ones.

"The lack of a law put people in the terrible position of having to break the law to protect the ones they love," said Ray Marky, a Tallahassee (Florida) prosecutor. "And women who are all alone have nowhere to turn."[193] Before legislation, Marky claims, stalkers were often dealt with by big brothers and fathers who put the problem to rest with a good beating. Marky stopped the stalking of his own daughter by sticking a shotgun in the stalker's face. The man never came back.

"The police would get a call saying the guy's coming over, even though there's a restraining order, and they'd tell the woman there's nothing they can do until he gets there," said David Beatty, director of public policy at the National Victim Center, talking about the typical police response before antistalking laws. "And then the next call they'd get is the neighbor saying, 'He shot her.'"[194]

Unfortunately, this lack of legal action against stalking remained for many, many years a common problem in police departments all across the United States. In Tampa, Florida, for example, a woman who wouldn't allow her abusive husband back into the house after his release from prison was soon stalked by him. She called the local police department over and over for help, but received little response from them. "I called so many times they finally told me to stop," the woman said. "They said, 'We're getting tired of you calling us.'"[195] The day after this conversation with the police, the woman's husband cornered her in a parking lot and stabbed her in the chest.

Of course, most readers will immediately wonder why the police would treat anything as serious as stalking so lightly. There are a number of reasons. Until very recently no state had a law against stalking (the first antistalking law was passed in 1990 in California), and so until some sort of violence took place in a stalking incident there was very little the police could do. Before the 1990s, a person could legally follow and harass someone, and the police were powerless. Often, the only protection avail-

able against stalkers, prior to antistalking laws, were protective and restraining orders, which to determined, obsessed stalkers meant very little,
and which they many times violated without a thought. For reasons I've
never understood, courts in the past would usually do very little to the
stalkers who violated these orders. Therefore, to stop what appeared to be
dangerous stalkers, concerned police officers, before antistalking laws,
often had to try to find some law the stalker had violated.

Before antistalking laws, the police would use charges such as menacing, making terroristic threats, making threats through the mail, and the
like. However, none of these charges included the more subtle acts of
stalking: the following, the implied threats, the sitting for hours outside
the victims' homes, the showing up wherever the victims went, and so
forth. The police had to wait until the stalking progressed to more serious
levels before they could act, which in some cases could take months or
even years, during which time the victims simply had to tolerate the
stalkers' behavior. Having to wait for the stalking to reach serious levels
also usually gave more time for the stalkers' obsessions to deepen and
intensify, making the stalkers just that much harder to stop when their
behavior finally did reach a critical level.

The primary reason, however, that police departments in the past
treated stalking cases lightly was because so many stalking cases involved
married partners, former married partners, or former intimate partners.
Officers usually didn't like to become deeply involved in these cases
because they found that prosecutors seldom would file charges due to the
very high likelihood that by the time the case came to trial the couple
would be back together and the incident forgotten (at least until the next
incident). Also, police officers didn't want to become deeply involved in
stalking cases because even when they made an arrest and the prosecutor
pressed charges, judges seldom meted out any significant sentences to
those found guilty.

Because many aspects of stalking behavior, such as the calling over
and over for a date or continually showing up wherever the victim goes,
appear by themselves to be innocuous, or at best only a nuisance, the courts
in the past, no matter what charges the police used, often did little or
nothing about stalkers. The sentence most courts would hand down for
stalkers, even those convicted of crimes such as menacing or making
terroristic threats, was a suspended jail sentence and usually probation. It
would take several horrible tragedies in 1989 and 1990 before the criminal
justice system finally began seeing stalking as a serious problem.

In 1989, the senseless murder of actress Rebecca Schaeffer at the hands of a stalker both stunned and horrified the people of California. Many wondered if this tragedy could or should have been prevented. Then, adding to the horror, stalkers killed four more women in Orange County, California, the following year, all within a 5-week period. All four women had sought help from the police, and three of them had gotten restraining orders against their stalkers, but to no avail.

The first of these four victims, a 19-year-old Orange County waitress, beaten by the estranged father of their 21-month-old child, unsuccessfully went to the police for help, finally asking them, "What does he have to do—shoot me?" Soon afterward, he did just that, killing her.

Less than a month after this murder, the boyfriend of an Orange County nurse, who had followed her to California from Europe and had been stalking her for 10 years, allegedly intentionally rammed his car into hers. The woman's car burst into flames, and she died in the fire.

Just 3 days later, former Olympic skater Patricia Kastle, stalked by her estranged husband, died from gunshots fired by her stalker, who then turned the gun on himself and committed suicide. The police found in the victim's purse a copy of a restraining order against her estranged husband.

Only 11 days after this, an Orange County woman died from gunfire at the hands of an abusive ex-boyfriend. The woman, after leaving him, first went to a women's shelter and then found a new apartment. The ex-boyfriend hired a private detective to locate the victim.

After reading about these cases, Orange County Superior Court Judge John Watson realized something had to be done. "This made me realize that the way the law was written did not allow us to protect these women," Judge Watson said. "In some of these cases, the police told the women there was nothing they could do until the man committed a criminal act. By then it was too late."[196]

Judge Watson helped write California's antistalking bill. Sponsored by State Senator Ed Royce, the bill passed the California legislature in 1990, and became law effective 1 January 1991. This law finally took the handcuffs off of the police in stalking cases, and allowed them to take action where before they couldn't. Much of stalking, particularly in the early stages, is psychological manipulation of the victim, meant to instill fear and terror, rather than physical assault (which was already against the law). Before California's antistalking law, this psychological manipulation, though repugnant and reprehensible, was not illegal, and consequently the police could do nothing about it. With the new law, though, they finally could.

Following California's example, and under intense pressure from both women's groups and voters, the other 49 states soon began passing legislation similar to California's antistalking law. "He stands outside and listens to my conversations," said a witness who testified before the Florida House Criminal Justice Committee, which held hearings on anti-stalking legislation in 1992. "He trails my dates. I tried to get a restraining order, but I was told that first he had to hurt me twice."[197]

A legal assistant to the Florida legislator who sponsored that state's antistalking bill added, "The frustration these victims had with the system was really upsetting. They come into your office crying or hysterical, saying their son or daughter or mother is going to be hurt and the law can't do a thing about it."[198]

On 13 October 1993, Maine became the last of the 50 states to make stalking illegal. Unfortunately, though passed by the various state legislatures, these state antistalking laws were often quickly put together and rushed through to passage. Because of this, many were poorly worded, vague, and either so overly broad that innocent people could easily be convicted of stalking or so narrow that no one could be convicted. Consequently, many of these early state antistalking statutes did not survive court challenges questioning their constitutionality. Opponents successfully claimed that these state antistalking laws violated the right of free speech, the right of free travel, and the right of free assembly.

"It's possible that an overzealous prosecutor could sweep in a lot of legally protected activity and speech while prosecuting someone for stalking," said Phillip S. Gutis, a spokesperson for the American Civil Liberties Union.[199]

In addition to the constitutionality question of many early state antistalking laws, a number of the laws contained other serious flaws. To qualify as stalking in some states a stalker had to actually physically follow the victim. Waiting outside the home, sending threatening letters, or making threatening telephone calls was not enough. Another state required that the stalker be confronted and told to stop the conduct before the stalking became illegal, which, based on many tragic incidents of confrontations with stalkers, could obviously be an extremely dangerous requirement. One state said that the stalker and the victim had to have shared an intimate relationship before the stalking became illegal. In some states, to constitute stalking, the victims simply had to be put in fear, whereas in others they had to be put in fear of great bodily harm—an important and risky difference.

In several other states, threats had to be explicitly made before the behavior counted as stalking. However, victims often find that the threats made by stalkers are implied, such as sending them dead flowers, animal carcasses, or pictures with the victims cut out. Other states required at least three or more episodes of threats, and still others required proof that the stalker intended to terrorize the victim. Intent, incidentally, can be difficult to prove in stalking cases, because the stalkers will insist, and probably believe, that they do not intend to terrorize their victims, only show them how much they love them. Because of these problems with the early state antistalking laws, courts threw out many cases, or local prosecutors declined to even take any cases to court. Consequently, most states rewrote the laws to make them more specific, clearer, and easier to enforce.

"The need for sound state antistalking legislation is overwhelming," said U.S. Senator William Cohen. "The crime of stalking is insidious, frightening, and, unfortunately, on the rise."[200]

Some state antistalking laws also had to be rewritten because the earlier versions left out important aspects of stalking. For example, in some states, only threats against the victim, and not threats against the victim's family members, counted as part of stalking. Also, many states found they had made the penalties for stalking too light on the first passage of the law, the crime often being only a misdemeanor, many times just a step or two above serious traffic violations. Most states, on the second and occasionally even third writing of the law, stiffened the penalties against certain types of stalking, many adding a felony stalking.

Because of the confusing, poorly written, and hard to enforce state laws against stalking, in 1993, the Congress of the United States finally directed the U.S. Department of Justice to develop a model antistalking law. The idea behind this assignment was that the model law would provide the various state legislatures with direction when formulating such laws in their respective states.

"In their haste to respond, the states may adopt something so broad as to be unconstitutional, or so narrow as to be virtually meaningless," said Senator Cohen, who sponsored the bill to draft model antistalking legislation.[201]

To assist in the drafting and development of this model antistalking law, the National Institute of Justice brought in the National Conference of State Legislatures, the American Bar Association, and the Police Executive Research Forum. In October 1993, the National Institute of Justice published its findings as to what a model antistalking law should contain.

The model law, in part, reads:

.

Any person who:

(a)   purposely engages in a course of conduct directed at a specific person that would cause a reasonable person to fear bodily injury to himself or herself or a member of his or her immediate family or to fear the death of himself or herself or a member of his or her immediate family; and

(b)   has knowledge or should have knowledge that the specific person will be placed in reasonable fear of bodily injury to himself or herself or a member of his or her immediate family or will be placed in reasonable fear of the death of himself or herself or a member of his or her immediate family; and

(c)   whose acts induce fear in the specific person of bodily injury to himself or herself or a member of his or her immediate family or induce fear in the specific person of the death of himself or herself or a member of his or her immediate family;

is guilty of stalking.[202]

What this model law does is take the vagueness out of antistalking laws because it defines specific criminal behaviors. It also removes the overly broad claims because it excludes constitutionally protected behaviors and outlaws only those behaviors that make up genuine stalking. Many people felt that some of the early state antistalking laws would have made a reporter going after a story, a bill collector attempting to collect a debt, or even a process server guilty of stalking. The model law eliminates that problem.

The group that formulated this model law also felt that different levels of stalking should merit different punishments. They felt that states should create a felony stalking for those stalkers who present a serious danger to their victims, or who are extraordinarily persistent or obsessive. In addition, as stalking is often characterized by a series of increasingly serious acts, the panel recommended that states establish a continuum of charges in their antistalking laws so that law enforcement could intervene in the early stages whenever possible. In other words, state laws should include legal sanctions against the minor acts committed during the early nuisance stages of stalking. States should make this behavior illegal and with a penalty demonstrating that society does not condone this behavior. With increasing levels of stalking the penalties should become sterner. This could possibly forestall some of the tragedies that occur because intervention comes only after a serious act is finally committed by the stalker.

In the sentencing of stalkers, the model law developers felt that states should put together a provision that allowed for incarceration, if needed, for any stalking conviction at any level. In addition, they said that states should establish a felony-level aggravated stalking, with an appropriate sentence, for those who continue to stalk even after being convicted of stalking. Also, the developers felt that the states should put into their release from incarceration options, both pretrial and at the conclusion of the sentence, restrictions and conditions that reflect the risk the stalker represents. In other words, they felt that the more dangerous the stalkers are, the closer they should be watched and controlled when released from custody, either on bail or at the conclusion of their sentence.

The sentencing concerns of the developers of the model law are, unfortunately, very real. During my research for this book, I found numerous cases in which a court, even though finding a stalker guilty of terrorizing a victim, only gave him or her a weak slap on the wrist, that is, if the case even reached the court. Much too often since the creation of state antistalking laws, when stalking complaints were taken by the police and an arrest was made, the complaints never made it past the prosecutor's office, which would decline to bring charges. For example, in the Gary Wilensky case, discussed in Chapter 6, after Wilensky had been arrested for stalking several children while wearing a wig and a black leather mask, the prosecutor dropped the charges after viewing a scrapbook that reportedly showed Wilensky's many good deeds. Like most stalkers, Wilensky, when he discovered he was not going to receive any negative sanctions for his actions, continued the stalking. According to the Bureau of Justice Statistics research paper *Prosecutors in State Courts, 1994*, of all prosecutor's offices across the United States in 1994, only 68 percent prosecuted any stalking cases, even though stalking occurred in 100 percent of the United States.[203] This problem often derives from the fact that, with stalking being such a new crime, prosecutors many times aren't sure how to proceed with the criminal prosecution, and so they don't.

Unfortunately, even in those cases in which the police arrest a stalker and the officers can persuade the prosecutor to press charges, far too many judges, who see these cases as private domestic or personal relationship problems, and who obviously don't understand the mental makeup of stalkers or the depths of their obsessions, set ridiculously low bonds for them. This usually only encourages the stalkers to continue their actions since it appears the criminal justice system views their offense to be very minor.

In an example of this, Menominee, Minnesota, police officers arrested the local fire chief for stalking his ex-girlfriend. As a condition of the fire chief's release from jail, a judge ordered him to have no contact at all with his ex-girlfriend. However, as with most stalkers, this order meant very little. Once freed, the fire chief called his ex-girlfriend several times and sent her mail. The police arrested the fire chief again, this time for felony stalking, but a judge once more released him. This time, while free, the stalker killed himself. Fortunately, this case is an exception because no one else was hurt.

According to the Bureau of Justice Statistics research paper *Pretrial Release of Felony Defendants*, 63 percent of all felony defendants are released on bail. Yet for those who are arrested while out on bail, 56 percent are released on bail again.[204]

"Before we had a stalking law, we used to have to tell victims there was nothing we could do," said Lieutenant Mike Smallwood of the Bibb County (Georgia) Sheriff's Department. "Now, we can lock them up, but they get out on bond. These women shouldn't have to be prisoners in their own free country, but no law enforcement agency has the manpower to guard a stalking victim twenty-four hours a day, seven days a week."[205]

Besides setting ridiculously low bonds, many judges, when juries convict stalkers, also mete out extremely light sentences, hardly sufficient to discourage future stalking. Too many judges simply don't understand the depth of the obsession that controls stalkers, or how stalking their victims is often the only objective these people have in life.

An incident I witnessed demonstrates how judges often view stalking not as a crime, but as only a relationship or domestic problem. While in court one day waiting for my case to be heard, I sat through a case involving a stalker. A woman testified that she had been followed, harassed, and beaten several times by a former boyfriend. After a short trial, the judge found the man guilty, but then sentenced him only to probation. As the woman was leaving the courtroom, obviously upset over the light-handed handling of her case, the judge said very loudly that if the victim and stalker got married he would drop the probation. This brought a roar of laughter from the courtroom, which is, I suppose, what the judge wanted.

Other examples of this light-handed treatment of stalkers are plentiful. In Minneapolis, in 1995, a court convicted former Minnesota Timberwolves's assistant coach Charles Davisson of stalking a local television news anchorwoman. Davisson admitted being in the woman's neighborhood, where neighbors complained they saw him peering into the woman's home, and twice he went to her television station to stare at her. He also violated a restraining order to stay away from the woman, whom he so unnerved by his stalking that she asked the television station to provide her with security.

Hennepin County Judge Pamela Alexander said that the evidence showed clear intent of Davisson to harass and put the woman in fear. However, the judge sentenced him to only 2 years of probation. Whether the judge was a Timberwolves fan or thought as the judge in the previous incident did I'm not sure.[206]

In Jacksonville, Florida, in 1994, the police arrested a stalker as he was purchasing items on a three-page list he had drawn up of the things he would need to kill a woman he was stalking. A person who knew the stalker secretly taped conversations with him in which the stalker talked about cannibalism, sexual torture, and the murder of the stalking victim. Regardless of these circumstances, a judge sentenced this extraordinarily dangerous stalker to only 9 years of probation and an order to get mental health treatment.

In Philadelphia, in 1993, a judge sentenced a convicted stalker to 5 years of probation. This came, however, only after the police had hunted the stalker down when he failed to show up for court after his first arrest. The man had been released by the judge with no bond, even though he had no known address.

In another case, a stalker so terrorized a Kansas City, Missouri, woman for 18 months during 1993 and 1994 that she spent her entire life's savings on security. The man received a sentence of just 1 year of probation. Within a few weeks of this sentence, however, the police arrested the man again when they caught him placing a ladder up to the wall of the woman's apartment building. The judge then sentenced him to 3 more years of probation.

"Some judges are still reluctant to consider stalking a serious crime," said Pat Corey, Assistant Solicitor in Aiken, Bamberg, and Barnwell Counties (South Carolina).[207] This is true even though South Carolina has one of the best antistalking laws in the country, with three levels of the crime: harassment, stalking, and aggravated stalking.

"Stalking causes a high level of fear that interferes with women's lives," said Professor Mary Brewster of West Chester University in Pennsylvania, who is presently conducting a study of stalking victims in Pennsylvania. "It forces drastic changes, inhibits their activities—what they do socially, the way they drive to work. But stalking is not always treated as a serious offense."[208]

Deputy District Attorney for Los Angeles Jane Shade adds, "I think the law should take into account the damage done to the victims in what amounts to, in some cases, psychological torture. In some cases the victims say, 'I wish he'd hit me or shoot at me and get it over with.'"[209]

Although some readers might argue that the prosecutors handling stalking cases should make judges understand the seriousness of stalking, these readers obviously don't understand the strict rules of evidence that courts operate under, or the hierarchy of a courtroom, in which the judge sits at the top of the pyramid. A prosecutor doesn't make a judge do anything. Fortunately, there is a solution that will correct the problem of judges who don't understand the psychological makeup or seriousness of stalkers, which will be detailed in Chapter 17.

Even more outrageous, however, when stalkers do receive a jail or prison sentence, many prison officials and parole boards regard them as harmless or, at most, as less harmful than average criminals. In Florida, a woman who stalked an ex-boyfriend and eventually shot him to death in a University of North Florida classroom served only 1 year of a 15-year sentence before being released from prison. In Indiana, a court sentenced Alan Matheney to prison for brutally attacking his wife. Even though incarcerated, he continued stalking his now ex-wife by making repeated death threats against her from prison. Despite this, prison officials considered Matheney a low-risk prisoner and eventually approved a 48-hour furlough for him. Before he was freed, however, prison officials made Matheney give them his word that he would stay in the Indianapolis area and not go to northern Indiana, where his ex-wife lived. Upon leaving prison on his furlough, Matheney immediately drove to his ex-wife's home in northern Indiana and murdered her.

This lenient treatment of stalkers isn't confined only to American courts. In 1993, in Germany, a stalker savagely attacked tennis star Monica Seles with a kitchen knife. The man, apparently obsessed with tennis star Steffi Graf, thought that by putting Seles out of action he would help advance Graf's tennis career. A German judge, Elke Bosse, after finding the stalker guilty of the knife attack, sentenced him to 2 years in prison, then immediately suspended the sentence and set the man free. I don't think anyone is sure why the judge did this, though most observers were stunned by her action.

In an effort to avoid this type of travesty, the United States now has two sets of stalking laws, state and federal. The federal law, called the

Interstate Stalking Punishment and Prevention Act, grew partly out of Senator Kay Bailey Hutchison's (Texas) experience with a stalker. In 1972, a man who worked as a volunteer in Hutchison's campaign for the Texas House of Representatives began stalking her, one time plunging an ice pick into Hutchison's photograph on a campaign poster.

The new federal law, signed by President Clinton on 23 September 1996, makes it a crime to cross a state line to stalk someone, and carries a penalty of 5 years in prison, which increases to 10 years in those cases involving serious injury or the use of a weapon, to 20 years for permanent disfigurement or a life-threatening injury, and to life in prison for those incidents that end in the victim's death. Unlike some state antistalking laws, the stalker doesn't have to commit an act of violence, or be a spouse or former intimate partner of the victim to be charged. Also, the victim doesn't have to have a restraining order against the stalker to press charges.

"Today we say loud and clear," said President Clinton on signing the antistalking measure, "if you stalk and harass, the law will follow you wherever you may go."[210]

Congressman Ed Royce, speaking of the new federal law against stalking, adds, "There are thousands of people trying to escape stalking by moving to another state, but there hasn't been any protection for them when they are followed. Now there is."[211]

Although most state antistalking laws went through a turbulent period of change and evolution, all states now have workable laws that can be used to stop stalkers. Along with these, there is now a federal law against stalking for those cases that cross state lines. However, just having these laws is not enough. They must be enforced by the police, prosecuted vigorously, and if the stalker is convicted, courts must mete out punishment commensurate with the crime. Only then can stalking in America be brought under control.

16

WHAT CAN A VICTIM DO?

Bonnie and Herbert Estep's divorce became final in September 1994. Soon afterward, Bonnie filed for a protective order against Herbert when he allegedly broke into her home, smashed her furniture, tossed out her clothing, and threatened her. In 1995, despite Herbert's continued stalking, Bonnie decided to begin living a normal life again, so she started dating Wesley Begley. Herbert, however, felt that Bonnie was "his property."

In November 1995, Wesley and Bonnie were driving in Bonnie's car when she suddenly spotted Herbert's car slip in behind and then begin following them. Several times when Bonnie stopped for a red light Herbert would jump out of his car brandishing a gun, dash up to her car, and begin beating on the windows. With her heart pounding, and in terror for their lives, Bonnie raced with Wesley to the state police post in London, Kentucky.

However, when Bonnie hurriedly parked her car next to the building in the state police post parking lot, Herbert raced his car in behind hers and blocked them in. Wesley jumped out of Bonnie's car, and, after a confrontation, he shot and killed Herbert with a gun he carried for protection.

"I think it would be fair to say that Mr. Estep was apparently jealous," said Wesley's attorney.[212]

Following the shooting, Wesley hurried into the state police post and told them what had happened. The police, after placing Wesley under arrest, examined the crime scene, and recovered a loaded pistol from Herbert's car. A grand jury declined to bring charges against Wesley, citing self-defense.

A Pierce County (Minnesota) court ordered Harry P. Weinberg, data processing coordinator for Pierce County, to stay away from his estranged wife, Ruth. This order was included as one of the conditions of his release from jail when freed on $5000 bail after being arrested on five felony charges involving his stalking of Ruth, confining her against her will, and assaulting her with his fists and a tire iron. The court ordered him to have no contact at all with his wife, their child, and her children from a previous marriage.

On 28 March 1994, police responded to Ruth's apartment on the report of a domestic disturbance. They found Harry lying on the living room floor, dead from a gunshot wound to the chest, reportedly fired by Ruth. The officers did not make any arrests, but instead said they would refer the case to the district attorney's office.

Dwight Samuels could not accept his girlfriend's decision to end their relationship. Instead, he began following, harassing, and threatening her. On 2 February 1995, Dwight showed up at his former girlfriend's apartment in Miami. She refused to let him in, and he began pounding on the door, and then finally kicked it in. However, when Dwight started to rush into the apartment, a family friend shot him five times, killing him.

➤   ➤   ➤   ➤

In Charlotte, North Carolina, Nancy Small and Tommy Laws both worked at the Drexel Heritage plant, Nancy as a clerk and Tommy in the cabinetmaking shop. Although at one time involved in a romantic relationship, Nancy had decided to end it. When Tommy tried to rekindle the romance, Nancy refused, and the stalking began.

Tommy allegedly began following Nancy, threatening her, and vandalizing her car by carving the word "traitor" into the paint and by cutting a brake cable. He also reportedly told Nancy he was going to find someone to rape her 20-year-old daughter. Nancy complained to company officials at Drexel Heritage that problems between her and Tommy were beginning to spill over into the workplace.

Despite this warning to company officials, Nancy and Tommy both attended an employee meeting on 22 June 1995. Nancy would afterward tell authorities that as they were leaving the meeting Tommy again began threatening her. A few minutes later, company employees called the police, who, on responding to the call, found Nancy standing over Tommy's dead body, a .25-caliber pistol in her hand. Reportedly, she was so hysterical and distraught she was still pulling the trigger on an empty gun when the police arrived.

As part of a plea bargain, Nancy pled guilty to voluntary manslaughter. Because the judge found the stalking to be mitigating circumstances, he sentenced her to 90 days in jail and a $350 fine. The judge credited Nancy with 77 days already spent in jail awaiting trial.

"She went berserk; she couldn't take it anymore," said Nancy's attorney. "She was battered mentally until she absolutely lost her mind."[213]

In the preceding four incidents, the stalking of these victims finally reached the point where they felt their lives were in imminent danger, or the intensity of the stalking finally reached the point where the victim snapped. By presenting these incidents, am I advising victims of stalking to carry weapons or take deadly action to stop the stalking? Of course not. Actually, as I will show later, carrying a weapon can often add even more danger for the victim. What I am doing is showing how very dangerous stalkers can be, and how very desperate and frightened the victims can become. In truth, knowledgeable stalking victims have the power to keep from being put into situations such as those in the incidents above, situations in which deadly actions are necessary to survive. If stalking victims follow certain safety rules and take certain precautions, such drastic actions would seldom become necessary. The much safer avenue is for victims to take action against stalkers or potential stalkers before the obsession has reached the point where the only way out is deadly force.

Naturally, the first step cautious people should take to greatly lessen the possibility of becoming a victim is not to become involved with individuals who exhibit any of the signs of a potential stalker. All contact with people who display any of these warning signs should be immediately and completely broken off before they have any emotional investment in you. A profile of who and what stalkers are was given in Chapter 2, but there are also specific warning signs of potential or future stalkers.

First, a very large percentage of the stalkers in this country are ex-spouses or ex-intimate partners who refuse to accept that a relationship is over. Because a very large number of these ex-spouses or ex-intimate partners, now stalkers, were abusive during the relationship, some of the signs of a possible future abusive spouse or intimate partner are the same signs of a possible future stalker.

The first sign of a person who could easily move from being an ex-intimate partner to a stalker is extreme jealousy and possessiveness. This trait manifests itself from practically the first encounter. The intense jealousy arises because many abusive spouses or intimate partners, and possible future stalkers, have low self-esteem. They feel very insecure about themselves and any relationship they become involved in. They almost immediately become convinced that, because of their own lack of worth, the people they are interested in likely aren't really interested in them and secretly want someone else. This is why so many abusers and stalkers keep their victims under constant surveillance.

"He was always accusing me of infidelity," said a woman stalked by her ex-husband. "If a man even spoke to me, he would accuse me of encouraging him. He would call me on the cellular phone when I went to the store, wanting to know how much longer I was going to be."

Because of this intense jealousy, when future stalkers are dating, they will often want to spend every second possible with the individuals they've become involved with, and will try to keep the individuals from having any contact at all with anyone of the opposite sex. They will often make the individuals they're dating account for every second when they're away from them. Although this possessiveness and wanting to spend every minute with them may at first seem intensely romantic, it soon becomes suffocating, and finally imprisoning. This possessiveness should be a clear sign of what will happen if the victims ever try to leave the relationship.

Another sign of a future abuser and stalker that should be taken just as seriously as extreme jealously is the **need for control**. Both domestic abuse and stalking are all about controlling another person's life through any means necessary, be it gifts and love letters or assaults and death threats. If you're considering becoming intimately involved with someone, you should ask yourself several questions first. Does the person you're interested in always have to have his or her way? Does the person try to tell you what you should wear, what you should buy, who you should associate with? Does the person become moody, sullen, and angry if he or she doesn't get his or her way? If you've answered yes to any of these questions, the chances of a good, solid, two-way relationship with this person are extremely thin. The person wants to control your life, and it will not get any better the longer the relationship goes on.

"He wanted complete control," said a former spousal abuse and then stalking victim. "He had to make all of the decisions about everything. If I decided something, he would do everything he could to stop it."

As discussed in Chapter 2, because abusive spouses and intimate partners who become stalkers have such low self-esteem, and often lack power anywhere in their lives except in their dominance of the relationship, all of their self-worth and identity is tied up in the control they exert over their partners. Their entire sense of being comes from the power they hold over their spouses or intimate partners. As a result, these individuals often panic once they find out they are about to lose this control when their partners take steps to end the relationship. The abusers' greatest fear is about to be realized, because without controlling their spouses or partners they will have no power, they will have no identity, they will be nothing. Consequently, they will follow, harass, threaten, physically assault, and take just about any other action necessary in order to get the victims to return to the relationship. Ex-abusers-turned-stalkers often feel that if they can't regain the control they previously had, then their lives are not worth living. Without this control they are a nonperson, someone with no power and no identity. These types of suicidal thoughts make them extraordinarily dangerous, and not just to themselves, but also to the victims, whom they may decide to take with them.

Future or potential stalkers, however, aren't always just abusive spouses or intimate partners, but may also be casual acquaintances, business associates, or occasionally even strangers. As discussed in Chapter 2, many of these types of stalkers lack a core identity, and so they try to latch on psychologically to their victims, feeling that having a relationship with their victims will give them identity and self-worth. For these potential stalkers, an important sign to watch for is that they **lack social skills**. These types of stalkers, regardless of the romantic scenarios they often have envisioned with their victims, can seldom establish and maintain a workable emotional relationship with anyone. They are many times the people in high school who never dated, and who, as adults, seldom have any kind of emotional relationship with those of the opposite sex. (As readers will recall from Chapters 7, 12, and 13, this is an exact description of stalkers Robert Bardo, Richard Farley, and Larry Stagner.)

Because these stalkers often lack a core identity, when the relationship they're demanding of their victims doesn't develop into the romantic scenario they envisioned, or what does develop eventually disintegrates, they have no sense of self to fall back on. Consequently, they cannot accept the rejection, and will continue pursuing the victims regardless of how many times they are rejected, telling themselves that they just have to try harder. Stalkers, though, it must be warned, can finally reach a point where they can no longer fool themselves about the possibility of a relationship. Then, when they must face the humiliation of having to admit that their romantic scenario will never be, they may strike out violently at their victims.

The point is that one of the worst, and most dangerous, things you can do is to accept a date, or even a friendly outing, with someone because you feel sorry for him or her. It is a troubling reflection on human nature, but by dating someone who appears desperate for a relationship you could be setting yourself up for tragedy. This is precisely what happened to stalking victim Christine Sloan, who in Chapter 4 described the beginning of her relationship with a stalker as a "pity date."

Also, individuals, before becoming emotionally involved on **any level** with a person, need to be on the lookout for **signs of any kind of obsessive behavior** in the person's life. Stalkers are often obsessive in other areas besides pursuing the stalking victims. Ask yourself: are there indications that the person has the tendency to fixate on things? Is he or she a compulsive spender, or is the person such an avid fan of some celebrity that he or she spends large amounts of money traveling to attend appearances or to purchase CDs or videos? While investigating this history of obsession, individuals also need to look at a person's emotional background. Are there signs that this person has become obsessed with someone in the past? If you find any stalking at any level in a person's background this should be a red flag waving frantically. Don't believe that it won't happen to you.

To reiterate, it is definitely in any individual's best interests to check out a person before becoming emotionally involved. Although such checking won't stop casual acquaintance or stranger stalking cases, it will stop the largest category of stalkers: former intimate partners. To do a background check you don't have to hire a private detective (though this isn't a bad idea), you can check on the person yourself. Find out who the person's close friends and acquaintances are. **Many stalkers do not have any close friends, and this should be taken as a sign of caution.** Ask the friends or acquaintances about other people the person has been involved with. If possible, talk with others the person has been emotionally involved with. Although you should expect a certain level of negativity from anyone whose relationship with the person didn't end amicably, still listen carefully, and if you hear about any episodes of stalking, pull away and have nothing at all to do with the person any longer, no matter how attractive. It isn't worth the risk. Don't give the person time to feel that he or she has an emotional investment in you.

This investigation into a person's past must be done as discreetly as possible, because if you find something that indicates stalking in the person's background you will want to pull away, and you don't want to make it more difficult by having the person believe you are interested in him or her. If the person, however, should discover that you are checking, and you find evidence of obsession or stalking, you must be firm in your resolve to end the relationship then and there—totally. This checking into the background of a person, although chancy, doesn't carry nearly the risk as does trying to break away from an obsessive person once he or she has fixated on you.

A final suggestion: trust your instincts. Police officers find that a large number of women who have been sexually attacked tell us the rapist had made them feel uncomfortable before the attack, but they weren't sure why and so they didn't do anything about it. Stalkers are very similar to rapists. Stalkers want to control their victims, to have power over them, just like rapists. And so, **if you meet someone who makes you feel uncomfortable, act on your feelings. Get away from the person and break off any future contact.**

What things should make you feel uncomfortable? You should become alarmed if you find that a person expressing interest in you has obtained personal information about you from sources you consider private. You should be concerned if the person seems to always be "coincidentally" showing up wherever you are, if the person appears to want to manipulate you into becoming emotionally involved, or if the person wants you to enter into a serious relationship before you really know each other.

Summarizing the signs to watch for that could indicate a potential stalker:

1   Extreme jealousy and possessiveness
2   A need for control
3   Lacking in social skills
4   Obsessive behavior
5   Makes you feel uncomfortable

But, of course, while all of the signs above are valuable, there is a greater fear many people have than being stalked themselves, and that is having their children stalked. However, like adult stalking, there are measures parents can take to protect their children.

1   Parents must be alert to any signs of an adult's preoccupation with their children. Often, the stalking of children is a precursor to the sexual molestation of them, and so parents should be extremely concerned whenever an adult seems to be paying an unusual amount of attention to a child, or speaks of a child in romantic terms.

2   Parents must listen to their children and be alert to any stories of strange people following them or constantly showing up wherever they are.

3   I know you don't have nearly the control you'd like to have over who your children associate with, but parents should still watch for the signs given above in any of their children's dates or associates.

Although many of the signs I've given so far are valuable for those not yet being stalked, what if you are already being stalked, perhaps on a minor level at present? Or what if you believe there's a possibility, but you are not certain, that you may have attracted the attention of a stalker? What steps can be taken to maximize your safety and also end the stalking?

First, don't blame yourself because someone else has a problem. Don't think that a stalker's behavior is your fault because you spoke to the person, had a casual lunch with him or her, or perhaps just smiled at the person. The individual's mental problems are not your fault. A normal person wouldn't become obsessed with someone over such a small event. Sometimes, however, family members and friends will blame victims of stalking for their victimization. Family and friends will sometimes ask: "What did you do to attract him or her? Why did you ever go out with him or her to begin with?" Ignore these people. It's not your fault.

"There was a part of me that thought I had encouraged him, but in actuality I had not," said a stalking victim. "You start looking at yourself and start asking yourself how you could have dealt with things more firmly."[214]

Although you shouldn't blame yourself for being stalked, you also shouldn't minimize the problem or laugh it off as just a lovesick crush. Never underestimate the danger of a stalker. This has been a fatal mistake for many stalking victims. The mental problems typical of stalkers do not usually just go away. They often grow worse with time. Stop the behavior as early as possible.

One of the most common ways that stalkers begin their intimidation of victims is through telephone calls, and for some stalkers telephone harassment is the limit of their stalking. So, one of the first things stalking victims should do is change their telephone number to an unpublished one, preferably under another name. I should warn, however, that while this is a good idea, and should be given a try, many stalkers have no difficulty at all in persuading someone, through some ruse, to give them your new telephone number, or they find the new number in other ways, such as through friends at agencies or companies that have access to this information. Once this is done, you can change your telephone number again, but likely it will have the same end result.

A better method for victims of stalkers who telephone them constantly is to keep their old telephone number and hook it up to an answering machine, and then to have the telephone company install a second telephone line and number. This way, individuals can still receive calls from those they want to talk to, and the stalkers' messages can be captured on tape for later use in the event a criminal case is filed. The stalker, because your answering machine still answers his or her calls, will have no reason to suspect you have another line and number.

For telephone stalking the easiest way to handle and stop it is simply not to talk to the stalker. Screening your calls through an answering machine can effectively cut off the stalker's contact with you. Telephone stalkers live and thrive off of the reaction of victims. If they don't get one they will often move on to another victim. As related in Chapter 10, Henry Blair tried to keep his victim answering his calls and talking to him by hinting that he knew where her missing daughter was. If he hadn't been able to keep her on the line, he likely would have moved on to someone else.

Unlike the steps taken to end telephone stalking, however, before taking steps to end other types of stalking, particularly those in which the stalker has made some type of personal contact, victims must first assess the situation as to its seriousness and danger. If you know the stalker, does he or she have a history of violence? Is there a history of mental problems or substance abuse? Has the stalker made threats or taken any threatening action? How motivated is this person, and, if you know, why did he or she pick you? If any danger signs are present, personal contact with the stalker is more hazardous than the likelihood that a firm refusal personally delivered will stop the stalking.

However, with minor stalking incidents that appear at present to be relatively nonthreatening, the sooner you tell possible stalkers that you have no, and never will have any, romantic interest in them, the less they have invested psychologically and emotionally in you. Yet, no matter how nice of a person you are, experts warn not to try to soften your rejection because stalkers can hear hope and possibility in almost anything nice you say, particularly if you try to soften the blow of rejection with phrases such as "Not right now," "Yes, I like you, but," "I need some time," or something similar. Don't "waffle-talk." Be blunt and to the point. Yet, allow the person to maintain his or her dignity. During almost 30 years as a police officer I have found that often you can force people who don't want to be violent into committing violence if you take away their dignity. A good response would be simply, "No thank you. I'm not interested," said in a plain, matter-of-fact tone. However, when confronting a potential stalker like this, always be certain you have a safety backup, such as doing it in a place where others are close by and can help you if necessary.

"It all depends on who's doing the confronting and how vulnerable the victim is," said Dr. Park Dietz. "If the confrontation makes the stalker more angry or focused and the victim has no safeguards, it's foolish to confront."[215]

Of course, readers might question the advice of having anything at all to do with stalkers, as you could just be encouraging their actions by talking with them. Although this can be true for the deeply obsessed stalkers who see any interaction with their victims as positive, if you don't tell people bluntly you are not interested in them, then they might justifiably feel that you are interested and only playing hard to get.

However, if blunt words don't work, the next tactic to try with individuals who have not yet shown any signs of being a serious threat, and for whom you don't want to deal with as extremely as involving the police, is to have no further contact at all with them. Don't respond to telephone calls or letters, and don't let the stalker believe he or she has upset you. Act as though the stalker doesn't exist. Stalkers gain control and power over their victims through fear and intimidation. **If you don't react to the stalker, then the stalker is not able to intimidate and control you, which is what he or she wants and craves.** Many stalkers are serial stalkers, and if they find they can get little or no response from you, they will often move on to another victim. But most important, don't give in to your natural urge to grab the telephone after the 25th time it has rung and scream at the stalker to stop it. Stalkers won't be embarrassed or ashamed by your reaction. Instead, they have just learned that it takes 25 calls before you'll pick up the telephone, and probably 100 before you'll go out with them. So, they will continue calling. Instead, ignore them.

"Continuing the dialogue is the biggest mistake you can make when someone is stalking you," said Lt. John Lane of the Los Angeles Police Department's Threat Management Unit.[216]

Also, never believe you can negotiate with stalkers. Don't assume that giving in a little bit to stalkers' demands, such as having coffee or a casual lunch, will, as they promise, bring the stalking behavior to a stop. **Stalkers want control, not compromise.** Although stalkers may appear to be happy to accept less than what they were after, this is only a beginning, a way to get more. You will hear from them again. Victims are much better off, after the initial rejection, having nothing at all to do with stalkers. Deeply obsessed stalkers will cling to any shred of evidence, no matter how tenuous, that the victims actually care for them. Truly obsessed individuals live for and thrive on any reaction from their victims.

"Any response that a woman gives him is going to be taken as basically a sign that she is interested in him," said Dr. David Spiegel, an associate professor of psychiatry and behavioral sciences at the Stanford University School of Medicine.[217]

Of course, during the time you are ignoring a stalker don't let down your guard. Although the stalker may appear to be only a nuisance, any stalker can be dangerous. Use extraordinary caution during this time because stalkers can move from gifts and claims of love to threats and acts of violence in a matter of seconds. The one thing that makes stalking so dangerous is its unpredictability. A victim never knows when or where a stalker will strike or when the violence level will suddenly escalate.

For your safety during the time you are ignoring a stalker, be certain all of your family and friends, your co-workers (particularly receptionists or others who monitor access to a work site), and your neighbors know about your situation so they can be extra eyes and ears for you. Give them either a picture or a description of the stalker, and, if known, a description and license number of any vehicle the stalker uses. This not only broadens the web of emotional support you will receive, but also gives you many more sources of information about what the stalker might be doing. In addition, if these people know that a certain person is stalking you, they will be less likely to give the stalker personal information about you. But most important, take extra precautions to be certain your home is safe from break-in, as stalkers sometimes break into their victims' homes to obtain information about them, or to surprise them when they return home. Also, use extra precautions when traveling outside the home. My book *Protecting Your Life, Home, and Property* (Plenum, 1995) can help you decide what security measures you need to take, both at home and when away. You must never give a stalker the opportunity to try to live out a fantasy by having close personal (and dangerous) contact with you.

"The stalker usually moves on to greener pastures, or disaster happens," said Dr. Ronald Markman, a psychiatrist and attorney.[218]

With this quote in mind, what you must do is make the stalker want to move on to greener pastures without deciding to harm you first. You must make the stalker believe that the amount of energy he or she is expending is not going to result in a return worth the investment. You also want to take every step necessary to avoid giving a stalker any opportunity to use violence if he or she becomes frustrated by being unable to contact you or become involved in your life.

According to the National Institute of Justice's research paper *Threat Assessment: An Approach to Prevent Targeted Violence*: "Violent behavior does not occur in a vacuum. Careful analysis of violent incidents show that violent acts often are the culmination of long-developing, identifiable trails of problems, conflicts, disputes, and failures." The paper says that violence is the product of an interaction among three factors:

1   The individual who takes the violent action
2   Stimulus or triggering conditions that lead the subject to see violence as an option, "way out," or solution to problems or life situations
3   A setting that facilitates or permits the violence, or at least does not stop it from occurring[219]

The first and most obvious point from the information stated above is that the less contact of any type you have with a stalker, the less the chances of any violence. Some victims, however, in the early stages of stalking, when the stalkers don't want to accept rejection—even when this rejection is given bluntly and to the point—believe they should confront the stalkers again and this time demand that they stop. This type of confrontation was even a requirement under one state law before stalking would be legally recognized as having been committed. However, this really isn't a good idea. Personal confrontations, after the initial rejection, can be extremely dangerous, and confrontations over the telephone are usually counterproductive. Some stalkers feel that just the act of the victims talking to them is a victory, and this many times increases their obsession. Even though the victims may have rejected them, a confrontation after the rejection shows the stalkers that they have gotten the victims to pay attention to them. They are now part of their victims' lives. And no matter how negative the victims' words, stalkers' minds can twist them to positive by convincing themselves the victims are just playing hard to get. Although this may not sound logical, remember: stalkers seldom rely on logic.

"The laws are just very small tools," said security expert Gavin DeBecker. "What really helps is to educate victims, to make them understand that straight talk won't work on crooked people."[220]

But what if no matter what you do or say initially to show you are not interested in any way in a person, he or she won't go away? What if you have taken every step possible to avoid contact, yet the person becomes obsessed with you anyway? What if the stalker won't seem to give up, and his or her actions, such as minor vandalism or messages that have turned vicious, begin to make you feel very uncomfortable? What should you do?

Call the police at the first act of serious stalking, such as property damage or threats that frighten you. Insist that the officers make a report. A stalking victim will need this because a conviction for stalking, by its legal definition, requires a series of acts, and victims must be able to show this "course of conduct" or continuation of behavior.

"A lot of people fail to make a report," said Sergeant Jan Meanix-Garza of the Houston Police Department. "Then six months later they call the police, and we have no evidence of prior problems. The problem in prosecuting these cases is often proving that a victim is being stalked."[221]

Columbia, South Carolina, attorney Christine Sloan, who suffered through 6 years of stalking, said, "Each case is unique. The one thing we know about stalkers is that there is no way to predict how they will act. The only conclusion I have reached is that they [victims] should get the police involved as quickly as possible."[222]

Getting the police involved early can often scare away less determined stalkers. Having a police officer contact them can occasionally break the resolve of stalkers who haven't much invested yet in the stalking. And if this doesn't work, victims are probably not that less well off because the stalkers are obviously so determined they wouldn't have let the victims off the hook no matter what they did.

As a police officer with many years of experience, I feel I need at this point to explain a few things about dealing with the police. Although you are likely frightened and upset by the stalking, do your best to talk to the officers calmly. This is important because if the stalkers are there they will very likely be calm, and, compared to victims who appear hysterical, will seem to sound believable when they say they don't know what the victims are talking about. Also, don't lie about or minimize your involvement with the stalker. If you lie, the police will not know what to believe when they find out the truth. If you have had an intimate relationship with the stalker, tell the officers so.

Police officers in Indianapolis, and most other cities, must make reports when citizens request them, **so do request that the officers make a report about the stalking.** Find out how you can obtain a copy of this police report or get a case number. You will need this to prove the stalking if a criminal case is pursued. Don't be bullied or persuaded out of making your complaint, and don't let the police downplay its seriousness or tell you no crime has been committed. Stalking laws are new and many officers may not be completely clear on them. Therefore, it would be to your advantage to obtain a copy of the stalking law in your state, and become familiar with it (also obtain a copy of the new federal law against stalking, just in case your circumstances meet its criteria). State antistalking laws can be obtained from your state attorney general's office. The new federal law can be obtained through the U.S. Attorney's office for your district or through your congressman's office. For individuals with access to the Internet, a copy of the federal law can be obtained at web address *http://law.house.gov/usc.htm.* Also, obtain and remember the names or badge numbers of the police officers you talked to about the stalking. You don't have to loudly demand this information, just look at the name tags or badges and remember the names or numbers. All of this information will be valuable later if you have to show a continuing pattern of behavior by the stalker.

If, however, you receive unsatisfactory treatment from the officers, or you feel that your complaint is not being taken seriously, go higher. Tell the officers you would like to have a supervisor come to the scene. If the officers will not do so, call 911 and ask for one. As 911 calls are recorded, few dispatchers will refuse to do this. Tell the supervisor your problem and that you would like to have a report made. If you still feel you are receiving less service than you expect, go higher and file a complaint. All police departments have a complaint mechanism for individuals who feel they are receiving less than satisfactory service. Use it. The job of the police is to serve and protect, and as a citizen you deserve protection, and should get it. Keep a record of everything you have done and everyone you have spoken to about the stalking. It can become valuable if your case later goes to court.

When, after filing your report, you are contacted by a detective from the police department, express your concern about the stalking and your desire to prosecute to the fullest extent. Find out exactly what the police department needs to make its case against the stalker, and then attempt to help the police get it. Aggressive, willing victims make police officers more aggressive and willing to help.

But what if after doing everything advised above, and even after calling the police, your stalker still appears very persistent and likely dangerous? What can you do then?

You may eventually want to obtain a restraining or protective order. These are court orders that restrict a stalker from having any contact with you. A restraining or protective order also puts the stalker on notice of your intent. An order should leave no question that you do not wish for more contact. Restraining or protective orders will stop some minor stalkers, those who have a stake in the community and fear the consequences of violating them. A word of caution, however. Protective orders are just pieces of paper, not some invisible armor. They will not stop, or even slow down, the very determined stalkers, and may infuriate them and drive them to take even more aggressive action. Don't ever believe that protective orders will actually protect you from someone with murderous intent. They won't. Remember, laws seldom deter mentally disturbed and obsessed people.

"I think that certainly these types of orders [protective] are effective in a number of cases," said Jeremy Fogel, supervising judge of Santa Clara County (California) Superior Court's family division. "If someone is determined to make your life miserable, it may not be effective."[223]

Why, if protective orders many times don't work, and may even cause a stalker to become more dangerous, should you get one? For several good reasons. First, as stated above, they do work on the less determined stalkers who fear the consequences of violating them. A protective order also shows your concern and fear of the stalker in the event the case later goes to court. In addition, having such an order gives the police the right to intervene and arrest the stalker if they catch him or her around you. Also, some states have made stalking a more serious crime, with stiffer penalties, if it is committed in defiance of a protective order.

Once you've obtained a protective order, make several copies of it and keep a copy in your home and a copy at your place of business. Also, carry a copy with you when you are out, just in case the stalker follows or approaches you. But **never** expect a restraining or protective order to provide safety by itself. To some stalkers these orders mean absolutely nothing.

"They never give up," said Sergeant Charles Drago of the Fort Lauderdale Police Department. "Without a law to interrupt them, they will either torment their victim out of his or her mind or they'll harm them."[224]

There are some stalkers, as Sergeant Drago points out, for whom the advice given so far is of minor value at best. There are stalkers, particularly former spouses and intimate partners, who are so desperate to regain the victim, or what they see as their lost dignity from the breakup, that they appear, and may well be, ready to use any action, including deadly force, to accomplish this end. And occasionally, casual acquaintance and even stranger stalkers can become so obsessed with establishing the romantic relationship they have fantasized about for so long that they are also ready to do anything, including commit murder if necessary, to accomplish their obsession. Victims in these circumstances must realize that the chances of something serious happening to them are very high, and so extra steps must be taken to ensure their safety.

There are basically two avenues a victim can take when dealing with a stalker who has reached the level where serious bodily injury and/or a homicide appear distinct possibilities. Neither of these avenues, incidentally, is depending on the police to protect you. There are simply not enough police officers to give stalking victims 24-hour protection. Also, these stalkers, even though appearing homicidal, have often not yet broken any laws that would allow the police to take them into custody. And even if the stalkers have broken laws, the violations are many times not serious enough to allow the court to hold them without bond. So often the police can be of little or no help. Instead, the solution to these deadly stalking situations rests with the victims.

The first solution possible for stalking victims who believe the stalker very likely will kill them if they don't take some kind of action is to attempt to disappear and establish a new identity. "I often tell my clients who aren't public figures to move, to change their phone numbers, to change their jobs," said security expert Gavin DeBecker.[225]

Of course, to make the above solution workable, stalking victims will have to discard everything connected with their past identities. Otherwise, stalkers can simply track them down in their new identities through family, friends, acquaintances, hobbies, interests, vocations (particularly if the victims have a job that required considerable schooling and therefore cannot change occupations without taking a huge pay cut), and anything else that ties the victims to their past life. If considering this solution, victims should remember what private investigator Leigh Hearon said in Chapter 14: that it is extraordinarily difficult to disappear and not leave a trace behind.

Still, some victims of stalking feel so threatened and vulnerable that they believe the only way to assure their safety is to completely erase their present life and start a new life somewhere else. Actually, for the worst cases of stalking this is a dream of many of the victims: to be able to just disappear and leave the stalker and the terror behind.

Although this may sound like a good idea to stalking victims, who have sometimes suffered through years of terror, in most cases it isn't practical. It is a daydream, like winning the lottery, of how great things could be. But how many people have jobs they can just give up without taking a tremendous pay cut? How many people are willing to give up forever all of the things they love and enjoy about their present life? How many people are willing to never again have any contact with family members and friends? How many people are willing to uproot their children from their friends and surroundings and make them start new lives?

If you aren't willing to do all of this, you are probably just going to make the situation worse, because if you don't completely change everything, a stalker can very likely find you again, and then all you have done, with all of the accompanying expense, has been for nothing. In addition, attempting to establish a new identity can be dangerous because once victims feel that they have successfully disappeared, they often let their caution down a bit, which can be extremely dangerous. The most determined stalkers will use every means possible to find you in your new identity. Stalkers have been known to travel thousands of miles and spend thousands of dollars in pursuit of their victims, and the smallest slip-up in your new identity can undo it all.

Also, when using the solution of changing identities, victims must worry about chance meetings. The book *The Most Wanted Man In America* tells the story of fugitive John William Clouser, who was on the FBI's Ten Most Wanted List for over 10 years. He managed to successfully elude capture for over a decade by totally discarding his old life and creating a completely new identity, with a new name, new Social Security number, new identification, new job, and new friends. Despite his thoroughness in designing his new life, and living thousands of miles away from his old home, one day he came ever so close to running into an old acquaintance. Fortunately for Clouser, he saw the acquaintance before the acquaintance saw him, but still these chance meetings do and will happen, and then suddenly all of the work and expense of creating a new identity goes for nothing.[226]

Victims who attempt this solution must also worry about coincidences. Recall from Chapter 13 how stalker Larry Stagner found his vanished stalking victim, Kathleen Baty, when he was coincidentally sent to deliver a pizza to her new, and up to that moment secret, address.

A real problem, therefore, with the idea of attempting to drop out of sight and create a new identity is that stalking victims who decide on this solution are still forced to look over their shoulders for the rest of their lives. They must always live with the fear that the stalkers have found some trace they left behind.

An article in *The New Yorker* tells of a woman who gave up an excellent career in retail and attempted to hide from her stalker by changing her address, telephone number, and so on. "Fearful that John will discover her, [Mary] never returned to the retail field. To this day, before she leaves the house she looks out the windows to see if John is waiting outside and watching for her." Is this the kind of life you want to live until either you or the stalker dies?[227]

A much better, and safer, solution is having the stalker incarcerated. This is not a permanent solution—stalking only stops definitely and permanently when the stalker dies—but it is the safest, and will give victims freedom during the time of the incarceration. An article in *Essence* magazine said, "The first step in keeping a stalker at bay is often the woman's [or man's] decision to prosecute."[228] Michael Lindsey, in *The Terror of Batterer Stalking*, says, "The only method of controlling these individuals is jail."[229] I agree totally. Only when stalkers are put in jail, prison, or a mental facility can the victims rest and feel secure. Only then can stalking victims really feel safe, and not have to constantly worry that the stalkers are hiding nearby and about to strike. Only then do stalking victims not have to worry whenever they hear a noise at night, or fear to go into their house because of the possibility that the stalkers are hiding inside.

Stalking victim Kathleen Baty, in an incident discussed in Chapter 13, said, "Each year that Larry Stagner is in custody is another year that I can live normally without fear."[230] Stalking victim Kathy Gerardi, in another incident related in Chapter 13, forged threatening letters from her stalker in an effort to get him put back into jail so that she would feel safe. A victim of serial stalker David DeGennaro, in an incident discussed in Chapter 11, said, "The only time I felt safe was when he was put away."[231]

These victims have found that using the law to incarcerate stalkers is the best solution to stalking. They have found that the only time a victim can truly feel safe is when the stalker has been sentenced to a jail, prison, or mental facility. However, after deciding to use this solution, don't expect the police to just step in, take over your case, gather the evidence, and arrest the stalker. Most police departments don't have that kind of manpower.

"We treat victims as clients," said Lt. John Lane of the Los Angeles Police Department's Threat Management Unit. "This is their problem. They will get help in managing their problem. But it's unrealistic to expect that life will improve just by filing a police report."[232]

Part of what Lieutenant Lane is saying is that as a victim of stalking you'll have to do much of the case building and evidence collecting yourself. If you want the stalker incarcerated, you'll have to be willing to do a bit of work. However, as demonstrated in the two incidents below, it can pay off.

A woman in Pembroke, Massachusetts, had been stalked for years by a man who made obscene and threatening telephone calls to her. She finally decided to do some detective work to bring the stalking to an end. First, she signed up for Caller ID service and had the telephone company install a second telephone line into her house. Following this, she spent several days driving around and compiling the addresses and telephone numbers of all of the pay phones near where she lived.

Her hard work paid off when the stalker called her again. The number, she discovered from her Caller ID, came from a pay phone in nearby Hanover, Massachusetts. While the stalker talked, the woman called the police on her second line. The stalker was still talking with the victim over the pay phone when the police arrived and arrested him.

In another incident, this one in Bradenton, Florida, a court sentenced Joey Alexander to 2 years in prison for harassing his former girlfriend, Robyn Runyon. After they broke up, Joey reportedly telephoned Robyn hundreds of times, one time threatening her and the next time apologizing and begging her to take him back. Robyn saved the tapes of his calls on her answering machine. The prosecutor said these tapes made the difference in her case.

"Many cases are never prosecuted for lack of evidence," said Bradenton Assistant State Attorney Paul Hudson. "Stalking situations often involve the victim's word against the suspect's and little evidence." He goes on to say, "The main thing is to call the police when things happen and to document everything. The fact that [victims] didn't call the police will sometimes be used against them later in court."[233]

To help in obtaining a conviction against stalkers, Hudson also encourages stalking victims to keep a log of the stalkers' telephone calls, and of any encounters with the stalkers, including dates, times, and witnesses to the encounters. In addition, save all answering machine tapes, and notes and letters from the stalker.

"People who think they're being stalked should call the police, file a restraining order, and keep copies of everything they have been sent," said Sergeant Ray Raimondi of the Pembroke Pines (Florida) Police Department. "The messages on an answering machine, faxes, letters, and even computer E-mail messages are all important to build a case."[234]

To make an arrest for stalking, police officers must have probable cause, or evidence, that the crime actually occurred, and stalking victims must often supply this. This is not that difficult, though, because, by the very nature of the crime, stalkers leave a considerable amount of evidence behind, such as messages on answering machines, threatening letters, confrontations when other people are present, and the like. Save and document everything for the police. To help build the case against their stalkers, victims should take pictures of any vandalism. In addition, victims should always keep an Instamatic-type camera or video camera handy and photograph the stalkers if they follow them or stake out their home. But very important, victims should handle anything received from stalkers carefully so as not to smear fingerprints, which can help prove later in court who was doing the stalking. However, don't do as police detectives on television and in the movies do: pick up items with a handkerchief. This is a Hollywood invention. Police officers don't really do that. This will smear fingerprints just as easily as using your bare hands will. Pick up papers by the corners and objects by rough parts that likely couldn't contain fingerprints anyway. Put everything received in clear plastic bags.

"Most people don't realize it because they feel so helpless and vulnerable, but the letters and phone calls that come in the early stages of stalking are now a criminal offense," said Linda Fairstein, head of the Manhattan District Attorney's Prosecution Unit. "Keep the tapes of the messages. Save the letters. Stalking generally escalates from there, and usually, it gets worse."[235]

Once the police do arrest a stalker, don't be afraid to talk to the prosecutor handling the case about requesting a high bond. Judges will often do this if it can be shown that the person would be a danger to the community if released. If you are in serious fear of the stalker, ask the prosecutor about any protection programs your community may have. As discussed in the next chapter, some communities utilize alarm bracelets, loan cellular phones, and have other safety programs.

Also, make the prosecutor's office aware of how serious you consider the stalking, and that you are willing to do whatever it takes to obtain a conviction. Ask the prosecutor handling your case what information or evidence is needed to get a conviction, and then help obtain it. A prosecutor's office that feels they have a victim who will stick with the case is much more willing to be aggressive in their prosecution.

However, readers may ask, what if no matter what you've done, from obtaining a restraining order to having the stalker arrested, he or she gets out on bail and appears now to be more dangerous than ever? What if after taking all of the steps I've advised so far the stalker becomes even more obsessed and progressively more violent, so much so that you know the next step could very possibly be your murder? What can you do?

First, don't even think about dropping the charges. This will not dampen the stalker's obsession and fixation with you. Actually, it will likely increase the obsession because it shows the stalker that when you are scared enough you can be manipulated. The only real solution to stalking is having the stalker incarcerated. So, until a court sentences the stalker to a correctional facility or mental hospital, you must begin practicing strict personal safety measures. These will reduce the chances that the stalker will be able to confront and intimidate or assault you.

Being safe means being prepared. Stalking victims who fear assault or murder should always be ready to escape to safety from anywhere they might be. No matter where you are, know all of the exits and other ways out. Also, know the stores that are open all night in your neighborhood, and know the location of the nearest police station or firehouse, places where you can seek safety from the stalker if necessary. And though not always foolproof, try not to go out alone.

To help you practice these safety measures, the next time you run into a police officer take a few moments to watch him or her without the officer knowing it. Watch as the officer enters a room or approaches a car, how his or her eyes scan everyone in the room or car, looking for things most individuals wouldn't notice, such as threatening postures, people with their hands not visible, or anything that appears out of the ordinary and unusual. Police officers do this almost unconsciously, and as a stalking victim you should too. Every place you enter you should automatically determine who is there, whether or not there is any danger to you, and all of the ways out.

Stalking victims who feel they are in serious danger of assault or murder should also put together an "escape kit" to keep in their car. This escape kit should contain items you will need in the event you have to flee your home quickly or find you can't return there. In this kit, besides the normal items a person would need who has to spend an evening or two away from home, such as toiletries and a change of clothing, should be money or credit cards, some identification, copies of any restraining orders and police reports, any necessary medications, and a spare set of keys. Along with the escape kit, you naturally must have a place to go, and this place should have already been decided.

Having an escape kit and a plan of where to go makes a person feel less vulnerable and helpless. With this advance planning a person is prepared and doesn't flee the house frazzled and bewildered, but with a purpose. You might also want to consider installing a "safe room" in your home. This is a room you can flee to if threatened, a room with a solid, preferably metal, door and frame that will take some time to force open. This will delay an intruder's entry long enough to give you time to escape the house or summon help. I discuss this concept in depth in my book *Protecting Your Life, Home, and Property* (Plenum, 1995).

A few other safety measures you should practice include varying the route to your job, and using a different grocery store and mall. Don't be predictable in anything you do. But most important of all, **every stalking victim should have and always carry a cellular telephone.** This can be an invaluable aid if, for example, you have a restraining order and your stalker follows you. Using it, you can call the police and keep them advised of the stalker's location. It can also be invaluable if the stalker attempts to stop your car or run you off the road (a very common occurrence). However, keep in mind that you must always know your exact location in case you suddenly need to call for help. In addition, a cellular telephone can be life-saving if the stalker breaks into your home and cuts off your regular telephone service by severing the wires or simply removing a telephone receiver from the cradle.

I realize that some victims might complain they cannot afford a cellular phone. I recently saw an advertisement for a cellular telephone meant to be used only in emergency situations (such as calling the police, the paramedics, or the auto club) that can be leased at substantially lower rates than regular cellular telephones. In cases, however, in which victims feel that even this would still be cost prohibitive, check with the local victim assistance organization to see if there is an agency in your community that will loan stalking victims a cellular telephone. If not, measure the expense of a cellular telephone against that of being seriously injured or murdered, a real possibility with the truly obsessed stalkers. How important is the cost then?

At this point in a stalking situation, when officers have arrested the stalker, but the case hasn't been heard in court yet and the stalker is free on bail, the police may be of some help in protecting you, but you simply cannot depend totally on them because they can't be everywhere with you, whereas the stalker may be. For many stalkers, their obsession is their life. There is nothing else. If these stalkers have reached the point in their obsession where they feel the only way they are ever going to have a relationship with you is to kill both you and themselves so that the two of you can be together forever in the hereafter (an amazingly common delusional thought with the most desperate stalkers), or, just as dangerous, they are willing to give up their freedom or life to kill you because they feel you have wronged them, you must immediately take the safety measures discussed above. Don't hesitate or put them off. Delays can mean disaster, as the following incident sadly shows.

➤   ➤   ➤   ➤

Friends say that Ann Weiland quietly suffered through an abusive marriage for 27 years. But then on a frigid day in January 1993 she finally fled from her home in La Crescent, Minnesota, and drove across the Mississippi River to her sister's house in La Crosse, Wisconsin. Although staying there for a while, Ann didn't want to endanger her sister, so she soon moved into a women's shelter. She also filed for divorce from her husband, Robert Weiland, and obtained restraining orders against him in both Minnesota and Wisconsin.

Interestingly, Robert had no police record in the first 52 years of his life, until Ann left him. After this he quickly racked up 13 arrests for violating restraining orders and bail jumping. Once, after the couple had separated, Robert allegedly broke into where Ann was staying and hid with a shotgun under the bed, waiting for her to return. Fortunately, Ann was out of town and the police came instead, arresting Robert.

Robert also reportedly called his wife over and over at the bank where she worked, and followed her in his car. He even drove around and around the women's shelter Ann stayed in, despite the fact that she had a restraining order against him.

"He had a total disregard for consequences," said a Wisconsin County Attorney.[236]

The police eventually arrested Robert for his harassment of Ann, and he pled guilty to violating the restraining order in Wisconsin. Because of aggressive action by the La Crosse County Attorney's Office, Robert received a 9-month jail sentence. However, this had little effect on him. He called Ann repeatedly from jail.

In September 1993, Ann met Burton Simon, and eventually they decided to get married. However, during this time, Robert had disappeared while on a jail furlough.

In March 1994, Ann and Burton applied for their marriage license. They planned, after their marriage, to move far away from Robert and his stalking of them. However, on the evening after obtaining their marriage license, as Burton pulled into his driveway with Ann in the car, Robert lay in wait for them. He fired six shots into Ann, one of them passing through her and into Burton. As Robert was reloading, Burton, even though seriously injured and in intense pain, floored the accelerator and rammed the car into Robert, who then fled the scene.

Nine hours later, when the police stopped Robert's car, he used the same gun to kill himself. Ann also died of the gunshot wounds.

The point of the incident above is that time is crucial. If you are being stalked, you must do something **right now!** Although Ann and Burton had planned to move out of the Midwest after their wedding, they waited too long. A stalker often makes it his or her life's work to stalk you. While you are busy thinking about taking some sort of action, the stalker is likely busy planning how to take control of your life, or maybe how to just take your life.

Victims must take immediate action, but they must also take every precaution possible because, until the stalker dies or is securely locked away, victims can never feel that they have a foolproof plan of safety. If you don't take every possible precaution, you must be prepared for the stalker to suddenly and violently crash back into your life, as the following incident dramatically illustrates.

Lisa Woodfin and Paul "Rusty" Smith had to elope in May 1987 because Lisa's family didn't approve of the marriage. Six years later, Lisa filed for divorce, claiming physical cruelty. In her divorce petition, Lisa said she feared for her life because her husband had both beaten her severely and pointed a gun at her.

Rusty, though, wouldn't be gotten rid of that easily. After their separation, he began stalking Lisa. Knowing only too well just how dangerous Rusty was, Lisa moved and got an unlisted telephone number.

However, on 9 July 1993, while Lisa shopped with a friend at a mall in Spartanburg, South Carolina, Rusty caught up with her. Lisa and her friend fled for their lives when they spotted Rusty, who yelled, "Where are you going to run to now, Lisa? Where are you going to run to now?" He shot both Lisa and her friend.

Lisa fell fatally wounded to the concrete parking lot. Her friend, shot in the face, also fell to the hot concrete. The friend, though, only injured, held her breath and played dead. When she heard a car door slam and then tires squealing out of the parking lot, she got up and ran into a nearby store for help.

"It sounded like someone was beating a hammer on the concrete," said one of the mall employees. "Then a woman came running in screaming for us to call the police, that someone had just killed her best friend and tried to kill her."[237]

Twenty miles from the mall, Rusty stopped at a pay phone. He called 911 and told the dispatcher he had just killed his ex-wife. Rusty also told the dispatcher that he would be waiting for the police at his home. Officers arrested Rusty and charged him with murder and assault and battery with intent to kill.

In the incident above, Lisa had taken several important precautions in an attempt to ensure her safety from Rusty. She had moved and obtained an unlisted telephone number. However, with many stalkers, especially the most deeply obsessed ones, this is not enough. Victims must do more. They must take **every** precaution possible, because if these stalkers cannot find out where you live, and cannot contact you on the telephone, they seldom just give up. Instead, they begin looking for you in other places they believe you will be, such as at a friend's or relative's home, at a health club you belong to, at your favorite restaurant, or, as in the incident above, where you shop. Don't be predictable, as Lisa was.

With the most obsessed stalkers, if you want to be as safe as possible until they are securely incarcerated, you can no longer go where you used to go. You can no longer go to your favorite ice cream store, your favorite movie theater, or your favorite mall. Until the stalker is securely locked away, you must change the complete pattern of your life. You can do nothing that is predictable.

Is this fair? Is it fair to make victims who may have done nothing more than become involved with the wrong people, or maybe as little as just come to the attention of the wrong people, give up all of the things in life they love and enjoy? Is it fair that their lives should be so totally disrupted?

Of course it's not fair. But the alternative is often a grisly murder. Stalkers are many times sick, totally possessed individuals, who, like Rusty in the incident above, are willing to see their own lives destroyed just to carry out their obsession. The United States, as a free country, does not have a mechanism for locking away these people until a court has found them guilty of a crime or has found that they are mentally ill and a danger to society. Consequently, this can be a truly frightening time for stalking victims.

Sometimes stalking victims become so frightened and terrorized that they consider carrying guns, knifes, chemical sprays, or electrical shocking devices for protection. Victims may consider signing up for self-defense courses with the hope that, if necessary, they will be able to successfully defend themselves against their stalkers.

There are a number of important things stalking victims need to know about self-protection and the carrying of weapons. First, carrying a weapon is useless if a stalker surprises you. Having a gun, knife, pepper spray, or electrical shocking device is of no value if the self-defense weapon is not out and ready to use. Also, firearms in particular can often be more dangerous to the owner than a stalker. A study done in King County (Seattle), Washington, for example, found that a gun kept in the home was 18 times more likely to be used against a family member than an intruder. As for chemical sprays and electrical shocking devices, these are not as effective as the manufacturers would want you to believe they are. For the electrical shocking devices to work they must be held against bare skin for several seconds, which is extremely difficult to do with a moving, struggling adult. Even police pepper sprays, which are stronger than those that can be purchased by the public, are not effective all of the time. They often have no effect at all on mentally disturbed people or individuals high on drugs. As for karate, judo, and other means of self-defense, these are also not as useful as they might seem. When I went through the Police Academy they taught us a number of these self-defense tactics. However, when I got out onto the street and tried to use them, I found that most didn't work nearly as well as they did in class, where my self-defense partner didn't jump around and fight back.

In addition, just carrying a weapon is not enough. You must be willing to use it. You must be willing to kill the stalker if necessary. Therefore, before considering buying and carrying a weapon, make the decision of whether you could use it or not, and if so, then obtain it legally and seek training in its use. Otherwise, you are just presenting the stalker with a weapon that can be taken away and used against you. Don't believe this won't occur because every year it happens even to people highly trained in the use of weapons. Between 1983 and 1992, 16 percent of the police officers in the United States killed by handguns were killed with their own gun that had been taken away from them or by a handgun taken away from another police officer. The victim in the following incident discovered just how dangerous carrying a weapon can be.

➤ ➤ ➤ ➤

Cathy Carlson, with good reason, felt an intense fear of her ex-boy-friend, Larry Langill. Because of this fear, she had moved to a new home, gotten a different telephone number, obtained a restraining order against him, and began carrying a knife for protection. Larry, however, knew where Cathy worked. On the evening of 16 April 1994, fearing that Larry might be waiting for her in the parking lot of the Cracker Barrel restaurant in Miami, where she worked, Cathy had police officers escort her to her car.

On the morning of 17 April 1994, an employee at a convenience store near the Cracker Barrel restaurant reported to the police that a suspicious man was sitting in their parking lot. The police responded to the call and found Larry sitting in his car. The officers checked on him, but the only thing they found was that he had a suspended driver's license. Restraining orders, unfortunately, didn't show up at that time on the police department's computer. Because Larry had parked his car and was not driving, there was nothing the officers could do. Although they watched Larry for a while to see if he would drive away, he instead walked over to the nearby Waffle House restaurant for breakfast. The officers left.

An hour later, an urgent call brought the officers back. They found Cathy, who had come to open the Cracker Barrel restaurant, dead, stabbed seven times in the chest with the knife she carried for protection. The police arrested and charged Larry with first-degree murder and aggravated stalking.

"I knew he was going to do it," said a friend of Cathy's. "He was violent and scary-looking all the time."

When asked by the police about Cathy, Larry reportedly said, "She broke my heart."[238]

Although I don't believe most victims of stalking should carry weapons in the belief that they will stop stalkers (as these weapons can be more dangerous to them than the stalkers), or try to stop their stalkers through violence, I will admit this has worked for some people. Even though I won't recommend it because of the dangers involved, I will show a couple of examples of how violence, or the threat of violence, has worked for some stalking victims.

In an article in *Ladies' Home Journal*, author Linda Stasi tells of her 2 years of terror while being stalked by a neighbor. Nothing she did could make the stalker quit and go away. Finally, in frustration and desperation, she went to a man whom she described as a "tough guy," and told him her problem. The next day he called her and said, "I explained a couple things to our neighbor. He won't bother you again."

And he didn't. The author said that afterward she accidentally ran into the ex-stalker in a store. When the man saw her he ran away from her as fast as he could.[239]

In another incident, this one in Miami, Florida, a 31-year-old ex-felon began calling a family's 13-year-old daughter and telling her of the sexually explicit dreams he was having about her. Out of desperation when other means wouldn't stop the stalker, the father borrowed a shotgun from a friend.

"I took the shotgun, and I was ready to use it," the father said. "I got out in front of my house and stood there. He jumped into his car and ran over my lawn and all of my bushes. But I never heard from him again."[240]

Even though proving successful in the few cases above, I don't recommend that stalking victims use weapons and violence because these methods pose extreme danger to the victims. Vigorously pursuing criminal prosecution is the safer, and more effective, method of stopping stalkers. The victims below, by using this solution, have been able to once more sleep soundly and leave their homes without fear, knowing that their tormentors are safely locked away.

In March 1997, a judge in Florida sentenced a man to 6 years in prison after convicting him of stalking a former girlfriend. Although the victim had obtained a protective order, the stalker ignored it, showing up constantly at the victim's job, hiding in some bushes near her home, throwing rocks at her, and trying to bribe her friends into giving him the victim's new address after she had moved to escape him.

In another case, Porter County (Indiana) Judge Roger Bradford sentenced 35-year-old Dillard Landis to 12 years in prison after a jury convicted him of stalking. For some time, Landis had been relentlessly pursuing a woman who wanted nothing to do with him. Even though a court issued an order for Landis to stay away from the woman, witnesses told the jury they saw Landis walking and driving around her home.

An Orange County (California) woman, after being convicted of stalking a man who had spurned her romantic advances, received a 4-year prison sentence. The stalker had threatened to burn down the man's house and snatch his young son. She also had the victim's telephone number changed and his electricity shut off without his knowledge.

In Media, Pennsylvania, a man pled guilty to stalking a 10-year-old girl. Testimony heard during the trial revealed that the stalker, while following the young victim in his car, made sexual remarks to her. The judge sentenced the stalker to a prison sentence of 3 to 10 years.

A man convicted of stalking a 16-year-old Pennsylvania girl received a prison term of 44 to 60 months. The stalker, after seeing the victim in a sportswear store, traced the license plate number of her car to an automobile leasing company. The stalker then broke into the leasing company office to obtain personal information about the victim from the lease agreement.

In Santa Ana, California, a man sent his former girlfriend dozens of letters and telephoned her hundreds of times after their breakup. He also punctured her tires and followed her in violation of a court order. When the stalker's attorney told the court that he felt the 4-year prison term imposed was too harsh because the stalker had done no physical harm to the victim, the judge responded, "There is a small step from piercing tires to piercing skin."[241]

A judge in Orange County, California, sentenced a man to 15 years of probation after convicting him of stalking a former girlfriend. Along with following her, the stalker broke into the victim's house and smashed out her car windows. While on probation, the stalker once again showed up at the former girlfriend's house, where the police arrested him. The same judge then sentenced the stalker to 35 years in prison.

Regardless of whatever method stalking victims use to protect themselves, however, through all of the upheaval that stalking brings to a person's life, one of the most important things victims need is the emotional support of both family members and friends. Being stalked is a terrifying experience and victims need to know that they have people who care and understand, and people who will help them. Often, however, family members and friends offer little support because, particularly in the early stages of stalking, they may believe the victim is overreacting to what appears to them to be only a lovesick suitor. Of course, later on these family members and friends are often horrified by the lengths the stalker has gone to, and may eventually be supportive. But a victim needs support from the beginning. If you know someone being stalked you can be a true friend by providing emotional support from the start. Don't minimize the situation or say the person must be imagining it. Be there when the victim needs you.

Another serious problem often encountered when stalking victims look for emotional support is that family members and friends who care about them find they are helpless to do anything to stop the stalking. They discover that attempting to persuade the stalker to stop, and even threatening the stalker, many times has no effect. Because of this feeling of helplessness, those individuals whose support the stalking victims need most may begin avoiding them. Avoidance is easier than feeling powerless and impotent. In this case, victims may want to join a group of other stalking victims to get the emotional support they need.

There are a number of groups who act as emotional support to stalking victims. The largest one is probably Survivors of Stalking, which I will talk more about in the next chapter. Victims can also contact their local victims assistance organization (usually affiliated with the local police department or prosecutor's office) for the names of any support groups in their area.

To stop the crime of stalking in our country, victims must first realize they are not powerless. For truly obsessed stalkers, the only thing that will stop them is incarceration. Fortunately, there are laws now in every state that can do this. Victims who have the knowledge of how to use these laws also have the power to free themselves from the nightmare of stalking. By being aware of the stalking law in your state, and working with the police and prosecutor, you can stop even the most obsessed stalker.

WHAT CAN SOCIETY DO?

"Somewhere, somehow out there in the system or in our city, there is a way to stop this from happening, either him or myself or someone else ending up dead," said Garcia Garrett, a victim stalked by her estranged husband, Darrell Wayne Garrett, who she insists "will kill me, or he will kill both of us, or he will kill himself."

Garcia speaks with the frustration felt by many stalking victims who for years found that the American criminal justice system simply did not have an answer for their problem. Our criminal justice system, as detailed in Chapter 15, often didn't treat stalking as a crime, but rather as a private matter, particularly if it involved a couple engaged in, or previously engaged in, an intimate relationship. Victims found that, at most, the criminal justice system treated stalking as a nuisance offense, seldom meriting serious punishment. But far too often, as we have seen, stalking incidents left unpunished and allowed to follow their own natural course end in violence and death.

From 1989 to 1995, police records show that Darrell Garrett amassed 18 charges in Kentucky stemming from his alleged harassment and threatening of four women, including Garcia. For all of these charges Darrell spent a total of only 130 days in jail (and much of this time on an unrelated shoplifting charge) and paid only $429 in fines, hardly fitting punishment considering the misery he put the four women through. Even though ordered by several judges to stay away from each of the four women, Darrell regularly violated these orders. The charges kept piling up, but the criminal justice system did little to stop Darrell.

On 1 August 1989, a woman who had had two children by Darrell filed a complaint and the police arrested him for harassment, criminal trespassing, menacing, and theft by unlawful taking under $100. Darrell paid $80 and the court dismissed the charges.

On 18 April 1991, another woman who had had a child by Darrell likewise filed charges for harassment. She claimed Darrell harassed her by calling her over and over at work and by following her. The court dismissed the charges, but with the stipulation that Darrell cause no more problems for the woman.

On 3 May 1992, the police took Darrell into emergency detention when he threatened suicide after a fight with Garcia. Garcia also told the police that Darrell threatened to kill her and her children.

On 10 June 1992, the police charged Darrell with terroristic threatening. He told Lexington, Kentucky, police officers he was going to kill his wife.

On 27 June 1992, the police arrested Darrell for threatening Garcia's children. They charged him with terroristic threatening and harassing communication. The police also added another charge, third-degree trespassing, because Darrell refused to leave Garcia's home. For all of the offenses committed during June 1992 Darrell spent only 9 days in jail and paid $132 in fines.

On 5 August 1992, the police arrested and charged Darrell with stalking Garcia, the first use with Darrell of Kentucky's newly passed antistalking law. Garcia told the police that Darrell had been chasing her, and that she feared he was going to kill her. Darrell, possibly because of the light-handed treatment he'd received from the criminal justice system, assaulted Garcia in the presence of the police, who then, along with charging him with contempt of court for violating a court order to stay away from Garcia, additionally charged Darrell with the assault. A judge sentenced Darrell to 30 days in jail for the incident.

On 7 November 1993, Darrell once again assaulted Garcia. "He threw me up against the closet door, up against a table, and up against the bunk beds," Garcia said. "He threw me down on the floor and started strangling me. He strangled me harder and harder. I couldn't breathe. When I finally came to my senses, he wasn't on top of me any more. He pulled out a little measuring cup. It had Clorox in it. He threw it all over me."[242]

Following this attack, the police arrested Darrell and charged him with fourth-degree assault and second-degree wanton endangerment. For this incident Darrell spent several weeks in jail before being transferred to a mental hospital. After Darrell had spent a short time in the hospital, though, hospital personnel released him without informing the police of what they were doing. Within a few days of Darrell's release from the hospital, the police again arrested him, this time for third-degree criminal trespass involving another woman he was allegedly harassing.

Fortunately, this story doesn't end as many other stalking stories do, with the stalkers going free or being put on probation, which they usually ignore, and the victims once more being forced to live in fear as the stalkers resume their activities with even more vigor. This case instead shows how the criminal justice system should, but unfortunately seldom does, work for stalking victims. Assistant County Attorney Kathy Stein persuaded the court that, in view of Darrell's past actions, the charges against him should be increased to felony level. The judge agreed, and increased Darrell's bond. He now faces up to 20 years in prison if convicted. It is a shame it took the criminal justice system so long to recognize the danger of stalkers like Darrell.

"It was the belief of everyone that the [original] charges were not appropriate," said Fayette County (Kentucky) Attorney Margaret Kannen-sohn.[243] She noted that since 1989 Darrell has faced 26 misdemeanor charges, 18 of which related to women he stalked. For added security, as Darrell had assaulted Garcia in the past, even in the presence of police officers, Captain Kathy Whitt, head of the Fayette County Sheriff's Department's domestic violence unit, escorted Garcia to court.

The above incident illustrates one of the most important things that society can do to stop stalking. Society must begin to see stalking as the serious crime it is. In particular, we must stop thinking of stalking as simply a nuisance or the act of a lovesick individual. Stalking is a crime, a dangerous crime committed by a disturbed person. It is a crime that, after forcing its victims to live in fear and terror for months or even years, many times ends in disaster.

This change of outlook about stalking won't come, however, without education. For society to have a much more realistic viewpoint about stalking, a nationwide educational campaign must be mounted. The campaign should aim at enlightening the public about what stalking really is, the kind of people stalkers actually are, how dangerous stalking can be, and the detrimental effects it can have, both physically and psychologically, on its victims.

A national educational program of this type and scope is certainly not without precedent. In the last decade there have been a number of campaigns aimed at showing the public the real threat of what were once considered "socially acceptable" crimes. For example, an aggressive, well-delivered campaign has for the last few years been trying to show the public that driving while intoxicated is not just a peccadillo that everyone commits now and then, but a serious, and often fatal, crime. A number of the campaign advertisements have shown the carnage of smashed vehicles and mangled bodies at wrecks caused by intoxicated drivers. Other advertisements have shown the burials of victims killed by intoxicated drivers and the families devastated by it. Just recently, a number of organizations that deal with domestic violence have also been running prime-time television advertisements meant to educate the public about the truth concerning domestic violence. Using the slogan, "There is no excuse," these advertisements are designed to make the public aware that domestic violence is not acceptable behavior, but a crime that wrecks families, psychologically damages children, and can result in serious injuries, even death. This same type of educational program needs to be developed about stalking. The public must be made aware of what stalking really is, and that it is not acceptable behavior, but a crime.

Of course, old stereotypes are hard to break, but through education the general public can be made to see that a stalker isn't just some overzealous suitor, or a lovesick former intimate partner who wants his or her partner back, but a dangerous criminal with dysfunctional personality traits or occasionally severe mental problems that can lead to injury and death. One of the major benefits of this public education would become apparent when selections are made for juries. This is important because juries must see stalkers for what they really are: criminals.

Attorneys defending stalkers often attempt to portray their clients not as criminals, but simply as lovesick individuals who have perhaps pursued too hard. This can many times work on jurors who recall times in their own past when they pursued someone ardently, and were heartbroken when they didn't win the person. However, through the public education suggested above, jurors will understand the difference between their own experience and stalking. Jurors will realize that pursuing another person doesn't involve 100 telephone calls a night, sitting evening after evening outside the person's home, and it certainly doesn't involve vandalism, assault, and threats of death. But only through education can we make the public aware of the stark reality of stalking.

This public education is a vital, realistic concern, because, in the Madonna stalker case discussed in Chapter 7, a female member of the jury that convicted Madonna's stalker said afterward that the deliberations took so long because the women on the jury had to convince the men that the crime Mr. Hoskins committed was stalking, not simply trespassing. According to her, the men had trouble understanding that Mr. Hoskins did not come onto Madonna's property just to be there, but rather to terrorize her.

Making the public aware of the reality of stalking is not enough, however. The public must then insist that the police and other members of the criminal justice system also think of, and treat, stalking for what it is. Unfortunately, this hasn't always been the case. In the past, many police departments took the stance that until a stalker physically assaulted a victim they wouldn't get involved. This is unacceptable.

Much of stalking involves psychological manipulation meant to intimidate and terrorize victims. The constant following, the threatening messages, the minor vandalism are all meant to frighten victims and make them easier to control. The police must become involved during these early stages of stalking, before any violence occurs.

All citizens must be able to depend on the police to defend and protect them. The public must insist that the police not be allowed to ignore any pleas for help from stalking victims simply because nothing serious has yet occurred. As shown in the following incident, police departments, by becoming aggressive, involved, and proactive, can stop stalkers and possibly prevent tragedies from happening.

After Neil Rosen had served 2 months of a 3-month sentence for stalking his ex-wife, correctional authorities released him from the Broward County (Florida) jail. Twelve hours later, because of heads-up, alert work by a unit of the local police department, officers put Rosen back in jail, charged with once more stalking his ex-wife, and they did this without injuries to anyone. The police, suspecting that the 2 months in jail hadn't dampened Rosen's obsession, decided to keep an eye on him after his release.

"We wanted to take proactive action rather than sit back and wait until he started stalking her again," said Sergeant Charles Drago of the Fort Lauderdale Police Department.

Soon after the authorities released Rosen from jail, his ex-wife began receiving hang-up calls. Her Caller ID service showed that the calls came from telephones in the same area where Rosen was at the time.

Later that day, Rosen drove to his ex-wife's apartment, in violation of his probation. Apparently unaware that officers of Fort Lauderdale's antistalking unit were following him, Rosen parked his vehicle behind his ex-wife's car, blocking it in, and then headed for her apartment. The police arrested him soon afterward.

"He seemed stunned that we were there," Sergeant Drago said.[244]

Every major police department in the United States needs, as in the incident above, a unit formed specifically to deal with stalkers. In July 1990, following the Rebecca Schaeffer murder discussed in Chapter 7, the Los Angeles Police Department formed the Threat Management Unit, the first unit in a major U.S. police department formed specifically to deal with stalkers. The few other units now operating in other police departments around the United States have modeled themselves after the Threat Management Unit. This Los Angeles unit has found that it is most successful when it deals with stalkers by both victim and suspect intervention. This means the police attempt to resolve a stalking case both by working with the victim and by intervening against the stalker.

Victim intervention by the Los Angeles Police Department's Threat Management Unit starts with education of the victims about stalkers and stalking. The members of the Threat Management Unit often find that victims, because of their lack of knowledge about stalkers and stalking, may unknowingly aggravate the situation, making it more dangerous than necessary. In their attempt to remedy the situation, stalking victims quite often try to verbally persuade the stalkers to leave them alone, a usually meaningless and occasionally dangerous act that may even increase a stalker's obsession because it shows the stalker that he or she has grabbed the attention of the victim and is now part of the victim's life. Also, victims many times don't see or react to the danger signals of stalking because they don't know what they are. The Threat Management Unit makes sure they do. This unit, besides educating the victims about stalkers, also makes the victims aware of the security measures they can take, both at home and at work, including changing phone numbers and residences. They also advise changing the time schedule of any regular activities the stalkers know about, such as jogging or walking the dog. The unit also provides the victims with information about the various support groups available in the community, and a number of self-defense courses victims can take.

Suspect intervention by the Los Angeles unit can include personal or telephone contact by a police detective with the stalker, which for low grade or early stalkers may often frighten them away. Intervention may also include arrest and detention of the suspect. Detectives have found that a few days behind bars can sometimes have a dramatic effect on stalkers who have never experienced the reality of incarceration. Of course, with others, those with deep obsessions or serious personality disorders or mental problems, this has little effect. In these cases, serious prosecution must follow.

A study completed in Los Angeles of an 18-month period found that aggressive intervention by the Threat Management Unit can be very effective in stopping stalkers. Researchers examined 102 cases, and in 57 of them found a total abstinence of stalking in the 6 months following the unit's intervention.

Fort Lauderdale, Florida, has established a unit similar to Los Angeles's Threat Management Unit. Called the Threat Abatement Group, this Fort Lauderdale unit also actively goes after stalkers. "They're going to stalk the stalkers until they get them in jail," said Charles Drago of the Fort Lauderdale Police Department.[245]

Although these two units are certainly commendable efforts, and have shown that active intervention by the police can stop some stalkers, it is not enough. Citizens in every community must demand that their police department institute a unit similar to the ones in Los Angeles and Fort Lauderdale. Units such as these, which are proactive rather than reactive, can save lives. Seriously obsessed stalkers must be kept under surveillance to prevent them from continuing their stalking. For any police department that argues that the manpower cost of this is prohibitive, I would pose the following question: If the police department knew there was a crazed terrorist loose in the community, would they keep him under surveillance? I can guarantee you they would. In the stalking incident at ESL, Inc. discussed in Chapter 12, seven innocent people died at the hands of a stalker, which shows that stalkers can be just as dangerous and unpredictable as crazed terrorists.

"To deal with the problem effectively, we've got to change attitudes in the criminal justice system and add some enforcement dollars," said Phil Gutis, spokesperson for the American Civil Liberties Union.[246]

To make such antistalking units work, however, police departments must be notified whenever a stalker is released from jail or prison. This means police departments and correctional personnel must share information regularly, which, as we shall see, they don't always do.

➤   ➤   ➤   ➤

On 6 December 1993, Louisville resident Mary Byron felt relatively safe from her former boyfriend, Donavan Harris, whom the police arrested 3 weeks earlier after he raped her at gunpoint on the basement floor of her parents' home. Mary knew the violence Donavan was capable of, and trembled whenever she thought of him, but she also knew the authorities had him safely locked away in jail on a high bond. The authorities had assured Mary they would notify her if he was released. Two days earlier, though, unknown to Mary, an unidentified woman posted Donavan's $25,000 bond. Unfortunately, the jail personnel who released Donavan didn't notify the police or the prosecutor of it, and no one notified Mary.

It was Mary's 21st birthday, and as she left her job at a local mall, her car filled with presents and balloons from co-workers, she found the parking lot teeming with holiday shoppers. Suddenly, Donavan, apparently unconcerned about all of the witnesses, and likely looking to Mary like some minion from hell, stepped in front of her automobile brandishing a gun. He shot her seven times in the head and body at close range as she sat in her car, killing her.

Almost 2 years later, a jury found Donavan guilty of both the murder and rape of Mary. The court sentenced him to 18 years on the rape charge, and life imprisonment on the murder charge, the sentences to be served consecutively.

➤   ➤   ➤   ➤

In response to this unnecessary death, the Jefferson County (Kentucky) Commonwealth Attorney's Office immediately announced they would institute a program of manually calling victims whenever jail personnel released their attackers. Although a worthy idea, this could only be done during regular business hours, Monday through Friday. But a person could be released from jail anytime day or night, and this program became only a stopgap measure. Jefferson County authorities knew they needed a more comprehensive program.

"We're going to crawl before we walk," said Jefferson County Commonwealth Attorney Mike Conliffe. "We know what we have in mind for business working hours, now we have to devise a plan for non-business working hours, i.e. weekends, holidays, and non-working nights."[247]

In December 1994, the Victim Information and Notification Everyday (VINE) program began in Jefferson County, Kentucky. "An inmate can be bailed out of jail at any hour of any day," said Jo Ann Phillips, director of victim advocacy for the Jefferson County Commonwealth Attorney's Office. "To provide the level of security offered by an automated system, someone would have to be on the phone to jail authorities at all times. There isn't enough time or money for that kind of staff commitment. The [VINE] system solves the problem by providing victims with a direct link to accurate inmate information."

The VINE program works through a computer that constantly monitors the jail's computer, and keeps track of the status of the jail's inmates. Whenever a change occurs in the status of one of the inmates, including a release from custody or a change of a court date, the computer automatically calls anyone registered with the VINE program and notifies them. The calls continue for 24 hours or until the person registered with the program enters a code.

Individuals registered with the VINE program are only required to give a telephone number, and no other personal information. Even the telephone number, though, is not retrievable from the system, and so anonymity is guaranteed. The VINE program makes most calls within 10 minutes of a change in status.

"I registered with VINE because I didn't want to be another Mary Byron," said a rape victim. "I wanted to be sure to know if he was out so that I wouldn't come home and find him hiding in my closet again."[248]

United States Attorney General Janet Reno has called the VINE program a model for the nation, and I certainly agree. Many stalkers, as shown by the incidents reported in this book, are not intimidated a bit by incarceration, and are many times very likely to continue their criminal activity, often intensified, once released from jail. For the highest level of personal safety, all stalking victims must know if their stalkers are securely locked away or out of jail. Stalking victims must know when to be extra vigilant. In 1996, Daviess County, Kentucky, also adopted the VINE program. VINE should serve as a model for every community in the United States.

Many times, stalking victims, wanting to forestall the chance of violence, will call police officers to the scene of stalking incidents that are still in the nonviolent or minor violence stage, expecting the officers to arrest the stalker. The victims are often disappointed in the police response, because if there are no restraining orders in effect and the officers do not witness the stalking, the police are usually powerless to do anything. In many states, stalking is a misdemeanor, and police officers must witness most misdemeanors in order to make an on-scene arrest. The stalkers, of course, when questioned by the police, will usually act as though they don't know what the victims are talking about, and if the stalkers haven't committed a felony, the police often can't do much. A number of states have solved this problem by giving police officers the authority to arrest in misdemeanor stalking cases, even if they don't witness the crime. Most states have already done this for misdemeanor drunken driving and misdemeanor domestic battery cases, and it appears to work well in the majority of incidents. All states should expand this authority to arrest for unwitnessed misdemeanors to include stalking.

Quite often, though, even when police officers become actively involved and arrest stalkers, victims find they are thrown into a confusing web when they have to deal with the many different prosecutors who handle their case at various levels of the prosecution. Often, at each stage of the prosecution, the arraignment, the pretrial motions, and the trial itself, a different prosecutor handles the case. When victims are shuffled from one prosecutor to another, each new one usually entirely unaware of what has transpired before his or her assignment to the case, the victims begin to feel that their prosecutor's office really has little empathy for them.

A number of communities have solved this problem through the use of a system called "vertical prosecution." This means that the prosecutor assigned to the case immediately after the arrest is the same prosecutor who handles the case entirely through the trial and sentencing. This not only makes for better court cases, as the assigned prosecutor becomes and remains intimately aware of all aspects of the case, but also makes the victims feel that the criminal justice system cares and is working for them.

To truly bring stalking under control, however, all segments of the criminal justice system must work together. Police officers must strenuously pursue and arrest stalkers, prosecutors must aggressively prosecute them, and judges must see and treat stalkers as the dangerous criminals they are.

Unfortunately, even when the police and the prosecutor's office do take stalking seriously, stalking victims often find that judges don't consider stalkers as dangerous. Consequently, they set low bonds for them or release them on their own recognizance, putting the stalkers back on the streets and doing little, if anything, to discourage their stalking.

In my own experience as a police officer I have seen far too many times how judges view stalkers as being minimally dangerous, and set their bail accordingly, then react with surprise when they find the stalkers arrested again, usually for a more serious offense. The judicial system needs to recognize that innocent people feel unprotected and unserved by their criminal justice system when stalkers are let out of jail because of low bonds or minimal sentencing.

"I don't care what you arrest for, it isn't necessarily going to result in a cessation of what's going on," said Lieutenant John Lane of the Los Angeles Police Department's Threat Management Unit. "It's got to be taken seriously by the judges, prosecutors, and the courts."[249]

Often, though, in the past this release of stalkers on a small bail came about because judges only had access to the local criminal record of stalkers, and didn't have access to the national criminal records. Consequently, judges often didn't know how dangerous the stalkers really were. Fortunately, Section 40601 of the Violence Against Women Act authorizes judges in stalking cases to now have access to the criminal and wanted person records from the national crime information databanks. However, even though now available, these are still not always used by judges. Communities should insist they are.

A factor further compromising the safety of stalking victims is that even when the police and prosecutor's office do take stalking seriously enough to go after and obtain a conviction, judges many times sentence the stalkers only to probation. This then leaves the stalkers free to continue their obsessive pursuit, which, as we have seen, many do.

"In my opinion, most of the state antistalking legislation is toothless," said FBI agent Jim Wright. "The first time, a stalker's hand merely gets slapped. The next time, it gets slapped a little harder, and the time after that a little harder than that. Boy, if it happens a fourth time, that's a felony. Well, many times it would be a felony anyway because it's a homicide."[250]

There are a number of reasons why judges sentence stalkers to probation rather than incarceration, one reason having to do with judges not realizing how dangerous stalkers really are. This often happens because, with the size and caseload of the court systems in large communities, once stalkers are released and then commit other crimes, they many times appear in front of different judges. Another important reason for the extensive use of probation with stalkers reflects the fact that in 1995, according to the Bureau of Justice Statistics report *Prison and Jail Inmates*, American jails and prisons held 1,585,400 people. What this statistic says is that our jails and prisons are filled to capacity, and many are operating above their top capacity level.[251] Judges don't want to send stalkers to prisons that are often so full that if the institutions do take them in correctional officials will likely have to turn other criminals loose; instead, they sentence the stalkers to probation. This is also the rationale many judges use for releasing pretrial stalkers on minimal bond or personal recognizance.

This, however, is not the solution that will solve the problem of stalking. Rather than being seen as a less dangerous crime, stalking must be seen by judges as the serious, and often deadly, crime it is. Appropriately high bonds for stalkers must be set, and those convicted of stalking must be given appropriate prison sentences, regardless of jail and prison overcrowding, and without having to turn other dangerous criminals loose. The only way to do this, of course, is to build more jails and prisons. And although some people may say that this is a simplistic solution to a complex problem, we must look for new solutions because the old ones aren't working. Certainly building more prisons and jails will cost money, but the amount is nothing compared to the cost, emotional and physical, of stalking to its victims. A government's first and foremost job is protecting its citizens, not pinching pennies, and we cannot allow election economics to stand in the way of safety for all citizens.

Not putting and keeping stalkers in custody, both pre- and posttrial, can also have the perilous effect of making them just that much more dangerous, as an arrest and quick release on bail, or a sentence of only probation after conviction, can make stalkers believe that the criminal justice system sees their offense as very minor. The following incident shows this effect.

Three months after Georgia residents Glenn and Ernestine O'Reilly divorced, the police arrested and charged Glenn with kidnapping and false imprisonment. The court released Glenn on bond, with one of the conditions of his bail being that he stay away from Ernestine. However, as with most stalkers, these types of promises are easily made and even easier broken.

The day after his release on bond Glenn began stalking Ernestine. He allegedly confronted her and her new boyfriend in a church foyer and loudly threatened that he would slit both of their throats if they continued their relationship. The police arrested Glenn for stalking.

With decision-making typical of many stalking prosecutions, the prosecutor worked out a plea agreement under which Glenn would plead guilty to two misdemeanor charges, for which he would receive probation, and the felony charges would be dropped. The judge hearing the case, however, refused to approve the plea bargain, insisting instead that Glenn either plead guilty to the felony stalking charges or prepare to go to trial on them.

"I don't think he's entitled to plead to a misdemeanor," said Bibb County (Georgia) Superior Court Judge Walker P. Johnson, Jr. "He tried to take advantage of a court allowing him out of jail."[252]

Because few judges react to stalking cases as Judge Johnson did, an obvious solution to part of the problem of stalkers being given low bonds or sentenced only to probation is education of the members of the judicial system about the risks and dangers associated with stalking. This is already being done with other issues. In Nevada, in 1993, for example, the Nevada Supreme Court closed all of the state's courts for one day and ordered all judges in the state to attend a training program on domestic violence. This type of judicial training should be expanded to every state, and it should include stalking. This is vitally important for the public's safety because, as we have seen in many of the anecdotes in this book, stalkers are extraordinarily dangerous, and not just to their victims, but also to the victims' families and even to innocent bystanders. Many times, the only thing that will stop stalkers is incarceration for a long period. Judges must be made to understand this. Judges must be educated about the depth of the obsession that drives many stalkers, and realize that they need to take serious and stern steps to stop stalkers. Section 40607 of the Violence Against Women Act authorizes such training for state judges, but states must take advantage of this.

"Attitudes are a long time changing," said Jane McAllister, founder of Citizens Against Stalking. "Stalking is sort of where the rape issue was twenty years ago. We need to do more education with magistrates and prosecutors."[253]

Fortunately, in some parts of the country the old attitudes about stalking are at last starting to change, and criminal justice officials are finally beginning to recognize the seriousness of this crime. In Illinois, Attorney General Roland W. Burris recently sponsored several conferences entitled "Stalking as a Crime: Relevant Laws and Their Applications." He held these conferences around the state of Illinois, in Chicago, Peoria, and Belleville. A few of the subjects covered in these conferences were: what constitutes stalking, evidence collection, reports, victim interviews, and strategies for successful prosecution.

"Because the laws are so new, law enforcement officials, judges, and others are trying to figure out how best to implement them," said David Beatty of the National Victim Center. "It's going to take some time to educate them and it may take some public pressure."[254]

In August 1996, the Annual Threat Management Conference convened in Anaheim, California. This conference, held every year, brings together hundreds of law enforcement personnel and others who deal with stalking. As with the conferences held in Illinois, they discuss the various aspects of stalking, and the best means for stopping it.

What these officials in Illinois and California are doing is commendable, but it is not enough. These types of conferences need to be held every year in every state, because, through them, individuals who work with stalking and stalkers can meet and exchange ideas and experiences, and through this can help each other.

"Conferences like this can help because people start talking to each other and, next thing you know, people are helping people," said Los Angeles Police Department spokesperson Greg Boles. "No one person can do everything—we're all in this together."[255]

As discussed above, one of the major problems with controlling stalkers is that individuals found guilty of stalking are often put on probation rather than incarcerated. Along with the other reasons already mentioned, judges sometimes do this believing that the stalkers, while on probation, will be closely watched and monitored, and that during their probation they will receive professional help. However, far too often stalkers don't receive the supervision or the professional help envisioned by the courts. The reason for this is that at the end of 1995, according to the U.S. Department of Justice, over 3,000,000 people in the United States were on probation.[256] This huge number obviously means huge caseloads for probation officers, and often very little personal attention to any one case. The answer to this problem is to hire more probation officers to supervise those stalkers whose crimes have not yet reached the level that would merit incarceration in a jail or prison, but who must be closely monitored to prevent them from continuing their obsessive behavior. Again, as with building more jails and prisons, I realize this will cost a considerable amount of money, but a government's first and foremost responsibility is its citizens' safety, and budget tightening and cost cuts should never affect this responsibility. Governments every year waste much more money than either of these proposals would cost.

A program recently launched in Indianapolis addresses the problem of having too many probationers for each probation officer. The chief probation officer for the county complained that his department simply didn't have the manpower necessary to keep an eye on all probationers. And so, in a pilot program, local police officers teamed up with probation officers and did home checks on high-risk probationers, finding, as expected, that a large number of them had violated their probation.

There are stalkers, however, for whom probation should never be considered, no matter how much personal attention probation officers could give them. For the public's safety, certain stalkers must be incarcerated, and incarcerated for a long time. The following incident demonstrates just such a case.

"This guy is your worst nightmare," said Assistant District Attorney Dan Hilford of accused stalker George Wayne Pendleton II. "He's the type that would focus on someone and fantasize that he was in love with her, and he's scary because he'd carry out [the fantasy]."[257]

Pendleton, accused of stalking two women, has been convicted of eight serious crimes in his 44 years. If convicted of the present charges, he could face life imprisonment through California's repeat offender law, which the District Attorney's Office decided to charge him under, an unusual development in stalking cases since only recently have stalkers been seen by many members of the criminal justice system as being dangerous.

According to court records, Pendleton has served several stretches in prison for rape, burglary, sodomy, false imprisonment, kidnapping, and oral copulation. The police most recently arrested him when a woman who claimed he was stalking her had her boyfriend hold him for the police. On investigating the case, police officers discovered another woman who also complained that Pendleton was stalking her. The woman said Pendleton approached her at her job, told her he had been watching her for months, and that he was in love with her. The woman later learned from her baby-sitter that Pendleton had been standing across the street from her home, watching it for hours. As can be seen from his record, Pendleton is not just a lovesick man pursuing someone. He is a dangerous criminal.

Stalkers like Pendleton, as shown by the convictions in his criminal record, can be extraordinarily dangerous individuals with a high propensity for violence. Unfortunately, when victims first meet criminals like Pendleton they often appear to be charming individuals, the same way many child molesters first appear to the victims and their families. Therefore, as many states have done with child molesters, every state needs to institute a registry of those individuals convicted of stalking. This registry, as are registries of convicted child molesters, should be accessible to the public and also fed into the FBI's national law enforcement computer, a system accessible to every police department in the United States. A registry of this type would assist individuals in checking out a person before becoming intimately involved with him or her (as discussed in the previous chapter), and would also assist any law enforcement personnel who may come in contact with the person.

Another registry that should be instituted in every state is a registry of all protective and restraining orders in effect, which should then be fed into the FBI's national law enforcement computer. Far too often, when a stalking victim travels from one jurisdiction to another the local police have no way of confirming that a protective order obtained in another jurisdiction is legally in effect. This can lead to serious consequences. Dangerous stalkers who should be arrested can very easily be turned loose. In the aftermath of the brutal murder of Kristin Lardner by an obsessed stalker who consistently violated court orders, an incident recounted in the book *The Stalking of Kristin*, Massachusetts computerized all records of restraining orders, along with violations of these orders (so officers could quickly identify not only violators but also repeat violators). Every state should do this.

A bill introduced in the U.S. Congress by Representative Ed Royce (California) would make local restraining orders valid anywhere in the United States. This bill, though well meant, shouldn't be needed because states are already required by the Violence Against Women Act to respect each other's protective orders. Few states are doing so yet because of the huge increase in access to each other's records that this would require. The federal government is presently running pilot programs of this requirement in several locations to test its feasibility. Feasible or not, the protection provided by such an order should not cease at state lines.

"If you look at every case where there was a long-term pursuit that ended in a homicide, you'll always find intervention in its history—usually a restraining order," said security expert Gavin DeBecker.[258] With a registry of these orders, a list of repeat violators of them, and all states recognizing each other's protective orders, some of these tragedies could be prevented.

Although many victims attempt to gain protection from their stalkers through some sort of restraining or protective order, others find they cannot afford even this meager protection. In the first incident related in this book, stalking victim Kim Springer, fearing for her safety, went to court to obtain a restraining order against her stalker, Mark Hilbun. She found, however, that she would have to wait until payday because she didn't have the necessary $182 filing fee. This is ridiculous. There should never be a cost for protection in a free country. That is the government's responsibility. Protection from violence is a right everyone should enjoy, not just those who can afford to pay for it. And although some jurisdictions will waive the filing fee of a protective order if the victim cannot afford it, that is not enough. All jurisdictions should waive the filing fee, or, better yet, there should be no fee at all.

Protective orders by themselves, however, are seldom the total answer. While researching numerous newspaper archives for this book I found many cases in which stalking victims obtained a restraining order that the stalkers then violated almost immediately. Yet, in those cases in which the police arrested the stalkers for violating these protective orders, the courts issuing the orders usually did little or nothing to punish the stalkers. Following this lack of punitive action by the court, and sensing an invulnerability, the stalkers often resumed the stalking with even more vigor, occasionally with fatal results.

A study completed in Massachusetts found that in only 18 percent of the cases in which the police arrested a person for violating a restraining order did a court sentence the violator to jail. Unfortunately, researchers completed this study in a part of the state considered a model area, so the real percentage is probably much less than this.

Why judges don't or won't punish individuals for violating a restraining or protective order has always been a mystery to me, as the person is directly flouting the court's authority. If a person did that in the courtroom, as I have seen done only twice during my career, judges would severely punish the offender, as they did in the two cases I witnessed. Judges must do the same with protective order violators. Stalkers must learn that if they violate a protective order they will go to jail. If judges would only do this regularly, they could increase the safety of stalking victims tremendously. In the National Institute of Justice booklet *Civil Protection Orders*, the authors say, "In jurisdictions such as Duluth and Philadelphia, where judges have established a formal policy that offenders who violate an order will be apprehended and punished, often with a jail term, both judges and victim advocates report the highest level of satisfaction with the system."[259]

Another problem stalking victims face is the complicated procedure necessary to obtain protective orders, particularly in an emergency situation. Colorado Springs, Colorado, has a protective order system that solves this problem and should serve as a model for the nation. If a police officer in Colorado Springs responds to a situation in which he or she believes a protective order is necessary, the officer telephones an on-call judge and explains the situation. If the judge agrees that an order is necessary, the officer fills out a blank protective order form, and, on authority from the judge, serves it on the stalker, ordering him or her to leave the victim alone. If the stalker doesn't, he or she can be arrested for violating the protective order. This order lasts until the end of the next court day, giving the victim time to apply for extended relief.

As discussed in Chapter 15, state antistalking bills often raced through their respective state legislatures and became laws much too quickly, consequently many times containing fatal flaws that caused the courts to throw them out for being vague, overbroad, or in conflict with First Amendment rights. Most state antistalking laws, however, have now been through two or three revisions to correct problems with constitutionality and difficulties in enforcement and prosecution. A study conducted by the National Institute of Justice, entitled *Domestic Violence, Stalking, and Antistalking Legislation*, has found that most state antistalking statutes are now surviving court challenges that they are vague, overbroad, or violate the First Amendment.[260] States, however, must continue this revision and refining, making the laws easier to enforce, and adding new forms of stalking as new technology becomes available. For example, who would have imagined computer on-line stalking 10 years ago? As the incident below shows, however, sometimes it takes a tragic and deadly incident before a state will examine and refine its antistalking law.

➤　　➤　　➤　　➤

Alexandria (Virginia) school teacher Karen L. Mitsoff had lived for a year with Fasseha Senbet before Mitsoff broke up with him. They started dating again several years later, but Mitsoff broke off the relationship once again, apparently angering Senbet. In retaliation, he broke into her apartment and confronted her with a revolver, telling her he was going to kill both of them. Mitsoff talked him out of it, and reported the incident to the police. Because this was the only incident the police knew of (Senbet had no criminal record, and Mitsoff hadn't reported any other incidents), the police couldn't charge Senbet with stalking, which, in Virginia, requires "a course of conduct," meaning a series of events. They instead charged him with burglary.

As the judge didn't know about all of the events surrounding the case, particularly of the threats to kill Mitsoff (since Senbet had been arrested for burglary and not threatening Mitsoff), he released Senbet on bail. Four days after his release from jail, Senbet killed both Mitsoff and himself.

In a city that prides itself in being progressive in its programs to prevent this kind of tragedy, Mitsoff's death showed an obvious gap in protection. As a consequence, the day after the murder/suicide the city of Alexandria set up a task force to see what could be done to prevent any future incidents of this kind.

"I'm sure every agency involved [in the Mitsoff case] would have liked to have the chance to try again and do a little bit more," said Commonwealth's Attorney John E. Kloth. "But although the Karen Mitsoff case was a tragedy, it was the basis of these changes, which may prevent violence in the future."[261]

The task force recommended providing judges at bail hearings with more information, such as the suspect's behavior at the time of the arrest, and whether a weapon was used. They also recommended that the state antistalking law be rewritten to heighten the punishment for stalking in Virginia. Stalking with a weapon, they said, should be made a felony.

Along with working on their antistalking laws, however, states also need to continue refining and passing other laws that work in tandem with antistalking laws. For example, in Minnesota, a recently passed law states that anyone convicted of stalking or violating a protective order must surrender all firearms for 3 years. A federal law, enacted in 1996, prohibits anyone convicted of domestic violence (which stalking can often spring from) from carrying a firearm. In Iowa, on the third offense of stalking comes a "presumption of ineligibility for bail." Although it can be dangerous for victims to have to wait for the third offense before stalkers are kept securely locked away, this is a start in the right direction. Another important addition needed in most state laws is that stalking in defiance of a restraining or protective order should be considered a felony, as should be the stalking of a juvenile by an adult. This would show stalkers that society has a special interest in protecting certain individuals, and that anyone acting in defiance of this protection must be willing to suffer severe consequences.

To truly protect victims, though, the penalties of all state antistalking laws must reflect the seriousness of the crime. Stalkers who relentlessly pursue and mentally torture their victims must, when convicted, be sentenced to substantial prison terms. This will give victims time to collect and rebuild their lives. Dr. Park Dietz, in an article in *The Charlotte Observer*, stated he believes judges should sentence stalkers to severe prison terms—10 years or more.[262] I agree.

As stated throughout this book, stalkers often suffer from mild to severe mental problems. Only when society finally recognizes this fact will we understand what to do with the many stalkers who are in need of serious psychiatric treatment: incarceration in mental hospitals. This is a problem, however, because in the 1980s many states closed their state-run mental hospitals. The idea behind these closures was to transfer most mentally disturbed individuals from these hospitals, which were often only holding facilities, to community-based mental health facilities, where the individuals would receive treatment. The problem, however, is that, whereas many of the state mental hospitals are now closed, most of the envisioned community-based mental health facilities were never built. Consequently, society now has many mentally disturbed and very dangerous individuals roaming the streets, and often preying on innocent victims. Yet, even for those stalkers committed to one of the remaining state mental hospitals, these facilities are often so crowded that administrators are always looking for a reason to release someone. Unfortunately, when in the controlled environment of a mental hospital and on medication, stalkers can appear deceptively lucid and say all of the right things, consequently getting themselves released. However, these stalkers often do not continue their medication once released, and revert to their old behavior problems.

The answer to this is that we must either build the community-based mental health centers envisioned or reopen the state mental hospitals. People with serious mental problems who are a danger to others should not be allowed to roam freely and terrorize innocent people.

Occasionally, however, the most persistent and dangerous stalkers, those most in need of serious psychiatric help, are sent to prison because of the lack of mental health facilities available. Once in prison, however, there is no assurance that the stalker will receive the psychiatric treatment necessary, or that even if the treatment is given the stalker will respond. As a consequence, parole boards quite often release stalkers at the end of their prison sentences in just as bad a mental state, or sometimes worse, than when first incarcerated. Often these individuals, even after a lengthy incarceration, immediately return to their earlier stalking behavior, many times with the same victims. The solution to this lies in having all states pass laws similar to the California law that allows the state to continue the incarceration of individuals past their initial sentence, should these individuals demonstrate a clear danger if released. Just recently, the U.S. Supreme Court upheld this and similar laws in several other states that allow the continued incarceration of sexual predators.

Thus far this chapter has considered how members of the criminal justice system—police officers, prosecutors, and judges—must work together and treat stalking as a serious crime. But there are other members of the criminal justice system who must also understand that stalkers should be considered high risk and dangerous individuals, and these are correctional officials. Unfortunately, as the following incident shows, these officials often treat stalkers as minor, low-risk offenders.

➤   ➤   ➤   ➤

"I am ready to play hardball now, are you?" the voice on the telephone challenged just 2 days after Leslie Wein had obtained a restraining order against her former boyfriend, Mark Bleakley. "Consider this an advanced warning. I'm not just coming after your possessions, you'll be the next thing damaged."

Wein had already received dozens of such telephone calls, which the police traced to Bleakley's place of employment. She had also had her tires slashed and acid thrown on her car. Following this, Wein had her dog stolen from her backyard, and, to torture the anxiety-ridden and heartbroken pet owner, the abductor left several Polaroid snapshots of the dog at her house. The dog later mysteriously reappeared tied to a pole outside Bleakley's attorney's office.

For many years the police would have been unable to take action against what was happening to Wein, but that was before California passed its antistalking law. The detective assigned to this case immediately saw that Bleakley's conduct fit well into the law's description of stalking. He arrested Bleakley and charged him with felony stalking after seeing

Bleakley drive by Wein's house, which he had staked out, four times. The detective believes that the arrest of Bleakley may have forestalled what appeared to be an escalation of violence against Wein. The detective found a .357 magnum revolver in Bleakley's home.

"The harassment of Wein got more brazen as time went on," said Detective Carlos Vidal. "Who knows what could have happened?"

Bleakley, even though arrested, continued to stalk Wein with telephone calls from jail. The calls stopped only after a court order finally took away his telephone privileges. Bleakley eventually pled no contest to the stalking charge, and received 1 year in prison and 5 years of probation, with the order to stay away from Wein. The judge credited Bleakley with 5 months he had already spent in jail awaiting trial and allowed him to serve the remainder of his sentence in a locked drug rehabilitation center. Bleakley blamed his behavior on the long-time use of steroids.

Although the police, the prosecutor, and the judge obviously saw Bleakley as a serious offender who needed to do hard time, correctional officials apparently didn't feel that way. After Bleakley had been in the drug rehabilitation center for several months he persuaded the personnel of the center to allow him to leave the facility unsupervised to pick up a car he was having serviced.

Immediately on leaving the facility, Bleakley raced to a health club that Wein belonged to, looking for her. The police arrested him.

"[He] was trying to track down his victim again," said Deputy District Attorney Robert Schuit.[263]

As shown by the incident above, the protection of stalking victims must come from every segment of the criminal justice system, from the police to the prosecutors to the judges to the correctional personnel. But even a committed criminal justice system can't protect a stalking victim every minute of every day. Fortunately, there are ways for a community to increase the protection available to stalking victims so that they do have a 24-hour defense.

To this end, a number of communities have implemented high-tech solutions in their effort to protect stalking victims and make them more aware of any possible danger. Several communities are now experimenting with having stalkers who are out of jail on probation, or on bail, wear electronic monitoring bracelets. These devices are presently being used in many communities for individuals on home detention (a form of incarceration in which courts sentence individuals to stay in their homes, rather than in jail). The electronic monitoring bracelet sets off an alarm and notifies the authorities if the home-detainee leaves his or her home. Cutting off the bracelet automatically sets off the alarm. For use in stalking cases, the victims have a monitoring device in the telephone at their home or workplace. If the stalkers come within a certain radius of the home or workplace the electronic monitoring bracelet sets off the device in the telephone, which then automatically calls the police, but also gives the victims warning and time to take the necessary safety precautions. For added protection, victims can wear pagers that will notify them if the alarm goes off while they're away from home, reducing the risk of being surprised by the stalker when they return home. These programs have been successfully tested in Indianapolis; San Joaquin, California; Dover, Massachusetts; and Arapahoe County, Colorado. They will soon be available in other communities.

"It's a very specific program aimed at breaking an obsession," said Michael Lindsey, cofounder of a program for male batterers, speaking of the electronic monitoring bracelet program in Arapahoe County, Colorado.[264]

Another use of modern technology, this one aimed at giving stalking victims the possibly lifesaving opportunity to immediately notify the police in the event a stalker finds and means to assault them, is presently being used in Leon County, Florida. Ninety-five cellular telephones have been donated to Refuge House, a women's shelter in Tallahassee. These telephones have been preprogrammed to call 911, and incoming calls are restricted to only those from law enforcement agencies and women's shelters. The cellular telephones are given to stalking victims who may need them to immediately seek help from the police in the event a stalker tracks them down. Several other communities are also considering this program.

One woman who received a cellular telephone because she fears being stalked again once her boyfriend is paroled said, "I know that someday I will have to face him. [The telephone] will save my life, because if he finds me, it will be a matter of life and death."[265]

In many of the incidents discussed in this book, stalkers have been able to locate their victims through personal information that shouldn't have been released to them. As discussed in Chapter 14, gaining or not gaining this information often makes the difference as to whether a stalker will continue the pursuit or not. It is therefore imperative that our society take a more active role in protecting personal information.

A rule every government agency should follow is that no personal information should ever be released to anyone (except under a court order) without the explicit permission of the person the information is about. In addition to this, every private business should have in place a set of responsible information-handling practices. Every business should have a written policy that outlines how it will handle and disseminate the personal information it stores, and not just personal information about its employees, but also personal information about its customers. This policy should be distributed regularly to the company's employees so that no one inadvertently assists a stalker. And even when personal information must be given out, companies should ensure that only the necessary information is given out, not the entire folder or record. Also, personnel records should be kept in a secure location and only be accessible on a need-to-know basis.

Unfortunately, with the proliferation of computer databases in American society, more and more personal information about each of us is shared among many private companies. As discussed in Chapter 14, whenever we buy something with a credit card, make a telephone call to an 800 or 900 number, or fill out an application, this information goes into a computer database that is often shared with many others without our knowledge or permission. Strict laws must be passed and enforced concerning the collection, use, and dissemination of this personal information, laws that protect possible stalking victims.

Although many victims may live in dire fear that their stalkers will somehow gain the personal information that will allow them to be found, those victims who have at one time shared an intimate relationship with their stalkers fear this even more because they usually know their stalkers' likelihood of violence. Regardless of the fear felt by these stalking victims, though, a nightmare that continues for them is that the stalkers many times have legal visitation rights with any children born of these relationships. How does a victim allow a former intimate partner, now a dangerous stalker, to safely pick up the children for visitation, particularly if the victim has moved to a new residence that the stalker doesn't know about? Also, how can a parent feel safe turning children over to a person who has shown a high level of dangerousness through becoming a stalker?

Duluth, Minnesota, has solved this problem with the creation, in 1989, of the Duluth Visitation Center. The center, which has facilities available for children of all age groups, can be used as the site of the child visitation if the custodial parent can convince a judge of the necessity of it, or the center can also be used as an exchange site for the children. The staff of the visitation center, when receiving a new family, draws up a contract for each parent specifying the terms of the visitation arrangements, such as the visits must take place at the center, no abusive language will be allowed, and so forth. Staff members are trained to watch the families using the center for any signs of abuse, and step in themselves to stop it, or call the police if necessary. Every community in America should have a visitation center.

However, because through such innovations as a visitation center stalking victims can often successfully conceal new home addresses, a large amount of stalking occurs at the workplaces of stalking victims, a location many victims cannot change. The following incident shows the danger of this.

A half-hour after the early shift at the Ford Motor Company plant in Plymouth Township, Michigan, began working, 43-year-old Michael Brattin walked up to his wife, Sandra, and shot her in the legs and stomach. The couple had been married for 16 years and were in the midst of divorce proceedings. Both worked at the Ford plant.

"I just heard shooting, just shooting," said one of the workers. "This is like family 12 hours a day, and we never thought it would happen here."

Sandra's new boyfriend, Michael O'Brien, saw what was happening, and he ran to her aid. The estranged husband turned the gun on the new boyfriend, shooting him three times and killing him. Other workers approached Brattin, but backed off when he pointed the gun at them. He then put the .40 caliber pistol up to his own head and killed himself.

"We have good security," said a Ford spokesman. "We can't police every single person every single time. These incidents do happen."[266]

As the Ford spokesman said, these incidents do happen, but unfortunately the incident above has become much too common in America. In Michigan, in just 5 months, three shootings of this type occurred at auto plants. Because these types of incidents are happening much more often today, businesses can no longer just stand back and say that stalking is a personal dispute in which the company will not intervene. Several high dollar lawsuits have shown that businesses can be held accountable for the safety of their employees against stalkers. Therefore, businesses must take a proactive role in preventing these kind of tragedies. They can do this through such means as obtaining their own restraining orders against the stalkers of employees, posting pictures of stalkers at receptionists' desks and other points of entry, sending notices of stalkers to all security people, and taking extra security precautions when a threatened employee is working.

"Unfortunately, what's happening is that with the increase of women in the work place, their estranged husbands and boyfriends know where to find them and so they often seek them out while they're working," said Dr. Don Hartsough, president of White River Psychology in Indianapolis.[267]

Some employers, however, seeing stalking as a serious safety issue for the entire company, react by adding even more problems to the lives of employees threatened by stalkers. According to a *Los Angeles Times* article, "Some employers deal with the issue simply—and frequently illegally—by firing or suspending the workers dogged by domestic problems" (which can include stalking).[268] Indeed, an article in the 12 August 1995 issue of the *Indianapolis Star* concerns how the ex-wife of Charles Barker, whom he kidnaped and took to Tennessee in the incident discussed in Chapter 12, was fired from her place of employment because of the incident. She is suing her previous employer.[269]

A survey of 248 companies in 27 states found many reports of domestic violence, stalking, and murder in the workplace. "A lot of work places are open and exposed to danger, which puts a lot of innocent people at risk," said Joseph Kinney of the National Safe Workplace Institute, which did the study. "However, stalkers are increasingly killing victims near workplaces, especially in parking lots or close to the place of employment."[270] Businesses must understand this and take the appropriate security precautions, and not just in the workplace, but also in parking lots and surrounding areas.

"In the airport, if you make a joke about a bomb threat, they'll take it seriously," said John Nacoletti, a police psychologist in Lakewood, Colorado, talking about stalking. "Corporations also need to have zero tolerance for this sort of thing."[271]

A tragic incident in Houston should make all businesses aware of what can happen if they don't take stalking complaints seriously and become involved in protecting their employees. A woman who had obtained a restraining order against a former boyfriend who was stalking her told her employer about it. Her employer paid no attention to her fears, and took no action. The former boyfriend came to the woman's place of employment with a gun and killed her. The employer and property management company settled with the woman's family for $350,000.

Some companies, however, are not just sitting back and ignoring threats to their employees, or waiting until tragedy strikes before doing something. They are taking action to prevent such tragedies. According to an article in the *Wall Street Journal*, Polaroid Corporation taps the telephones of employees who fear an attack, escorts them to and from their cars, and will even post security guards at their homes if necessary. Polaroid Corporation also obtains restraining orders in the company's name to keep stalkers away.[272] Another proactive company, when finding that a receptionist's estranged husband was threatening her, didn't have to do anything expensive, but simply moved her to another location. A few days later, the estranged husband smashed his truck through the lobby, crashing into the empty desk where his wife had previously sat.

Besides government agencies and corporations taking action against stalkers, private individuals can also do their part to help stalking victims. An article in the *Indianapolis Star* tells of a grass-roots organization in southern Indiana that comes to the aid of women who are being stalked. Called Crisis Connection, this organization is a group of rural residents who open their homes to victims of domestic violence and stalking. It sprang up because of the lack of women's shelters in rural areas. Victims who need help call an 800 number and talk to a hotline volunteer. If the victim needs a safe place to stay immediately, she and any children are met at a neutral location and driven to one of the "safe houses." Crisis Connection serves approximately 220 families every year.[273]

In April 1995, another grass-roots organization for stalking victims sprang up in Tampa, Florida. Called Survivors of Stalking (SOS), this organization was founded by a former stalking victim, Renee Goodale, who discovered that there was little support and assistance available when she was being stalked. SOS offers the victims of stalking peer support and counseling, and access to information on possible lifesaving solutions. The organization maintains a stalking referral service and an Internet information page. They also offer a number of seminars every year on how to deal with stalking and stalkers, and are considering holding on-line stalking-victim support meetings. Since 1995, the organization has helped over 2000 people with information and referrals. When I joined this organization, they sent me a very helpful booklet entitled *Stalking and Harassment: Ending the Silence That Kills*. Their address is:

Survivors of Stalking, Inc.
P. O. Box 20762
Tampa, Florida 33622-0762
1-813-889-0767
www.soshelp.org
E-mail: soshelp@soshelp.org

A similar organization exists for electronic stalking victims. Called CYBERANGELS, this organization, formed in 1995, assists individuals harassed or stalked on the Internet or by E-mail. Their Internet address is *www.cyberangels.org*.

If our nation is ever to prevent the many tragedies that accompany stalking, all of society, including government agencies, private businesses, and ordinary citizens, must become involved in stopping it. They must begin acknowledging and treating stalking for what it is: a serious crime with often fatal consequences. Society must demand that stalkers not be treated as pitiful, unwanted lovers, but instead as the criminals they are.

➤   ➤   ➤   ➤   ➤

A FINAL THOUGHT

During my 30 years as a police officer I have dealt with thousands of crime victims, and have felt a deep compassion for the majority of these people, who have been robbed, raped, shot, swindled, beaten, and burglarized. Yet, by the time I saw these victims, the crime was over and the healing process had already begun.

With stalking victims, however, the crime wasn't over with, but continued on and on. Victims of stalking say the experience is like a prolonged rape, a never-ending and terrifying loss of control over one's life. **Stalking is one of the most psychologically crippling things that can happen to a person**. Being stalked takes away a person's freedom, a person's security, and often a person's will to live.

I hope I have shown throughout this book that the best way to fight back against and stop stalking is through knowledge. When the public finally comes to see stalkers not as lovesick suitors, but as the dangerous criminals they really are, pressure will be brought onto police agencies, prosecutors, judges, and correctional workers to also see and treat stalkers as serious criminals. Only then can stalking be stopped. Stalkers must not be allowed to roam free in society to intimidate and terrorize innocent people. America will only be a free country when everyone is free to live his or her life unafraid.

> ➤ ➤ ➤ ➤ ➤

REFERENCES

1. Rene Lynch, "Postal Worker Recounts Life of Fear," *Los Angeles Times* (30 April 1994), p. A-28.
2. Frank Messina and Eric Lightblau, "Ex-Mail Carrier Kills 2 in O.C.; Attack Follows Similar Incident in Michigan," *Los Angeles Times* (7 May 1993), p. A-1.
3. Lynch.
4. "Former Postal Worker Convicted of Murder, Attempted Murder for Rampage," *The News-Times* (7 August 1996), p. 1.
5. Claire Serant, "Stalked," *Essence* (October 1993), p. 76.
6. Ibid., p. 73.
7. Patty Shillington, "The Mind of the Stalker; The Terror of the Stalked," *The Miami Herald* (4 July 1993), p. J-1.
8. "Stalker! Stalker!" *E! Online* (1996), p. 1.
9. George Mair, *Star Stalkers* (New York: Kensington Publishing Corp., 1995), p. 110.
10. Linden Gross, *To Have or to Harm* (New York: Warner Books, 1994), p. 37.
11. David Grossman, "Erotomania," *Vanity Fair* (September 1991), p. 191.
12. Howard Kohn, "The Stalker," *Redbook* (April 1993), p. 108.
13. Mair, p. 63.
14. Ibid., p. 218.
15. William Sherman, "Stalking: The Nightmare That Never Ends," *Cosmopolitan* (April 1994), p. 198.
16. Gross, p. 9.
17. Ibid., pp. 11–12.
18. Margaret S. Stockdale, "The Role of Sexual Misperceptions of Women's Friendliness in an Emerging Theory of Sexual Harassment," *Journal of Vocational Behavior* 42 (1993), pp. 84–101.
19. Michalene Busico and Michael Oricchio, "Obsessions Are Hard to Predict—Or Control, Experts Say," *San Jose Mercury News* (18 February 1988), p. F-1.

20. Kohn, p. 133.
21. ABC News, *20/20*, 10 January 1992.
22. Michael Lindsey, *The Terror of Batterer Stalking* (Littleton, CO: Gylantic Publishing, 1993), pp. 2–4.
23. Sherman, p. 199.
24. Kohn, p. 131.
25. Thomas W. Marino, "Looking Over Your Shoulder," *Counseling Today* 38 (October 1995), pp. 1–21.
26. "Stalking," The National Victim Center (1995), p. 3.
27. Dave O'Brian and Richard Scheinin, "When Love Is Twisted Into Anger and Hate," *San Jose Mercury News* (16 June 1989), p. C-1.
28. Mair, pp. 17–18.
29. Shillington.
30. Kohn, p. 133.
31. Nelson Price, "The Object of Obsession," *Indianapolis Star* (19 June 1996), p. G-2.
32. "Stalker! Stalker!" p. 3.
33. Ibid., p. 7.
34. Ibid., p. 4.
35. Kiley Armstrong, "Why, in the Name of Love, Is Stalking on the Increase?" *Philadelphia Inquirer* (10 December 1992), p. F-7.
36. Helen Guthrie Smith, "Police, Victims Take New Steps To Stop Stalkers," *Long Beach Press-Telegram* (9 November 1992), p. A-1.
37. Price.
38. Matt Nelson and Anne Bretts, "Weeks Before Fiery Suicide Foretold Tragedy," *Duluth News-Tribune* (9 December 1995), p. A-1.
39. Gross, p. 177.
40. Shillington.
41. Ibid.
42. Serant, p. 76.
43. Pam Lambert, "Judge or Be Judged," *People* (23 November 1992), p. 74.
44. Bill Romano, "Guilty of Stalking Judge's Daughter S.F. Lawyer Says He Had Not Intended To Frighten His Love Interest Or The Sunnyvale Jurist," *San Jose Mercury News* (4 September 1993), p. B-1.
45. James Franklin, "Actor Charged With Stalking," *Washington Post* (21 November 1996), p. B-1.
46. "Actor Farentino Charged With Stalking Tina Sinatra," *Long Beach Press-Telegram* (7 August 1993), p. A-7.
47. "Woman Sentenced to Five Years in Prison for Stalking Man," *Source* (16 May 1996), p. 1.
48. "9-Year-Old Accused of Stalking Schoolmate," *The New York Times* (8 March 1996), p. A-21.
49. Andrea Muirragui Davis, "Bluffton Wife Lived in Fear," *Fort Wayne News Sentinel* (14 December 1994), p. A-1.
50. Diane Craven, *Female Victims of Violent Crime*, U.S. Department of Justice (Washington, D.C.: U.S. Government Printing Office, 1996), pp. 1–3.

51. Melita Schaum and Karen Parrish, *Stalked* (New York: Pocket Books, 1995), pp. 56–57.
52. Ibid., p. 58.
53. Gross, p. 120.
54. "Stalking," p. 3.
55. Patrick Scott, "Gunman Accused of Stalking," *The Charlotte Observer* (6 January 1995), p. A-1.
56. Patrick Scott and Ken Bell, "Gunman Shoots Woman, Self," *The Charlotte Observer* (5 January 1995), p. Y-1.
57. Diana Jean Schemo, "Woman, Stalked for Year, Is Slain by Ex-Companion, Who Also Kills Himself," *The New York Times* (27 May 1993), p. B-7.
58. Pam Maples, "Under The Gun," *Indianapolis Star* (11 July 1993), p. F-4.
59. Pam Maples, "Bring Violence Home," *The Miami Herald* (13 June 1993), p. M-1.
60. Ibid.
61. Julio Ojeda-Zapata, "Former Client of Attorney Now Stalking, Haunting Him," *Saint Paul Pioneer Press* (21 October 1993), p. A-1.
62. "Senator's Wife Pleads for Anti-Stalking Bill, Tells of Ex-Employee's Threats," *San Jose Mercury News* (18 March 1993), p. A-7.
63. Mary Rogers, "Ex-Senator, Family Enduring Ordeal With Stalker," *The State* (21 March 1993), p. E-5.
64. "Nowhere To Hide," *People* (17 May 1993), p. 64.
65. Gail Gibson, "Woman Slain At Gas Station in Wayne County," *Lexington Herald-Leader* (28 November 1995), p. A-1.
66. Ibid.
67. Chuck Carroll, "Single Date Turns Into Stalking Nightmare of Calls, Threats," *The State* (7 February 1993), p. B-1.
68. Ibid.
69. Ibid.
70. Dr. Susan Forward, *Obsessive Love: When It Hurts Too Much to Let Go* (New York: Bantam Books, 1991), p. 23.
71. Ronet Bachman and Linda Saltzman, *Violence against Women: Estimates from the Redesigned Survey*, U.S. Department of Justice (Washington, D.C.: U.S. Government Printing Office, 1995), pp. 3–4.
72. Stuart Silverstein, "Stalked by Violence on the Job," *Los Angeles Times* (8 August 1994), p. A-1.
73. "Survey Says..." *Law Enforcement Technology* (February 1997), p. 16.
74. Sherman, p. 199.
75. Steve Wilstein, "Celebrities at Risk from Stalkers," *Akron Beacon Journal* (8 January 1994), p. A-1.
76. Mike Dooley, "Man Pleads Guilty to Stalking," *Fort Wayne News Sentinel* (14 June 1996), p. A-6.
77. Marino, p. 1.
78. Regina Anderson, "Stalking Remains Widely Unreported," *Montana Kaimin* (1996), p. 2.
79. Claire Safran, "A Stranger Was Stalking Our Little Girl," *Good Housekeeping* (November 1992), p. 185.
80. Shillington.

81. Christine Evans, "Can't Run, Can't Hide," *Bradenton Herald* (20 March 1992), p. A-1.
82. "Women Winning Legal Help Against Stalkers," *Chicago Tribune* (16 April 1992).
83. Shillington.
84. *Sally Jessy Raphael*, "He Was After Me," Transcript #1633 (9 January 1994).
85. Theresa Saldana, *Beyond Survival* (New York: Bantam Books, 1986).
86. "Star: Attacker's Parole 'Unbelievable,'" *The Miami Herald* (6 June 1989), p. A-16.
87. Mike Tharp, "In the Mind of a Stalker," *U.S. News & World Report* (17 February 1992), p. 28.
88. Mair, p. 26.
89. "Stalker! Stalker!" p. 2.
90. Tharp.
91. Gross, p. 164.
92. "Man To Be Tried on Charges of Murder in Actress' Slaying," *San Jose Mercury News* (6 December 1989), p. F-1.
93. Mair, p. 39.
94. Tharp.
95. Daniel Goleman, "Dangerous Delusions: When Fans Are a Threat," *The New York Times* (31 October 1989).
96. Elizabeth Snead, "Fame and Fear: Celebrities Face Rise in Stalking Incidents," *San Jose Mercury News* (3 September 1996), p. D-1.
97. "Stalker! Stalker!" p. 6.
98. Mair, p. 88.
99. Schaum, p. 44.
100. "Stalker! Stalker!" p. 2.
101. Doris Bacon, "When Fans Turn Into Fanatics, Nervous Celebs Call For Help From Security Expert Gavin DeBecker," *People* (12 February 1990), p. 105.
102. Terry Mulgannon, "People Who Harass Celebrities Are Lonely, Troubled and Smart—and They Often Don't Care Who It Is They Stalk," *E! Online* (1996), p. 2.
103. Gross, p. 162.
104. "Material Girl Is Material Witness," *Long Beach Press-Telegram* (4 January 1996), p. A-3.
105. Snead.
106. "After Court Order, Madonna Faces Accused in Stalker Case," *The New York Times* (4 January 1996), p. A-18.
107. Linda Deutsch, "'I Felt Incredibly Violated,' Madonna Testifies At Trial," *The Detroit News* (4 January 1996), p. 1.
108. "Material Girl Is Material Witness."
109. Jeff Meyer, "Both Sides Rest in Madonna Stalker Case," *Long Beach Press-Telegram* (6 January 1996), p. A-7.
110. Duke Helfand, "No Rest for Victims of Stalking," *Los Angeles Times* (5 January 1996), p. 1.
111. Mair, p. 41.
112. Helfand.

113. Wilstein.
114. "Obsessed Fan Admits Threatening Actress," *San Jose Mercury News* (1 September 1990), p. A-2.
115. Bill Hewitt and Dianna Waggoner, "Justine Bateman Becomes the Latest Celebrity to be Menaced by an Obsessive Fan," *People* (25 September 1989), p. 113.
116. Judy Lundstrom Thomas and Gail Randall, "Anti-Abortion Group Publicly Unmasks, Warns Clinic Doctor," *The Wichita Eagle* (22 August 1993), p. A-1.
117. "Shooting Suspect Wrote Fan Letters to Griffin," *The Miami Herald* (22 August 1993), p. B-5.
118. "Abortion Doctor Shot In Both Arms," *Bradenton Herald* (20 August 1993), p. A-1.
119. Testimony by Susan Hill before Subcommittee on Crime and Criminal Justice, U.S. House of Representatives, 21 September 1994.
120. Sandra G. Boodman, "Abortion Foes Strike At Doctors' Home Lives," *Washington Post* (8 April 1993), p. A-1.
121. Brian Harmon, "'Ambulatory Picketing' Raises Issue of Stalking," *The Detroit News* (25 January 1996), p. 1.
122. Phil Long and Martin Merzer, "Abortion Physician Shot Dead," *Bradenton Herald* (11 March 1993), p. A-1.
123. Kenneth E. Lamb, "For Killing In Name of Life, He Gets Death," *The Miami Herald* (7 December 1994), p. A-1.
124. Glenda Holste, "It Wasn't Just Isolated Zealots Who Made Climate Right For Violence At Clinics," *Saint Paul Pioneer Press* (12 August 1994), p. A-12.
125. Diana Penner, "Anti-Abortion Group Will Hold Protest Here and In Muncie," *Indianapolis Star* (18 February 1995), p. B-4.
126. Liz Doup and Peggy Landers, "Clergy: Killings For God Insane," *The Miami Herald* (15 March 1993), p. C-1.
127. David G. Savage, "High Court Upholds Free-Speech Rights of Abortion Foes," *Indianapolis Star* (20 February 1997), p. A-1.
128. Karen Branch, "Political Activist or Stalker?" *The Miami Herald* (23 August 1995), p. B-1.
129. Karen Rafinski, "Cable Employee Charged With Stalking Customers," *The Miami Herald* (8 September 1995), p. A-1.
130. "Victim of Stalker, Judge Wants Help From Law," *Saint Paul Pioneer Press* (20 February 1993), p. A-1.
131. John McGauley, "Police Ask State To Disarm Trio," *Fort Wayne News Sentinel* (6 May 1994), p. A-1.
132. Michael Siconolfi, "An Employee Fired By Kidder Peabody Casts a Pall of Fear," *Wall Street Journal* (29 April 1994), p. 1.
133. Dorothy Gilliam, "When Hate Moves In Next Door," *Washington Post* (16 December 1995), p. B-1.
134. Ray Martinez, "FDLE Documents Tell a Tale of Planned Murder for Hire," *Tallahassee Democrat* (10 March 1995), p. A-1.
135. Jill Smolove, "Voice of the Torturer," *Time* (18 December 1995), p. 51.
136. Ibid.
137. Ibid.

138. Manny Garcia, "Tragic Stories Were Agent's Porn," *The Miami Herald* (21 February 1996), p. B-1.
139. Gail Epstein, "A Pattern of Cruelty by Telephone," *The Miami Herald* (19 February 1996), p. A-1.
140. Garcia.
141. Manny Garcia, "Agent: I Was On the Brink of Suicide," *The Miami Herald* (5 March 1996), p. B-1.
142. "Phone Stalkers: Hooked on Terror," *USA Today* (8 January 1996), p. A-1.
143. Connie Piloto, "Man Accused of Stalking—Via Faxes," *The Miami Herald* (12 May 1996), p. SE-15.
144. Peter H. Lewis, "Persistent E-Mail: Electronic Stalking or Innocent Courtship?" *The New York Times* (16 September 1994), p. B-18.
145. Ibid.
146. Ibid.
147. Judy DeHaven, "High-Tech World Faces Low-Life Realities," *The Detroit News* (10 January 1996), p. 1.
148. "Female Users Take Measures to Avoid Online Harassment," *Salt Lake Tribune* (14 May 1996).
149. Kay Lazar, "In Six Women's Testimony, Fear Is Common Thread," *Philadelphia Inquirer* (6 January 1994), p. B-2.
150. Kay Lazar, "Sentenced For Stalking 35 Women A Levittown Man Got 1½ to 3 years," *Philadelphia Inquirer* (18 March 1994), p. B-3.
151. Doug Donovan, "Judge Approves Work Release For Convicted Stalker," *Philadelphia Inquirer* (11 August 1995), p. N-1.
152. Denise Marie Siino, "Stalking Their Prey," *Los Angeles Times* (12 November 1996), p. 1.
153. Busico.
154. Susan Hogan and John Allard, "Trail of Fear, Violence Ends In Murder-Suicide," *The State* (5 November 1995), p. A-1.
155. Robert Hoiles, "Women Survive Stalking Nightmare," *Akron Beacon Journal* (7 November 1996), p. C-1.
156. Joanne Griffith Domingue, "Accused Molester Has 10-year History of Stalking, Harassing Girls, Police Say," *Los Altos Town Crier* (11 September 1996), p. 1.
157. Ann W. O'Neill, "Farley Testifies, Says Obsession Began With Love At First Sight," *San Jose Mercury News* (21 August 1991), p. A-1.
158. Kirstin Downey and Jeanne Huber, "ESL Gunman 'A Nerdie Kid,'" *San Jose Mercury News* (20 February 1988), p. A-1.
159. Bob Trebilcock, "I Love You To Death," *Redbook* (March 1992), p. 103.
160. O'Neill.
161. Trebilcock, p. 112.
162. Ibid.
163. S.L. Wykes, "Judge Hears Tape At Farley Hearing," *San Jose Mercury News* (15 July 1988), p. B-1.
164. Ibid.
165. Trebilcock, p. 114.
166. Kirstin Downey, "What Made Farley Tick?" *San Jose Mercury News* (18 February 1988), p. A-1.

167. Ann W. O'Neill, "Farley Gloated at 'Fun' Killings, Negotiator Says," *San Jose Mercury News* (13 August 1991), p. B-1.
168. George McLaren, "Man Sentenced to Die for Killing Ex-Girlfriend's Grandparents," *Indianapolis Star* (27 November 1996), p. B-1.
169. Robert Kaiser and Valarie Honeycutt, "Gunman Kills 3 in Mercer," *Lexington Herald-Leader* (10 November 1991), p. A-1.
170. Mike Santangelo, "Cop Is Killed by 'Predator,'" *Newsday* (19 October 1996), p. A-5.
171. Marlene Aig, "15 Hour Seige Ends," *The Bakersfield Californian* (22 March 1996), p. 1.
172. Ibid.
173. Dale Sandusky, "Domestic Conflict Ends in Death," *New Albany Tribune* (28 July 1996), p. 1.
174. Shirley Streshinsky, "The Stalker and His Prey," *Glamour* (August 1992), p. 238.
175. Ibid., p. 265.
176. S.L. Wykes, "Woman Irate Over Stalker's Sentence," *San Jose Mercury News* (4 October 1990), p. B-1.
177. Streshinsky, p. 267.
178. Edwin Garcia, "Stalker's Release Puts Cops On Alert," *San Jose Mercury News* (25 January 1996), p. A-1.
179. Michael Oricchio, "Prisoners of Obsession," *San Jose Mercury News* (13 March 1988), p. L-1.
180. Ibid.
181. Jennifer Wing, "Stalking-Victim Study Will Probe For Similarities," *Philadelphia Inquirer* (25 March 1996), p. B-2.
182. "Woman Kills Herself Prior To Stalking Trial," *San Jose Mercury News* (12 January 1994), p. A-4.
183. Jeffrey Toobin, "Stalking in L.A.," *The New Yorker* (24 February 1997), p. 73.
184. "In A Small Town, Terror—and Then a Scandal," *GT Online* (1996), p. 1.
185. Schaum, p. 103.
186. Loretta Green, "He Took Her Freedom, Threatened Her Life," *San Jose Mercury News* (7 May 1993), p. 5.
187. Jeffrey Rothfeder, *Privacy For Sale* (New York: Simon & Schuster, 1992).
188. Tracy Thompson, "When the Eager Lover Becomes the Relentless Stalker," *Washington Post* (17 April 1994), p. A-1.
189. Sherman, p. 199.
190. Susan Bennett, "Database Prowlers Changing America," *The Miami Herald* (21 March 1994), p. A-1.
191. Statement by Congressman Bob Franks, Press Conference on Children's Lists, 22 May 1996.
192. Nina Bernstein, "Personal Files Via Computer Offer Money and Pose Threat," *The New York Times* (12 June 1997), p. A-1.
193. Cindi Ross Scoppe, "Florida Woman Hopes Law will Deter Stalker," *The State* (15 April 1992), p. A-5.
194. Tamar Lewin, "New Laws Address Old Problem: The Terror of a Stalker's Threats," *The New York Times* (8 February 1993), p. A-1.

195. Scoppe.
196. Miles Corwin, "When the Law Can't Protect," *Los Angeles Times* (8 May 1993), p. A-21.
197. Christine Evans, "Can't Run, Can't Hide," *Bradenton Herald* (20 March 1992), p. A-1.
198. Ibid.
199. Constance L. Hays, "If That Man Is Following Her, Connecticut Is Going to Follow Him," *The New York Times* (5 June 1992), p. B-1.
200. Renee Cordes, "DOJ Recommends Tough Antistalking Law," *Trial* 29 (December 1993), p. 81.
201. Maria Puente, "Legislators Tackling the Terror of Stalking," *USA Today* (21 July 1992), p. 9A.
202. U.S. Department of Justice, *Project To Develop a Model Anti-Stalking Code for States* (Washington, D.C.: U.S. Government Printing Office, October 1993), pp. 43–44.
203. Carol J. DeFrances and Steven K. Smith, *Prosecutors in State Courts, 1994*, U.S. Department of Justice (Washington, D.C.: U.S. Government Printing Office, 1996), p. 3.
204. U.S. Department of Justice, *Pretrial Release of Felony Defendants, 1992* (Washington, D.C.: U.S. Government Printing Office, 1994).
205. Audrey Post, "I Want My Life Back," *The Macon Telegraph* (1 October 1995), p. A-1.
206. "Former Timberwolves Assistant Guilty of Stalking," *Saint Paul Pioneer Press* (21 September 1996), p. E-3.
207. "Police: Stalking Law Is Tough to Enforce," *The Charlotte Observer* (8 October 1996), p. Y-2.
208. Wing.
209. Dana Parsons, "Tougher Law Gives Hope Stalking Case May Be Closed," *Los Angeles Times* (24 July 1994), p. B-1.
210. Todd S. Purdum, "Clinton Signs $256.6 Billion Defense Bill," *Indianapolis Star* (24 September 1996), p. A-4.
211. David Phinney, "Clinton Signs O.C.-Born Bill Outlawing Stalking," *Los Angeles Times* (24 September 1996), p. A-3.
212. "Man Gunned Down in Police Parking Lot Had Been Stalking Ex-Wife, Attorney Says," *Lexington Herald Leader* (12 November 1995), p. B-6.
213. Robin Uris, "Guilty Plea Entered in Slaying of Stalker," *The Charlotte Observer* (21 November 1996), p. C-1.
214. Oricchio.
215. Mulgannon, p. 8.
216. Helen Guthrie Smith, "Steps You Can Take To Obstruct Stalkers," *Long Beach Press-Telegram* (9 November 1992), p. A-8.
217. Oricchio.
218. Smith, "Police, Victims Take New Steps To Stop Stalkers."
219. Robert A. Fein et al., *Threat Assessment: An Approach To Prevent Targeted Violence*, U.S. Department of Justice (Washington, D.C.: U.S. Government Printing Office, 1995), p. 3.
220. Puente.

221. Serant, p. 132.
222. "Anti-Stalking Law Adds Tougher Fines, Sentences," *The State* (19 June 1995), p. A-10.
223. Michael Oricchio, "Going To Court Can Be Effective, But It Can Also be Risky," *San Jose Mercury News* (13 March 1988), p. L-6.
224. Shillington.
225. Toobin, p. 79.
226. John William Clouser and Dave Fisher, *The Most Wanted Man In America* (New York: Stein and Day, 1975).
227. Toobin, pp. 73–74.
228. Serant, p. 132.
229. Lindsey, p. 5.
230. Streshinsky, p. 267.
231. Donovan.
232. Gross, p. 201.
233. Ellen Moses, "Stalker Sentenced To Prison," *Bradenton Herald* (1 July 1996), p. L-1.
234. Piloto.
235. Sherman, p. 201.
236. Michele Cook, "A Man of Violence Extinguishes a Life, A Couple's Dreams," *Saint Paul Pioneer Press* (3 July 1994), p. A-1.
237. Suellen E. Dean, "Woman Slain at Spartanburg Mall," *The State* (10 July 1993), p. B-1.
238. "Stalked Woman Is Brutally Killed," *The Miami Herald* (19 April 1994), p. B-1.
239. Linda Stasi, "Someone Is Stalking Me," *Ladies' Home Journal* (January 1997), p. 32.
240. John Barry, "Your 13-Year-Old Daughter Is Being Stalked," *The Miami Herald* (12 March 1996), p. C-1.
241. Anna Cekola, "Man Sentenced to 4-Year Term in Stalking Case," *Los Angeles Times* (23 July 1994), p. B-1.
242. "Wife Says She Can't Escape Death Threats, Harassment," *Lexington Herald-Leader* (6 January 1995), p. A-1.
243. Thomas Tolliver, "Husband Faces Stiffer Charge in Assault Case Action," *Lexington Herald-Leader* (7 January 1995), p. A-1.
244. Amy Vernon, "Convicted Stalker Back in Jail Less Than a Day After Release," *The Miami Herald* (10 March 1993), p. BR-1.
245. Connie Piloto, "Lauderdale Cops to Follow Stalkers," *The Miami Herald* (15 July 1995), p. BR-8.
246. Joanne Furio, "Can New State Laws Stop the Stalker?" *Ms.* (January 1993), p. 91.
247. "Louisville Man Pleads Not Guilty In Slaying," *Lexington Herald-Leader* (18 December 1993), p. B-3.
248. "Notification Network Alerts Victims of Release Dates," *Law Enforcement Technology* (November 1996), pp. 52–55.
249. Lolo Pendergrast and Patrick Scott, "The Mind of a Stalker," *The Charlotte Observer* (10 January 1993), p. Y-1.
250. Gross, p. 192.

251. Darrell K. Gilliard and Allen J. Beck, *Prison and Jail Inmates, 1995*, U.S. Department of Justice (Washington, D.C.: U.S. Government Printing Office, 1996).

252. Eric Velasco, "Macon Judge Rejects Plea Bargain in Stalking Case," *The Macon Telegraph* (25 September 1996), p. A-1.

253. "VA. Stalking Statute Still Confuses Law Officials, Victims," *The Virginian-Pilot* (29 December 1994), p. B-3.

254. Interview on National Public Radio Program *All Things Considered*, 31 March 1996.

255. David Haldane, "Officials Hear Arguments for U.S. Anti- Stalking Law," *Los Angeles Times* (29 August 1996), p. 1.

256. U.S. Department of Justice, *Probation and Parole* (Washington, D.C.: U.S. Government Printing Office, 1996).

257. Danna Dykstra, "Repeat Stalker Faces Life in Prison Without Parole," *San Luis Obispo County Telegram-Tribune* (31 August 1996), p. 1.

258. Gross, p. 195.

259. Peter Finn and Sarah Colson, *Civil Protection Orders*, U.S. Department of Justice (Washington, D.C.: U.S. Government Printing Office, 1990), p. 2.

260. U.S. Department of Justice, *Domestic Violence, Stalking, and Antistalking Legislation* (Washington, D.C.: U.S. Government Printing Office, 1996), pp. A1–A11.

261. Cheryl L. Tan, "Tougher Stalking Law Urged For Va.," *Washington Post* (11 July 1997), p. V-1.

262. Pendergrast.

263. Michael Connelly, "Ex-Boyfriend Jailed Under 'Stalking' Law," *Los Angeles Times* (10 June 1991), p. B-1.

264. "Bracelet on Stalker Gives Warning to Potential Victim," *Lexington Herald-Leader* (19 September 1992), p. A-4.

265. Barbara Ash, "Donated Cellular Phones Give Victims Hope for Help," *Tallahassee Democrat* (16 May 1996), p. B-3.

266. Tom Coyne, "Man Opens Fire at Ford Plant, Killing Wife's Boyfriend, Self," *Indianapolis Star* (8 January 1995), p. A-5.

267. Eileen Ambrose and Peter Key, "Deadly Attacks in Workplace More Common," *Indianapolis Star* (21 October 1995), p. C-1.

268. Silverstein.

269. "Suit Accuses Company of Firing Victim in Abduction," *Indianapolis Star* (12 August 1995), p. B-3.

270. Paul Nowell, "Domestic Violence Also Workplace Issue," *The Charlotte Observer* (24 November 1994), p. A-58.

271. Shankar Vedantam, "Experts: Workplace Violence Is Predictable," *Long Beach Press-Telegram* (15 September 1995), p. A-5.

272. Joseph Pereira, "Employers Confront Domestic Abuse," *Wall Street Journal* (2 March 1995), p. B-1.

273. "Rural Volunteers Offer Safe Havens for Battered Women," *Indianapolis Star* (14 November 1995), p. D-4.

INDEX